THE IMPERIAL JAPANESE ARMY

THE INVINCIBLE YEARS

OSPREY
PUBLISHING

BILL YENNE

THE IMPERIAL JAPANESE ARMY

THE INVINCIBLE YEARS

1941-42

First published in Great Britain in 2014 by Osprey Publishing,
PO Box 883, Oxford, OX1 9PL, UK
PO Box 3985, New York, NY 10185-3985, USA
E-mail: info@ospreypublishing.com

Osprey Publishing is part of the Osprey Group

A CIP catalogue record for this book is available from the British Library

ISBN: 978 1 78200 932 0
E-pub ISBN: 978 1 78200 982 5
PDF ISBN: 978 1 78200 981 8

Index by Mark Swift
Cartography by Peter Bull Art Studio
Typeset in Adobe Garamond Pro and Trajan Pro
Originated by PDQ Media, Bungay, UK
Printed in China through Worldprint Ltd.

14 15 16 17 18 19   10 9 8 7 6 5 4 3 2 1

Osprey Publishing is supporting the
Woodland Trust, the UK's leading
woodland conservation charity, by funding
the dedication of trees.

www.ospreypublishing.com

Front cover: Japanese troops celebrate
victory. (Corbis)
Back cover: Japanese soldiers attacking,
December 1941. (Getty Images)

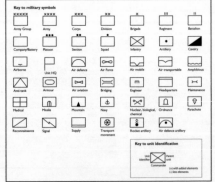

CONTENTS

Allied Forces and the Japanese Offensives

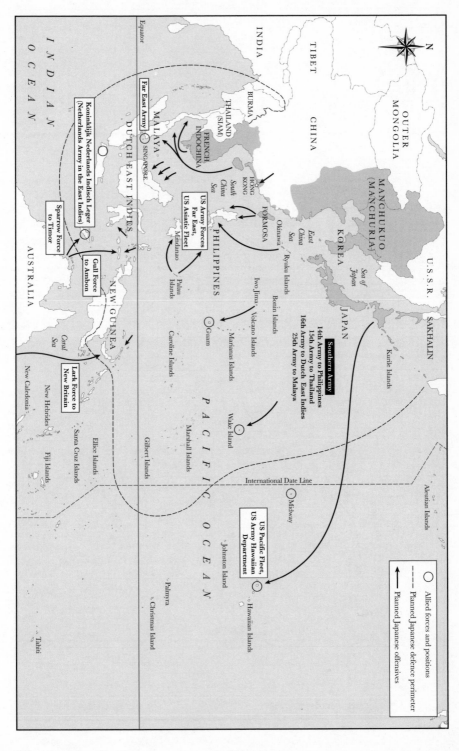

Operations Across Southeast Asia, December 1941

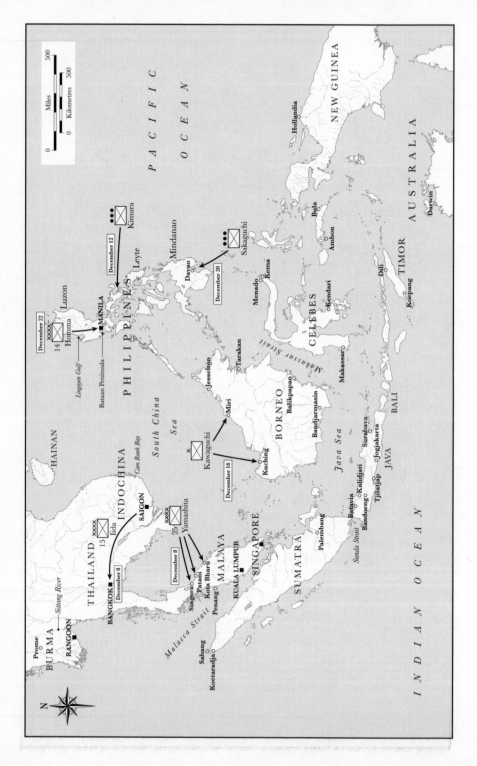

Operations Across Southeast Asia, January 1942

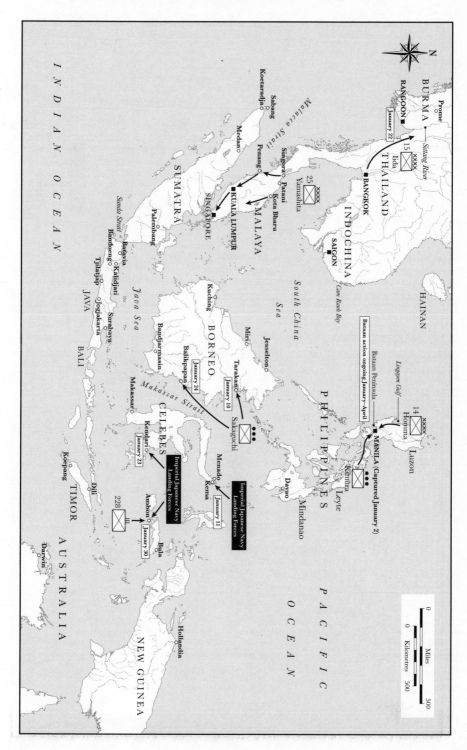

Operations Across Southeast Asia, February 1942

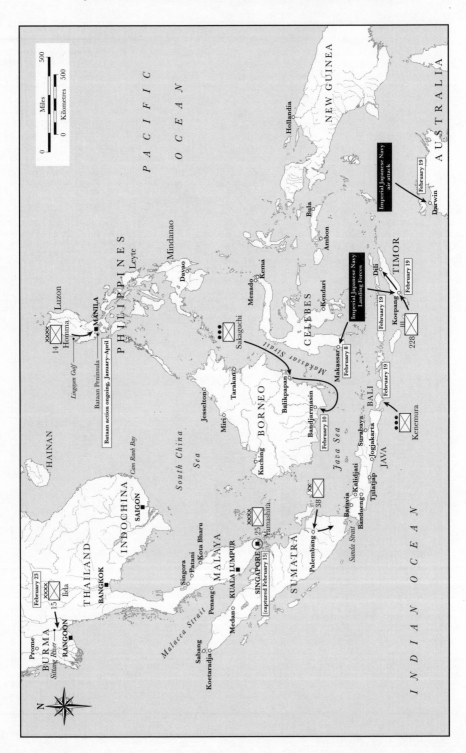

Operations Across Southeast Asia, March 1942

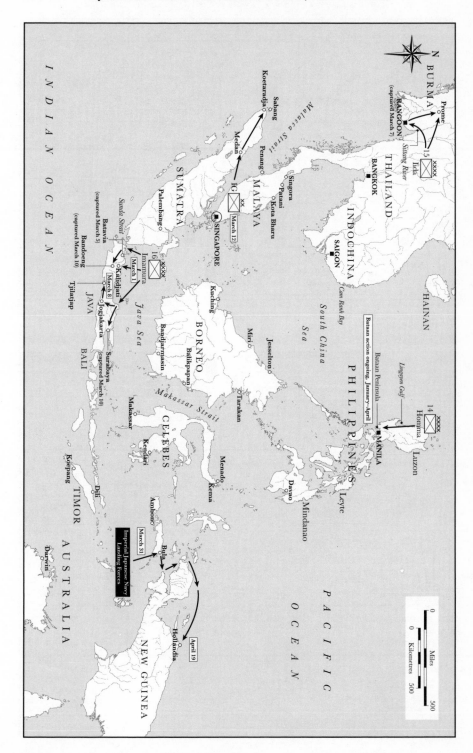

Operations in Malaya (left) and Singapore (right)

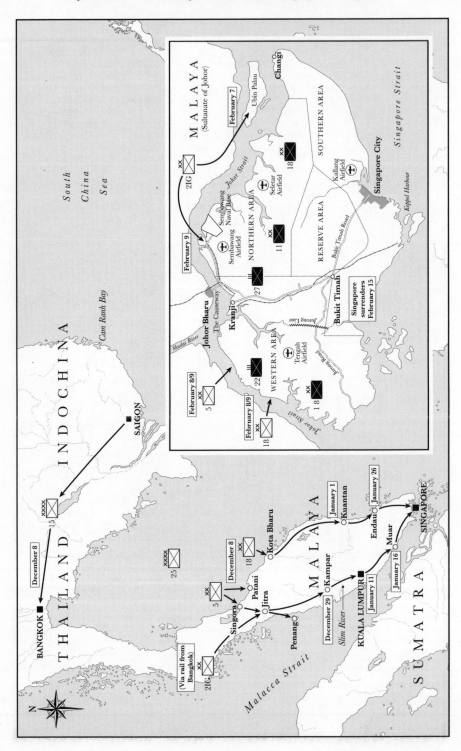

Operations in the Philippines

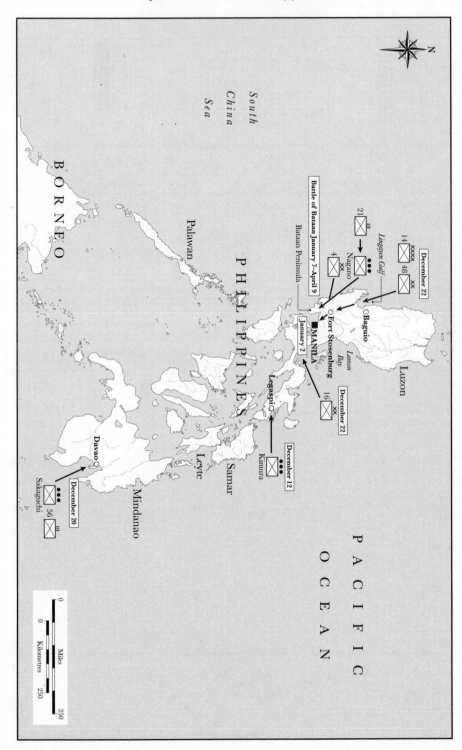

Operations in the Dutch East Indies

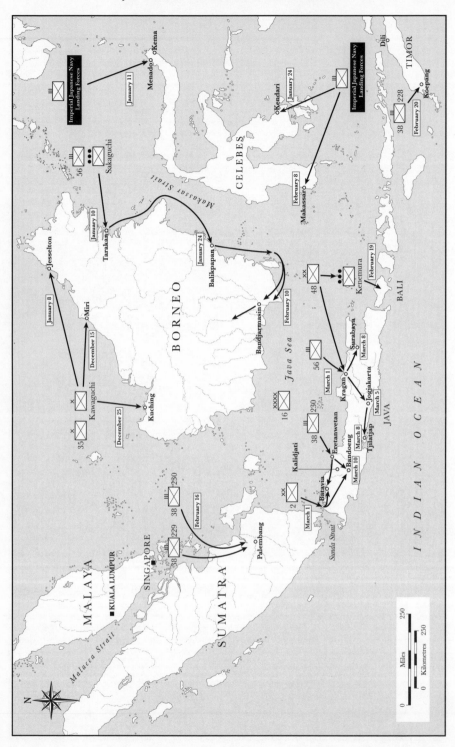

Operations in Burma

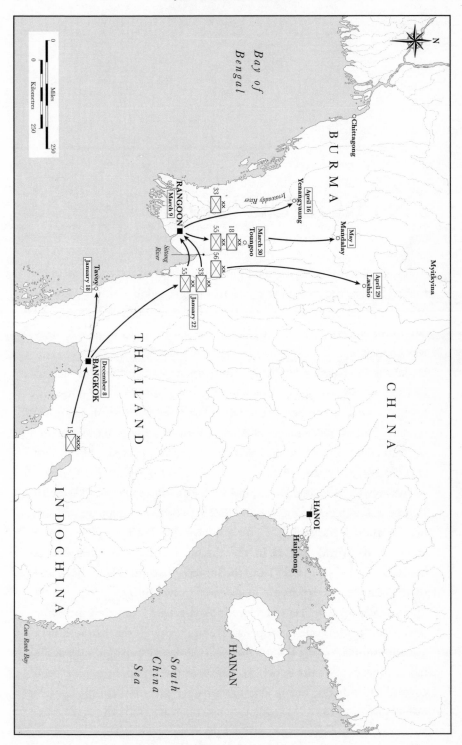

INTRODUCTION

This is the story of an unstoppable army that shocked the world, an army that reigned as the most powerful across half the globe. This is the story of the Imperial Japanese Army, the IJA or Dai-Nippon Teikoku Rikugun, and of the time between late 1941 and the start of 1943 when this army was invincible.

Just as the German blitzkrieg stunned its opponents and its victims in 1939–40, so too did the Japanese "blitzkrieg" of 1941–42. While the former is well remembered, the latter has since faded from historical memory. Yet, the six countries of Western Europe conquered by Germany in 1940 comprised a land area that was only a third the size of the land area conquered by the IJA through the first half of 1942. The German offensives which crushed Poland in 1939 and swallowed most of Western Europe in less than two months in 1940 have been well documented and heavily studied. Meanwhile, historians have also devoted a great deal of attention to World War II in the Pacific, focusing on naval battles between the US Navy (USN) and the Imperial Japanese Navy (IJN), and on the island campaign from Guadalcanal to Iwo Jima.

However, history has often overlooked a land campaign involving operations of equivalent scope and complexity – the extraordinary accomplishments of the IJA. Elements of this land campaign, such as the fall of Singapore or the American defeat in the Philippines, have been covered individually, but in this narrative we present a comprehensive overall picture of the remarkable Japanese offensive land campaign across

Southeast Asia and the surrounding archipelagos of the Philippines and the Dutch East Indies.

The motivations which led to this aspect of World War II are complex, and the roots can be traced back into the mists of ancient times. Legend holds that long ago, 2,600 years ago, Japan was ruled by an emperor named Jimmu, who in present memory is as mythical as he is real, and who may or may not have existed as more than just a heroic ideal. From Jimmu came the doctrine of *Hakko ichiu*, which is understood as meaning "eight corners of the world under one roof," or sometimes translated as "four corners and four walls under one roof." This idea was revived and interpreted in a Japan bent on dominance in the Far East in the 1930s to mean that the "eight corners of the world" were the eight cardinal and ordinal compass points of "Greater East Asia," and the "one roof" was that of Japan. From this flowed the idea of the Greater East Asia Co-Prosperity Sphere (Dai-to-a Kyoeiken), a concept that became more than merely foreign policy, developing into a clearly enunciated plan for a political and economic reality under which the nations in the region would be in orbit around Japan like planets around the sun.

The aggressive geopolitical vision within the Japanese Empire had come into being at the end of the nineteenth century, and had been expressed in the context of two points of their expansionist doctrine, Hokushinron, the Northern Road, and Nanshinron, the Southern Road. Like yin and yang, these represented a contrary, but complementary, duality. Within the halls of the military and political strategic leadership in Tokyo, where strategic thinkers planned Japan's wars, both Nanshinron and Hokushinron had passionate advocates who opposed the other with equal passion.

Beginning with the Sino-Japanese War in the 1890s, and continuing through the Russo-Japanese War, the Northern Road doctrine had dominated Japanese foreign policy. It had guided the annexation of Korea in 1910, and before that of the island of Taiwan off the coast of China.

In the 1930s, the Northern Road doctrine had carried Japan into the second Sino-Japanese War, and had taken the IJA into Manchuria, into northern China, and into border wars with the Soviet Union.

The Southern Road led toward Southeast Asia, a place where Japanese foreign policy had little experience, but where European powers had been dominant for more than a century. Turning south, in order to bring Southeast Asia into the Greater East Asia Co-Prosperity Sphere, Japan risked – and in some quarters even welcomed – a large-scale war with the great powers from across the globe. While the Hokushinron advocates continued to believe that Japan's destiny lay on the Northern Road, the pendulum was swinging the other way. The Nanshinron believers were now in the ascendancy.

The decision, for which the Nanshinron believers were the driving force, to take the Southern Road at the end of 1941 led to the events which are the subject of this book.

The Japanese troops who carried out Japan's war on the Southern Road were briefed ahead of time that their mission had implications that were beyond the geopolitical, and beyond mere nationalism. Their role was to liberate Greater East Asia from the old colonial masters and bring it all under the emperor's divine roof.

As they went off to war on the Southern Road, the IJA soldiers were each given a booklet entitled *Read This Alone: And The War Can Be Won*. In its opening pages, it described the mission for which these solders were fighting:

> We Japanese have been born in a country of no mean blessings, and thanks to the august power and influence of His Majesty the Emperor our land has never once, to this day, experienced invasion and occupation by a foreign power. The other peoples of the Far East look with envy upon Japan; they trust and honor the Japanese; and deep in their hearts they are hoping that, with the help of the Japanese people, they may themselves achieve national independence and happiness.

Japan was about to go to war on the Southern Road, as it had gone to war in China, under the assumption that the other peoples of the Far East looked "with envy upon Japan," that they trusted and honored the Japanese to bring them happiness and prosperity.

However, just as there existed a contrary, but complementary, duality in the geopolitical role of Hokushinron and Nanshinron, so too there were a yin and yang to the application of the Greater East Asia Co-Prosperity Sphere. On one hand, there was the altruistic ambition of replacing white masters with Asiatic masters. Opposing this idealistic yin there was the practical yang. It takes no stretch of the imagination to understand that when a totalitarian empire articulates a policy that contains the word "Co-Prosperity," the "prosperity" in question is its own. Japan needed the vast resources of Southeast Asia, especially the great oil reserves of the Dutch East Indies, to fuel its expanding domestic economy, and for its restless war machine.

As the date of the war they had planned drew near, Emperor Hirohito and his generals hoped for success on the Southern Road, but knew that this was by no means a sure thing. However, neither they, nor those who would soon oppose them, could have imagined how *very* successful they were about to be. These would be the invincible years.

PROLOGUE

Colonel Masanobu Tsuji of the IJA walked through the gate of a small former brigade headquarters complex near the city of Taihoku (now Taipei) on the island of Taiwan, which had been part of the Japanese Empire since 1895. It was the first day of 1941, and hot and muggy despite being the middle of winter. Tsuji was used to the chilly weather of Nanking (now Nanjing), where he had served until he was "exiled."

His transfer from China felt to Tsuji like an exile, and it was. He complained often of having been "driven out" of his post with the staff of the 400,000-man China Expeditionary Army (Shina Hakan Gun) to a minuscule post in a remote backwater far from the action. He complained that after 18 years as an officer, he now commanded only 30 people, and they included mainly typists and file clerks, not samurai.

The recently activated Taiwan Army Number 82 Section was the smallest unit Tsuji had yet to experience in his career, but it was growing. As he walked through the gate, his ears were filled with the sound of hammers, and his nostrils with the smell of newly sawn lumber.

Born on October 11, 1901 in Ishikawa Prefecture on the Sea of Japan, Masanobu Tsuji had graduated from the Imperial Japanese War College (Rikugun Daigakko) in 1931, and had served most of his active-duty career in China or on the Manchukuo border during the wars with the Soviet Union in the 1930s. Tsuji was aggressive and obstinate by nature, and proud of it. He knew that this rubbed people up the wrong way, but he was proud of this as well. He only rubbed people up the wrong way when *he* thought they needed rubbing, and when no one else in the hierarchy had the courage to do it.

According to John Toland, in *The Rising Sun*, Tsuji

> made a commonplace of eccentricity; once he had burned down a geisha house filled with fellow officers in a fit of moral indignation. With his roundish face, bald head and small, blinking eyes, he looked like the typical staff officer, but his brilliant maverick spirit inspired fanatic devotion in the younger staff officers. They revered him as Japan's "God of Operations," the hope of the Orient.

Toland reports that some of Tsuji's superiors did not share the ardor of the junior officers for Tsuji. He mentions that Lieutenant General Hitoshi Imamura, the deputy inspector general of IJA training, one of the most respected officers in the service, and later the wartime commander of the 16th Army, "saw the genius in Tsuji – but also the madman."

Within the IJA, there existed a subculture of the officer corps who were practitioners of the art of *gekokujo*, but Tsuji was a master. *Gekokujo* is a form of passive-aggressive institutional insubordination, dating back to the Warring States Period of the fifteenth century, which roughly translates as "the lower overcomes the higher," or "lesser ranks lead from below." Essentially, the bottom line of *gekokujo* was that "the end justifies the means." *Gekokujo* was one of those things lurking beneath the surface of the organizational culture that had long been tolerated because those ends which were justified by the means included a passionate, unyielding devotion to the empire and the emperor.

However, the practice had become abruptly less tolerable after it had served as a justification for the "February 26 Incident" in 1936, when a cadre of insubordinate *"gekokujan"* IJA officers attempted a coup against the Tokyo government. Though the coup failed, it resulted in a role for active-duty military officers in the heretofore civilian cabinet, and this would effectively open the door to a military-dominated Japanese government.

Tsuji's banishment had been precipitated not by *gekokujo*, but by guilt through association with his role model. This man, who was a grand master of the art of *gekokujo*, was the pugnacious and implacable General Kanji Ishihara (also written as Ishiwara), the officer who had been among those who engineered the 1931 Mukden Incident which gave Japan the pretext to invade and occupy Manchuria. The Japanese government was as stunned as the Chinese by how quickly and successfully Manchuria was occupied and turned into the puppet state of Manchukuo.

Had his ploy failed, Ishihara expected to be court-martialed – or worse – but his *gekokujo* served him well and succeeded, earning him the adoration of his troops, a permanent following, and the reluctant congratulations of his government. Failure is an orphan, but success has many willing fathers, and Ishihara came away from Mukden with many willing sons, including Tsuji.

In turn, Ishihara promulgated his East Asia Federation or East Asia League (Toa Renmei Undo), an "Asia for Asiatics" policy that was a precursor to the Greater East Asia Co-Prosperity Sphere concept. The Toa Renmei Undo doctrine imagined that Japan and puppet Manchukuo should ally themselves with China against non-Asian influences in Asia, especially the Comintern and the Soviet Union. While the pan-Asian component of the doctrine may have dovetailed with the official vision of a Greater East Asia Co-Prosperity Sphere, when Ishihara went so far as to propose that Japan should stop fighting China, that was the last straw. There was no future in China for IJA officers who considered the basic mission of the China Expeditionary Army to be flawed. Ishihara was relieved of his duties and placed on the retired list. If he had not been a leader of long service who had a great deal of respect within the officer corps, he might not have been allowed merely to slip away.

Tsuji, meanwhile, was also recalled to Tokyo. As far as the IJA was concerned, there was no place whatsoever in its ranks for Ishihara after China, but for Tsuji, it was another matter. He had the markings of an insubordinate, but the generals in Tokyo recognized that he had the makings of a *useful* insubordinate.

When he learned of their plans for him, Tsuji was astonished. He was one of those staff officers who lived and breathed Hokushinron, the Northern Road doctrine. He had spent much of his career fighting the Soviets along the frontier between Manchuria and Siberia, and even when he was in China, he kept one eye looking north.

When he took up his post at Taihoku at the beginning of 1941, he learned that the task before him at Number 82 Section was the direct opposite. He was now destined to walk the Nanshinron, the Southern Road. The architects of Tsuji's exile had placed him in charge of drawing up the first-ever contingency plans for IJA operations in Southeast Asia. Tsuji writes in his memoirs:

> Japanese soldiers were familiar only with the intensely cold regions of Manchukuo. None of them had any understanding of the meaning of the words "squall" or "jungle," much less any experience of these things. Consequently it was essential to begin to collect fundamental data for military operations in tropical areas … Even among the commissioned officers chosen for the staff there was not one who had had any real experience of the tropics.

Moreover, Tsuji was stunned that this unprecedented task given to the tiny Number 82 Section headquarters carried a virtually impossible deadline. As he explains,

> to this unpretentious and promiscuously chosen household was allotted the task of collecting, in approximately six months, all conceivable data connected with tropical warfare – the organization of Army corps, equipment, campaign direction, management and treatment of weapons, sanitation, supply, administration of occupied territory, and military strategy, tactics, and geography.

Six months to reorient an army for a type of warfare not previously imagined? How could this be done? Only by assigning the job to someone with the tenacity of an angry dog, the man with the "brilliant maverick spirit." There was method in the decision to assign this task to the aggressive and obstinate Colonel Masanobu Tsuji. The unit was officially under the command of Colonel Yoshihide Hayashi, but by all accounts Tsuji was its driving wheel.

Number 82 Section was also known, officially and benignly, as the Taiwan Army Research Department, but to its officers, it was the "Doro Nawa Unit." Roughly translated, Doro Nawa is a figure of speech that means catching a thief and thinking later about a rope to bind him. An analogous figure of speech is "putting the cart before the horse." It was the perception of Tsuji and his fellow officers that, having abruptly embraced the Nanshinron strategy, the Imperial General Headquarters had imposed a ridiculous timetable for its implementation.

It was the task of the Doro Nawa to train an army and design a strategy for operations never before envisioned or undertaken by the IJA, and to do it in half a year – when plans for operations against the Soviet Union had been developed and refined over more than a decade.

Tsuji and his fellow planners scratched their heads in dismay, pondering the problem and asking seemingly imponderable rhetorical questions. "What alterations had to be made in the organization of troops and the type of weapons and equipment used on the Siberian and Manchurian battlefields at twenty degrees below zero to meet requirements for fighting in the dense jungles of the tropics?" Tsuji wondered. "How should tactics and strategy used against the Soviet Union be revised for action against British and American armies?"

Winston Churchill begins his book *The Hinge of Fate*, the third volume of his massive history of World War II, with the assertion that Japan had "long prepared" for the campaign in Southeast Asia. Indeed, this was widely assumed by Allied planners throughout the war. In fact, the plans were compiled in a remarkably short time.

Through January and into February 1941, in the tropical heat to which he knew he must accustom himself, Tsuji pored over every bit of information that he could find about Southeast Asia. To his newly constructed headquarters, he called in civilians who had worked in Southeast Asia with Japanese firms – from the Ishihara Mining Company to the Taiwan Bank. He brought in professors from the Japanese university in Taiwan who could brief his team on tropical diseases and hygiene. He even sat down with an old sea captain who had sailed the waters of the Dutch East Indies and Malaya, to learn what he could about the nuances of weather, winds, and tides.

By the middle of February, it was time to evaluate tactics with a practical exercise. Sailing from Taiwan, clad in tropical weight uniforms and carrying gear which Number 82 Section had guessed would be compatible with tropical operations, a small contingent of IJA troops invaded Kagoshima Prefecture on Kyushu, the southernmost prefecture among the main islands of Japan.

Tsuji recalls that "the project was not characterized by either originality or peculiarity" but hastens to add that the maneuvers "brought together talented officers from all quarters, including naval staff men. During the two week period they came to know one another by sight and became friendly. Later these acquaintanceships were to prove of tremendous value on the battlefield."

A larger, second round of amphibious landing exercises was scheduled four months later on Hainan Island, off southern China, which had been used as a staging base for operations in southern China, as well as for operations related to the occupation of French Indochina.

These exercises went forward in June 1941, utilizing troops drawn from the IJA's 23rd Army, a garrison command recently formed in Fuchow, and not the units that would be used in the actual operations in Southeast Asia. These had yet to be determined. The maneuvers were aimed at refining more than merely amphibious landing techniques. They were, as Tsuji later writes,

> designed to work out a technique for an attack and a long-range penetration of approximately one thousand kilometers [625 miles] into enemy territory – the distance from southern Thailand to Singapore – and were to take into account the probability of strong resistance along the whole route of the attack and the fact that all bridges would be destroyed and roads damaged by the enemy.

Tsuji and his staff evaluated everything from how to pack horses into the hold of a ship to the endurance of troops on a sea voyage. In the case of the latter, he crowded men "three to a mat" and left them aboard ships for a week with a limited ration of water. Once ashore, Tsuji put the troops through their paces, studying the best means for moving quickly through a jungle. His engineers, meanwhile, were tasked with rapidly destroying and rebuilding bridges under primitive conditions.

Given that amphibious operations were relatively new for the IJA, Tsuji recalls that there were many unknowns to be investigated. As American planners of amphibious operations were soon to learn,

> the most difficult problem of all was to determine methods of disembarking men and equipment on open beaches with due regard for dangerous coral or hidden and sunken rocks; but eventually after considerable trouble satisfactory routines were evolved. Our study of these matters was carried out with the utmost seriousness; it was as a sword smeared with blood.

On the evening of June 22, Tsuji and his fellow officers were sitting down to a meal of boiled rice and salted fish at their encampment on Hainan. They had just lopped open some coconuts to drain their juice, when the wireless operator ran up to their table with news of Operation *Barbarossa*, the German invasion of the Soviet Union.

To officers who still held a grudge against their Axis partner for having concluded the 1939 pact with Stalin – Japan's mortal enemy – Germany's abrupt violation of this treaty was just as confusing. Citing an understanding that came from experience fighting the Soviet armies, Tsuji claims in his memoirs that he could see Hitler's folly:

> I, at that time, felt intuitively that a dark shadow had come over the future of Germany, which had consistently disregarded international good faith. War must have a morality and a reason which is understandable at home and abroad. From a propaganda standpoint Hitler's attack placed the Soviets in a one-hundred-per-cent more advantageous

position. Putting aside all questions of international morality, however, and looking at the position from a purely strategic aspect, the question arose whether the German nation had any real prospect of victory when confronted simultaneously by the Anglo-Saxon and Slav races.

Of course, Tsuji's memoirs were written ten years later, with the hindsight of knowing how Hitler's campaign against the Soviets had finally climaxed.

Two days later, Tsuji received a wire ordering him to come to Tokyo as soon as the Hainan exercises concluded, and to serve as a staff assistant on the Headquarters General Staff.

PART I

ONE FOOT ON THE ROAD

CHAPTER 1

TWO YOUNG WARRIORS AND THE EMPEROR'S ARMY

The tide of events that led Japan to the precipice of global war in 1941 was part of the evolution of a nation which, having joined the world out of the mists of millennia of isolation in the previous century, sought to be a dominant player in the world. The force underlying this momentum was the Dai-Nippon Teikoku Rikugun, the IJA.

At the turn of the twentieth century, the Japan that had emerged from those mists in the mid-nineteenth century was reorienting itself conceptually from a passionately inward-looking society to one which just as fervidly reached outward into Asia. Even the country's name implied that it was an object separate from, but nevertheless viewed from Asia. Japan was and is known formally as Nippon (or Nihon), roughly meaning the land in the east, as seen from continental Asia: the land lying in the direction of the rising sun, hence the emblem on its flag. The Nippon which was reinventing itself at the turn of the twentieth century was no longer merely the insular Nippon, but Dai-Nippon Teikoku, the Empire of the Rising Sun.

Two boys, whose lives are interwoven into the course of this narrative, were born into this time, and grew into manhood as soldiers of the Dai-Nippon Teikoku Rikugun, the Army of the Empire of the Rising Sun. The lives of these two men, soldiers of equally determined ambition, but widely opposite dispositions, are closely intertwined with the history of that army. The fiery and assertive Hideki Tojo was born in bustling Tokyo on December 30, 1884. Less than eleven months later, on November 8, 1885, the taciturn and circumspect Tomoyuki Yamashita was born amid the ancient, misty cedar forests in the mountain valley village of Osugi Mura on the island of Shikoku.

Hideki Tojo was the third of the seven sons of Hidenori Tojo, an officer in the IJA who would ultimately retire as a lieutenant general in 1908. Yamashita was the second of the two sons of Sakichi Yamashita, a country doctor. While young Tojo aspired to the family business, young Yamashita remained content with life in the misty rural forests of Shikoko. It was his older brother who was earmarked for their father's trade, although Tomoyuki imagined himself practicing medicine in Tokyo, rather than in a remote and rural corner of the smallest of Japan's four main islands.

By the time he was 12, however, Tomoyuki Yamashita was living with an uncle in Kochi on the Shikoku coast and enrolled at the Kainan middle school, a military school where samurai warriors had been trained in feudal times. For Japan and its army, the era of feudalism was not so far in the past as in Europe. Indeed, that era had only just ended, and ended abruptly, in 1868, when Hidenori Tojo and Sakichi Yamashita were young men.

For nearly seven centuries after the decline of the emperor to mere figurehead status, he had sat on his Chrysanthemum Throne in Kyoto, while Japan had been ruled by shoguns. Nominally appointed by the emperor, the shoguns had originated as regional warlords who derived their power from their respective hereditary fiefdoms, and maintained their control by surrounding themselves with a knightly caste of samurai.

Even after the Warring States Period gave way to the unified Tokugawa Shogunate in the seventeenth century, the regional lords wielded considerable power in their individual spheres of influence.

Just as the emperors remained sequestered behind their palace walls in Kyoto, essentially out of touch with nearly everything that transpired in Japan, the nation itself remained deliberately isolated from the rest of the world. The Tokugawa Shogunate, whose political power dominated most of Japan for more than 260 years, found its undoing in contact with the outside world. In the early nineteenth century, a series of visits by Westerners seeking to open a trading relationship, culminating in those of USN Commodore Matthew Perry in 1853–54, acquainted the Japanese with an outside world of which they were unaware. In turn, there was a growing number of Japanese who advocated opening Japan and embracing Western-style industrialization. This came to a head in the collapse of the Tokugawa Shogunate in November 1867, and the Boshin War – the War of the Year of the Dragon – in which the isolationists were defeated, and the emperor restored as the dominant ruling power of Japan. When he ascended to the throne, his supporters termed the teenaged Prince Mutsuhito as Emperor Meiji, or the Enlightened Ruler. It would be Meiji, and those around him, who would dramatically reorient introspective Nippon, the land of the rising sun, into Dai-Nippon Teikoku, the *Empire* of the Rising Sun.

The new emperor abolished feudalism, introduced democratic reforms, and moved his seat of power from Kyoto to the city of Edo, formerly the seat of the Tokugawa Shogunate, renaming it Tokyo, meaning "Eastern Capital." While the literal Chrysanthemum Throne remained in Kyoto, Japan would continue to be referred to as the "Chrysanthemum Kingdom," or "Chrysanthemum Empire," and the emperor adopted a stylized chrysanthemum flower as the official imperial seal. Emperor Meiji, who ruled for 45 years until his death in 1912, also opened this empire to the West and undertook a rapid industrialization process, and a modernization geared to European standards.

Among the changes was the creation of modern armed forces. At the time of the Meiji Restoration, the Tokugawa Shogunate's navy was the largest in the Far East, but in 1869 the emperor formed his own Imperial Japanese Navy, or Dai-Nippon Teikoku Kaigun, importing European engineers to help design and build modern warships. These, in turn, defeated the remnants of the Tokugawa navy that had not already defected to the emperor. Meanwhile, the transformation of a disunified gaggle of medieval shogunate militias into a single, unified IJA came in 1871.

As he had utilized French engineers to help design his warships, Meiji imported British naval officers to help him design his navy. With Britain then the world's preeminent sea power, there was no question that the emperor wanted the British as the architects of his navy. He initially brought in French military advisors to help organize and build his army, but after France was defeated in the Franco-Prussian War, he naturally switched to having Prussian officers mentor his new army. In fact, the Meiji government was modeled on that of Prussia, with the emperor wielding considerable power, and the military being beyond civilian control and answering directly to the emperor himself.

As Sakichi Yamashita was hiking through the deep cedar forests and climbing the mountain trails of Shikoko to visit his patients, Hidenori Tojo was climbing through the ranks of Emperor Meiji's new Imperial Army. He was not a samurai, but a young man of humble peasant stock who yearned to be one.

The IJA was born at exactly the right time for this aspiring warrior, who gravitated happily to the Prussian discipline which reminded him of what he knew of the ancient *bushido* code of the samurai. Though the feudal state had gone away, the *bushido* doctrine of unswerving loyalty and devotion to the deified emperor as an emblem of the state still permeated the institutional culture of the IJA as it would through the years leading up to World War II.

Ironically, Hidenori's first major operational career highlight was his participation in suppressing the 1877 Satsuma Rebellion, which was led by Saigo Takamori (aka Takanaga), the man who is often referred to as "the

Last Samurai," and upon whose life the 2003 film *The Last Samurai* was loosely based. This rebellion was by an army of former samurai whose role in society had been rendered obsolete by the Meiji Restoration and the end of feudalism. While many former samurai migrated into the officer corps of the IJA, there were those who refused to adapt themselves to this new way. They formed a stronghold in the Satsuma region of Kagoshima Prefecture, and resisted change. Their fierce but noble and short-lived rebellion culminated in the September 24, 1877 battle of Shiroyama, portrayed in the film, in which Takamori died.

After Shiroyama, Hidenori Tojo moved through the ranks, devoting more and more time to his Prussian-inspired military career, and his wife raised her boys in the vacuum created by a largely absent father.

Young Hideki Tojo grew up in parallel with Meiji Japan, its army, and his father's career. By the time he started school, the emperor commanded a modern military force that was second to none in the Far East in terms of numbers, efficiency, and discipline. This, in turn, became the instrument of an initial phase of empire-building operations that culminated in the invincible years of early World War II.

When Hideki was nine years old, his country went to war with the once and future Asian superpower, China. The issue at hand was control of Korea, which was independent, but part of China's sphere of influence. For two decades, Meiji had arm-twisted and wheedled the reclusive Koreans to open trade with the Chrysanthemum Empire, just as outsiders once had done to Japan. It was partly for security reasons and partly that Japan coveted Korean coal and iron ore to feed its industrial machine. Japanese wars then, as they would be in 1941, were at least partially about natural resources.

Nevertheless, despite a trade treaty signed in 1876, Korea remained in China's orbit. Finally, in 1894, it was time to send in Asia's largest modern army. China's Qing Dynasty (then called the Manchu Dynasty), which had succeeded the Ming Dynasty 250 years earlier, had been as unwilling to accept Western-style modernization as pre-Meiji Japan, and as a consequence, it was no match for the 120,000-man IJA.

Invited into Korea to meet the Japanese invasion, Chinese troops were soundly defeated in a series of battles in September 1894. At sea, the IJN, though outnumbered, defeated the disunified Chinese fleets decisively.

By the time that the war ended with the Treaty of Shimonoseki in April 1895 and Hidenori Tojo came home in triumph, Japan had defeated and humiliated China, occupied Korea (which was formally annexed in 1910), and was in the process of an unopposed occupation of the island of Taiwan, which was accomplished by October. Originally named Ilha Formosa (Beautiful Isle) by the Portuguese in the seventeenth century, Taiwan had been home to the short-lived Republic of Formosa before being absorbed by Japan in 1895, and the names "Formosa" and "Taiwan" were used interchangeably throughout the early twentieth century, including by the Japanese.

During the war, Japan had also occupied the strategic Kwantung Peninsula (now Guandong), northwest of Korea. Under the terms of the Treaty of Shimonoseki, Japan was given full sovereignty over Kwantung, although, under pressure from Germany, France, and Russia, the Japanese were forced to give it back to China almost immediately. With Kwantung back in their hands, the Chinese leased the port of Lüshun, at the tip of the peninsula, to the Russians, who craved this concession as a warm-weather port on the Pacific. They promptly renamed it Port Arthur and built a large naval facility there. Japan was learning that it would have to be more than merely the preeminent military power in the Far East.

In 1899, only four years after losing the Sino-Japanese War, the Chinese faced further disgrace during the Boxer Rebellion. When a society of anti-Western martial arts practitioners (known as "Boxers" because of the drawing of a fist on their banner) began attacking foreign diplomatic compounds in Beijing, an international military coalition intervened to put them down. Austria-Hungary, Britain, France, Germany, Italy, Russia, and the United States all sent troops. So too did Japan. In fact, the 20,000-man detachment from the IJA's 5th Division, under Lieutenant General Motoomi Yamaguchi, was the largest contingent of them all. Because China's dowager empress and her court had sided with the Boxers, who were defeated so decisively, the credibility of the Qing regime went into a long slow decline. The Qing Dynasty, and more than four millennia of imperial rule in China, collapsed in 1912.

For two imaginative teenage boys in military school, the decade that began in 1894 was an exciting time. For Hideki Tojo and Tomoyuki Yamashita, it was an era of sabres, uniforms, flags, and what appeared at home as a time of easy and glorious victories for the IJA.

As John Deane Potter writes in his biography of Yamashita, in 1899, when Tomoyuki "came home for the summer holidays to his mountain village, he confided to his mother, with whom he had always been very close, that he wanted to be a soldier. It was perhaps the best time in Japan's history for a boy to make such a decision." For Hideki Tojo, that auspicious decision had already been made for him.

In the meantime, the emperor had formed six new cadet schools across Japan to broaden the base of the IJA officer corps. Potter points out that although this corps was still dominated by an entrenched elite, "the shrewd liberal Emperor Meiji was beginning to throw the higher ranks open to selected candidates from the middle class."

The young and impressionable cadets were especially taken with news of the Boxer Rebellion, and beamed with pride as they learned that Japanese soldiers had served on equal terms with Europeans for the first time. They were in awe as the troops returned from Beijing. Looking through Yamashita's young eyes, Potter writes:

> After the rebellion was over, they returned to [Hiroshima], swaggering proudly along the streets in their black jackets and French kepis. They were splendid figures, the infantry in red trousers, the cavalry in green, and the artillery in yellow. When they came to lecture the cadets on their experiences, their audience listened breathlessly.

In 1904, a decade after the war against China had begun, Japan once again found itself engaged in a major conflict, this time against the great Russian Empire. The centerpiece of the disagreement was control of Manchuria, that vast region of northeast China with a land area three times that of Japan which was rich in coal and minerals, as well as possessing great expanses of farmland and potential farmland. It was coveted both by the Japanese, who eyed it from neighboring Korea, and by the Russians, who looked towards it from their port city of Vladivostok and who manipulated the area economically.

The first phase of the Russo-Japanese War involved the Japanese capture of the Russian base at Port Arthur, and the reoccupation of the Kwantung Peninsula. A decisive defeat of the Russian Army at the Manchurian city of Mukden (now Shenyang) in March 1905, followed by an equally decisive defeat of the Russian Navy at the Tsushima Straits between Japan and Korea two months later, decided the outcome. US President Theodore Roosevelt earned the sixth Nobel Peace Prize for negotiating the settlement that ended the war with the Treaty of Portsmouth in September 1905.

As part of the cessation of hostilities, Japan reacquired Kwantung and received control of Port Arthur, which was now renamed Ryojun. In 1906, the IJA established the Kwantung Garrison to defend this region and parts of Manchuria occupied by the IJA. This was a move that might have been a footnote worth omitting were it not for the fact that this contingent, renamed the Kwantung Army in 1919, was destined to become an immensely influential political power center within the IJA.

The defeat of the Russian Empire, a major European power many times Japan's size had now transformed the Chrysanthemum Empire into a world power. As with the disgracing of China a decade earlier, this victory was a crowning achievement for Emperor Meiji, whose country had been just a quirky, globally irrelevant, little kingdom when he had assumed the throne.

For the two young cadets, and all their colleagues, who graduated from the Imperial Japanese Army Academy (Rikugun Shikan Gakko) and received their commissions in 1905, the end of the war came much too soon. Lieutenant General Hidenori Tojo had led a brigade to glory during the war, but by the time that newly minted Second Lieutenant Hideki Tojo reached Manchuria, there was nothing left but the mopping up.

Basking in the glory of their homeland's new prestige and status on the world stage, Lieutenants Tojo and Yamashita continued up the career ladder, where the next rung for officers serious about advancement was the difficult competition to get into the Imperial Army War College (Rikugun Daigakko) in Tokyo. The two men graduated in 1915 and 1916, respectively.

With their careers on track, these two young officers had an opportunity for courtship, and ultimately marriage. Yamashita married Hisako Nagayama, the daughter of a retired general, while Tojo wed Katsuko Ito.

As these events were taking place, the outside world, the world which Japan had joined and in which it now had a prominent role, had tumbled into World War I. In the early days of August 1914, before anyone realized that this was about to be the bloodiest war to date in human history, declarations of war were an almost pro forma diplomatic exercise for all of the major powers of Europe. Japan, with its newfound prominence, also entered the fray.

Japan's military modernization had been mentored by both the British and the Germans, so sides had to be chosen. The Chrysanthemum Empire chose the former, despite the fact that this also allied them with the despised Russian Empire. Another irony was that German was then considered the elite military language by the IJA, and a required course at the War College. At the very moment that their country was declaring war on Germany, Hideki Tojo and Tomoyuki Yamashita were diligently becoming fluent in the German language.

By 1914, the sickly and inept Emperor Yoshihito (later called Taisho), eldest son of Meiji, was two years into his reign, but in light of his mental disabilities and his absence from public view, the shots were being called by Prime Minister Okuma Shigenobu and Foreign Minister Kato Takaaki. They recognized that while Japan had no role to play in Europe, the principal theater of the conflict, enormous opportunities presented themselves in the Pacific, where the Germans had a substantial number of outposts.

A partial list of the German islands which were to be occupied by Japan during World War I reads like a page taken from a history of

World War II – Kwajalein, Peleliu, Saipan, Tinian, Truk. Germany had purchased the Marshall Island archipelago from Spain in 1884, and bought the Carolines and the Marianas from the Spanish after the Spanish-American War of 1898. They were all seized by the IJN in the autumn of 1914, and mandated to Japan as League of Nations trust territories in 1920. This marked Japan's first steps on Nanshinron, the Southern Road.

In the meantime, on the Asian mainland, the IJN and IJA also seized, after a week-long siege in November 1914, the German enclave of Tsingtao (now Qingdao) on the coast of China.

When the war, then called the "Great War" or the "World War," was over in 1918, so too was the Russian Empire. In the wake of the 1917 Russian Revolution, the largest contiguous empire on earth dissolved into chaos and civil war. When the call went out for an international intervention, both the US Army and the IJA found themselves side by side, intervening in Siberia. The Americans pulled out in 1920, the Japanese lingered until 1922 before reluctantly withdrawing. In that year, the chaotic remnants of the old Russian Empire of the Tsars coalesced into a new Russian empire known as the Union of Soviet Socialist Republics.

The idea of a permanent Japanese occupation of Siberia east of Lake Baikal had been a topic of discussion by Japanese strategic planners for years. In the coming decades the Russian, now Soviet, frontier in Siberia, which lay on Hokushinron, the Northern Road, would be a principal area of operations for the IJA.

However, Hideki Tojo and Tomoyuki Yamashita would be headed west, not north, in the wake of World War I. With their recently acquired fluency in German, they were going to Europe, and for the first time in their careers, they would be serving together.

Initially posted to the Japanese Embassy in Switzerland in 1919 as military attachés, the two young captains also toured the continent, visiting wartime battlefields and spending a great deal of time in defeated Germany and Austria. Tojo remained in Europe for two years, Yamashita for three. During this time, the two men crossed paths with several individuals who, like themselves, would rise to prominence in Japan during World War II. These included Shigenori Togo, a future foreign minister, and two future generals, Tetsuzan Nagata and Yoshijiro Umezu, a future chief of staff of the IJA.

Meanwhile, the hyperinflation epidemic which would ravage Germany in the 1920s was only just beginning, but its effects were startling to the two Japanese officers. According to John Deane Potter, who had access to Yamashita's diaries, Yamashita prophetically told Tojo that "if Japan ever has to fight any nation, she must never surrender and get herself in a state like this."

After Europe, both men returned to Japan, where they were promoted to the rank of major and assigned to the Imperial General Headquarters in Tokyo. After a stint as a lecturer at the War College, Tojo was further promoted to lieutenant colonel in 1924. Two years later, he was assigned to the Military Affairs Bureau of the War Ministry.

Tomoyuki Yamashita, meanwhile, was having trouble at home. One of his in-laws had used him to guarantee a business loan, on which the relative defaulted. Yamashita took the fall with him, and lost his house on the eve of being assigned to return to Europe as the military attaché at the Japanese Embassy in Vienna. Furious with his wife for her role in the financial shenanigans, Yamashita left her in Tokyo as he traveled to Austria. It was here that he met and began an extended affair with the daughter of a German general, a woman known to history only as "Kitty."

In 1928, while Yamashita was wooing Kitty, Tojo, now a colonel, became head of the IJA Mobilization Section. The man who was called "the Razor" because of his sharp mind and decisive actions was clearly a rising star within the service.

At the turn of the decade, both men were back in Tokyo, where Tojo became commanding officer of the 1st Infantry Regiment, while Yamashita took over the 3rd Infantry Regiment. Both men were earmarked for bigger things, and had been given operational commands as a means of filling out their résumés, which would have been incomplete if filled only with staff experience.

Also at the beginning of the 1930s, events beyond the insulating walls of the Imperial General Headquarters were building toward enormous changes in Japan, her government, and her society. As Tojo and Yamashita had walked the streets of defeated Germany in the early 1920s, smugly commenting on the difficulties of its people, Japan had been enjoying an era of great prosperity. However, as is so often the case, economic boom was revealed to be an economic bubble. While the United States and victorious Europe were enjoying the Roaring Twenties, the Japanese economy stumbled firstly after the Great Kanto Earthquake of 1923 devastated Tokyo, and again when the Showa Financial Crisis of 1927 devastated the Japanese banking system. It was to falter for a third time when the Crash of 1929 brought on the Great Depression and devastated the entire global economy.

In the meantime, Japan was suffering from an absence of solid leadership at the top of its political system. Prime ministers came and went with increasing frequency, often serving for less than a year in office, while the passing of the astute and insightful Emperor Meiji had left much to be desired at the very top. By 1919, the mentally challenged Yoshihito had essentially stopped conducting any sort of official business, but it was not until 1921 that his 20-year-old eldest son, Crown Prince Hirohito, was named to rule as the *sessho*, or prince regent. Young Hirohito finally ascended to the throne as emperor in 1926, when Yoshihito died.

Whereas Hirohito's grandfather had possessed an intuitive understanding of leadership principles, and of his own empire, Hirohito was untrained in anything but the ceremonial trappings of his office as a god-like ruler. He had been kept as isolated from his empire as his empire had been from the rest of the world before the Meiji Restoration. Within this vacuum, all manner of mischief would be possible. However, as naive as he was, at least he had not inherited his father's mental frailties.

Hirohito's reign was formally designated in advance as the "Showa" period, an intended era of "abundant benevolence," and "enlightened peace." It would be anything but.

CHAPTER 2

TWO SENIOR OFFICERS AND THE EMPEROR'S ARMIES

In 1930, Colonel Hideki Tojo and Colonel Tomoyuki Yamashita found themselves among the cadre of officers at the heart of the IJA in its headquarters in Tokyo during exciting, if ominous, times. As the Japanese civilian government was growing progressively weaker against the backdrop of a revolving door of increasingly ineffective prime ministers, the importance of the disciplined and powerful military services was on the rise.

However, this was also a time of flux within the IJA, and a time when the Kwantung Army in China was emerging as a major center of authority whose power was to rival that of the Imperial General Headquarters. Both Tojo and Yamashita would serve tours with the Kwantung Army at important junctures in their respective careers.

In describing the restless and militant Kwantung Army of the early 1930s, you might say that it was almost a rival army to the IJA itself, or you might even omit the use of the word "almost." It was as though the Kwantung Army existed as an expression of *gekokujo* toward the Imperial

General Headquarters. Indeed, the leadership of the Kwantung Army was characterized by *gekokujo* masters like the uncompromising General Kanji Ishihara.

By 1930, it had already moved beyond its role as a garrison force in the Kwantung Peninsula to become the major player in Manchuria. During the coming decade, the Kwantung Army was to be the catalyst for independent actions in Manchuria and China that would define Japanese foreign policy and lead Japan toward World War II.

China, technically a republic since the fall of the Qing Dynasty in 1912, was still a disunified basket of competing fiefdoms trying to remodel itself as a modern world power. By this time, the Nationalist, or Kuomintang, forces headed by Chiang Kai-shek (now spelled Jiang Jieshi) had succeeded in defeating most rival warlords and consolidating power through much of China. While they still faced a serious challenge from a Chinese Communist insurgency, led by Mao Tse-Tung (now spelled Mao Zedong) and Chou En-lai (now spelled Zhou Enlai), Chiang's Republic of China government was now widely recognized in the world as the legitimate government.

As Chiang wrapped himself in the cloak of international legitimacy, and consolidated his power within China, one important area that was still out of Kuomintang control was Manchuria, that treasury of natural resources over which the Japanese and Russians had bickered and lusted since before the turn of the century. Since the time of World War I, Manchuria had been ruled by the warlord Chang Tso-lin (now spelled Zhang Zuolin), known as "Marshal Chang," with the tacit support of the Kwantung Army. Chang had once been so powerful as to pose a threat to Chiang himself. Moving beyond his own borders, he had even occupied Beijing in 1926. However, as Chiang Kai-shek now closed in, Chang retreated, and by 1928, he was faced with losing Manchuria itself.

The leadership of the Kwantung Army, then commanded by General Chotaro Muraoka, being Chang's patron, considered themselves to have the responsibility for dealing with the situation. Acting independently, without the Imperial General Headquarters authorization, but within the arrogant spirit of *gekokujo*, the Kwantung Army assassinated Marshal

Chang by blowing up his train in June 1928. However, they grossly underestimated the magnitude of Chang's importance, and the magnitude of the void left by his absence. It was not the Japanese, but the Chinese Nationalists (via Marshal Chang's son Chang Hsueh-liang (now spelled Zhang Xueliang) functioning as their puppet), who filled the vacuum.

No one in Tokyo, from the Imperial Palace to the Imperial General Headquarters, wanted to see a vacuum in Manchuria into which either Chiang's Nationalists or the Soviet Union could flow, but their hands were tied. However, for the Kwantung Army, it was merely a setback that could and would be rectified.

When he assumed command of the Kwantung Army in August 1931, Lieutenant General Shigeru Honjo ordered his troops to develop contingency plans for full-scale operations to make sure that things went Japan's way next time. Kanji Ishihara, along with Colonel Seishiro Itagaki, went to the drawing board, drafting a detailed plan for the armed conquest of Manchuria by the Kwantung Army. Itagaki carried this to Tokyo and made a presentation to Imperial General Headquarters. This being consistent with overall Japanese strategy for Manchuria, the plan was approved, although Itagaki was admonished that the Kwantung Army should not initiate a full-scale invasion without a serious provocation by the Chinese. To the IJA leadership, this meant waiting until the Chinese made a move. To Itagaki and Ishihara, this meant that a provocation must be created.

They concocted the plan to blow up a segment of the Japanese-owned South Manchuria Railway near Mukden and to blame it on the Chinese. The blast, detonated on September 18, 1931, did so little damage that the tracks remained passable, but it accomplished its intended goal. A provocation is a provocation. By the end of the following day, before either Imperial General Headquarters or the Kwantung Army Headquarters could respond, a small contingent of Japanese troops had swiftly attacked a vastly superior Chinese force, defeated them, and occupied Mukden. In the wake of September's "Mukden Incident," events unfolded quickly. The Kwantung Army succeeded in occupying much of Manchuria within a month, and at the end of February 1932, with the Japanese capture of the major city of Harbin, Chinese resistance to the invasion was formally suspended. As for Seishio Itagaki, he continued to advance through the ranks of the IJA, and by 1936, as a lieutenant general, he became the chief of staff of the Kwantung Army.

By March 1, 1932, the IJA, together with pro-Japanese factions within Manchuria, had formally declared Manchuria as the independent kingdom of Manchukuo, meaning "Manchu State," though this new puppet state was not recognized by the Japanese government until September. To rule Manchukuo, the Japanese sought out Puyi, who had been the last emperor of Qing Dynasty China. Then known as the Manchu Dynasty, the imperial family had a special connection to Manchuria, because, as the name suggests, it was considered to be their traditional homeland.

Puyi had ascended to the throne in 1908 at the age of two, but after the Chinese monarchy was overthrown in 1912, he had spent most of his 26 years living within the confines of the Japanese enclave at Tientsin (now Tianjin). He was now more than ready to rule, even it meant being a Japanese puppet ruler of the new Manchu State.

Initially, both the civilian and military leadership in Tokyo were surprised and distressed by the invasion of Manchuria, which had taken on a life of its own and was unfolding almost more quickly than it could be followed. In the early days of the action, the Imperial General Headquarters had ordered General Honjo to restrict his operations to southern Manchuria, but he ignored the orders, allowing their own momentum to guide his fast-moving troops. The government of Prime Minister Reijiro Wakatsuki fell in December 1931 as a result of the invasion, which the prime minister opposed. He was succeeded by Tsuyoshi Inukai, who took exception to the IJA imposing a puppet government on Manchuria under their own initiative, although he was powerless to stand up to the unstoppable energy of militarism.

Though it started with a pitifully small charge of dynamite, the Mukden Incident was a shot heard around the world. International condemnation of Japan was resounding – albeit without teeth, a bark without bite. In the United States, Secretary of State Henry Stimson declared the Stimson Doctrine, which said that the United States would recognize no Japanese territorial gains. In February 1933, when the League of Nations condemned Japanese aggression in Manchuria, Japan's delegation, led by the American-educated diplomat Yosuke Matsuoka, responded by dramatically marching out of the League chamber. The nation that had tried hard – and successfully – to become an integral part of the world community, was once again isolated. In the perception of many around the world, Japan was now an outlaw nation.

———

In Japan, meanwhile, the conquest of Manchuria and the transformation of it into the vassal state of Manchukuo had become the object of civic pride. The tide of public opinion had become a tsunami of nationalism in which criticism of the Manchukuo affair was considered tantamount to treason. In the midst of economic hard times, the Kwantung Army had given the people a glowing success story. The unstoppable momentum of militarism was sweeping the streets and the popular media, brushing aside moderate voices everywhere. On May 15, 1932, three weeks after turning 77, Prime Minister Tsuyoshi Inukai welcomed several young IJN officers at his official residence. They removed their shoes and sat with the old man on his *tatami* (a floor mat). Moments later, gunshots rang out and he lay in a pool of blood.

An attempted coup, launched simultaneously, failed, but the assassins and conspirators received lenient sentences. It was *gekokujo* in the extreme, but it helped set the course for the future. Viscount Makoto Saito, a retired admiral, became Japan's next prime minister, ushering in an era of *de facto* military rule that would continue through World War II.

In the meantime, the ranks of the IJA had themselves become divided into factions. At one extreme was the *kodoha*, or Imperial Way Faction, a coterie of young officers which came together around the outspoken Lieutenant General Sadao Araki. Their spiritual leader had commanded the 6th Division in the Kwantung Army, and became minister of war in December 1931.

The term *kodoha*, first mentioned by Araki in September 1932, described a form of institutionalized *gekokujo*, a sort of militarist utopianism. With the ancient *bushido* code as a basic belief, *kodoha* imagined a Japan in which the armed forces ruled all facets of society, answering only to the emperor and to the glory of an ever-expanding empire. Under this notion, the military would supersede civilians throughout the Japanese government, and usurp control of the Japanese industrial infrastructure from the *zaibatsu*, the family-run vertical conglomerates such as Mitsui, Mitsubishi, and Sumitomo.

Meanwhile, the Imperial Way Faction had the support of like-minded officers within the IJN where there was widespread dissatisfaction with civilian governments for having signed the 1922 and 1930 naval treaties under which Japan agreed to reduce naval tonnage to less than that of either the United Kingdom or the United States. The naval tonnage limitations on the world's naval powers were set for the United States, the United Kingdom, and Japan at a 5–5–3 ratio, which placed Japan at a disadvantage. The treaties were flashpoints of dissatisfaction for many officers within the IJN.

The disciples of *kodoha* were willing to resort to revolution on their road to their utopia. Though Araki and his immediate followers played no role in the "May 15 Incident," he described the participants as "irrepressible patriots."

In tacit opposition to the Imperial Way Faction, was the *toseiha*, or Control Faction. Like the *kodoha*, the *toseiha* believed in an enthusiastic devotion to emperor, as well as the strict militarist control of Japanese society and expansionist empire building. Where they differed was in method. They were methodical in their quest for power, preferring to work within the system, rather than to resort to open revolt.

Hideki Tojo and Tetsuzan Nagata, with whom Tojo had served in Europe, became the leading exponents of the way of *toseiha*. Neither had any use for *gekokujo*, a practice which Tojo called "unpardonable." The two men, both now major generals, believed in a growing Japanese empire, but they knew that a total war would require the kind of cooperation with the *zaibatsu* and civilian politicians that was unthinkable under *kodoha*.

In 1935, however, Tojo left the capital and the IJA's intramural politics. The commander of the Kwantung Army, General Jiro Minami, had personally requested that Tojo come over to Manchukuo to serve as the commander of his Kempeitai (military police) operations. The uncompromising Minami ruled his fiefdom with an iron fist, and Tojo became his enforcer. At first, Tojo lamented being sent away from the center of power in the capital, but he soon realized that experience in a field command would be useful to his career. He grew into the job. A strict disciplinarian by nature, the military police role very much suited him, while allowing him an understanding of the secret police that would serve him as he moved up the rungs of power.

While Tojo embraced politics like a second calling, Tomoyuki Yamashita avoided them. While Tojo was outspoken and sought political connections, the more contemplative Yamashita followed the path of a traditional military officer. He supported the idea of greater glory for the IJA, but had an aversion to the lack of discipline among the *kodoha* adherents. At one point when he commanded the 3rd Regiment, a junior officer came to him while fundraising for the *kodoha* cause. "I may give you sympathy and aid," Yamashita told him, "but not money." Like Tojo, Yamashita adhered to a view of discipline within the ranks which allowed no room for institutionalized *gekokujo*.

In the wake of the Inukai assassination in 1932, there had been numerous incidents of factional violence, including the murder of Tetsuzan Nagata himself by a *kodoha* fanatic in 1935. However, the major showdown between *kodoha* and *toseiha* came in February 1936 with the revolution which was called for in the *kodoha* creed. A coup launched by around 1,500 conspirators attempted to sweep the government of centrists.

It would later be called the "February 26 Incident," or the "Young Officers Revolt," but the conspirators called it the "Showa Restoration," naming it after Emperor Hirohito's reign, designated as "Showa," and using the term "Restoration" to show that they wished a restoration of strict imperial rule that was like nothing seen in Japan since the Meiji Restoration.

Targeted for assassination was a long list of politicians that was headed by Prime Minister Keisule Okada. An admiral in the IJN reserve, he had supported the 1930 London Naval Treaty while he was on active duty. Okada escaped and went into hiding, but General Jotaro Watanabe, inspector general of IJA training, one of the most important posts in the IJA, was killed in a gun battle inside his home while his nine-year-old-daughter watched. The rebels even planned to occupy the Imperial Palace.

Major General Tomoyuki Yamashita, in his capacity as chief of military affairs at Imperial General Headquarters, and therefore responsible for mobilization, learned of the coup at 6:20 am when he received a frantic phone call from the Ministry of War. Their building was surrounded. When Yamashita reached the home of War Minister Yoshiyuki Kawashima, the rebels were already there, and demanding that he take their demands for a total military state to the emperor. They imagined that he would support the revolt when he learned that they were still fiercely loyal to him personally – even if not his government, which they perceived as weak.

Yamashita accompanied Kawashima to the Imperial Palace, where Yamashita suggested that the mutineers would respect Hirohito's orders if he demanded that they stand down. He flatly refused to negotiate with the rebels. Yamashita wound up in the unenviable position as mediator between the Ministry of War and the rebels, working vainly to defuse the situation. After four days, the emperor finally took Yamashita's advice, ordering the revolting officers back to their barracks. It worked. No officer would disobey the emperor, no matter how much of a *gekokujan* he was.

Both Okada and Kawashima survived the coup, but resigned a few days later, replaced respectively by Foreign Minister Koki Hirota and Count Hisaichi Terauchi. A general and a *kodoha* follower, Terauchi was the son of Field Marshal Count Masatake Terauchi, who had served as both prime minister and minister of war earlier in the century. The younger Terauchi would play a key role on the Southern Road during World War II.

More than 100 men, mostly non-commissioned officers, were court-martialed for their roles in the February 26 Incident, but most of the heads that rolled were figurative. There were numerous forced resignations, but only 19 death sentences. According to separate accounts later related by Ben-Ami Shillony and Richard Storry, Hisaichi Terauchi remarked that if all the officers who had supported the mutiny had been forced to resign, there would not have been enough high-ranking officers left to replace them.

While his colleague Yamashita was in the thick of things, Hideki Tojo watched from afar, monitoring the dispatches as he paced the floor in Manchukuo. In his post as Kempeitai commander for the Kwantung Army, the anti-*gekokujo* Tojo was tasked by General Minami with using his far-reaching police powers to ensure that the Kwantung Army remained loyal to Imperial General Headquarters and did not join in the mutiny. It was an ironic turn considering that the Kwantung Army and the IJA had spent most of the previous decade at odds with one another.

Tojo was so effective in executing his duties that he was promoted to lieutenant general by the end of his years abroad, and was chief of staff of the Kwantung Army by March 1937. As for Yamashita, his role as middleman during the Young Officers Revolt had ingratiated him to neither side, and he readily accepted the offer of a transfer to Korea to get out of the political maelstrom in Tokyo.

Today, the Young Officers Revolt is probably the most overlooked major turning point on the road to World War II. It sent shock waves through the IJA and altered the culture within it. The hard line that existed between the *kodoha* and *toseiha* blurred and faded. The former faction had seen the folly of open revolt, while the center of gravity among the more methodical *toseiha* bloc drifted even farther toward hardcore militarism.

Among the civilian politicians, the center of gravity drifted from the cautious pacifism represented by the assassinated Tsuyoshi Inukai to the aggressive empire-building philosophy represented by Fumimaro Konoe, who took office in June 1937. The revolving door of weak prime ministers between Inukai and Konoe tacitly – and necessarily, given the political climate of the times – paid lip service to the military, but for Konoe, militarism was fundamental to his view of a powerful and assertive Japan. Konoe reached back into Japan's mythical past to the reign of the legendary Emperor Jimmu, who had conceived the ancient principle of *Hakko ichiu*, or "the eight corners of the world under one roof." This became an important principle of Konoe's doctrine of *Shintaisei*, or New Order, which he first described in December 1938, and which guided Japanese foreign policy over the coming years. For Konoe, the one roof was Japan, the eight corners were Asia. In 1940, Japan celebrated the 2,600th anniversary of Jimmu's rule by, among other things, erecting the 120-foot Hakko Ichiu Pillar in the city of Miyazaki on Kyushu, Jimmu's ancient capital. This edifice, which still exists as the centerpiece of a peace park, became a monument to Japanese expansionism.

In June of 1940, Japanese Foreign Minister Hachiro Arita gave a name to the Asia under Japan's roof that was to be formed under the New Order declared by Konoe. He called for a self-sufficient bloc of Asian nations led by Japan and free of Western powers which he termed the Greater East Asia Co-Prosperity Sphere (Dai-to-a Kyoeiken).

CHAPTER 3

THE FIRST BRIDGES ON THE ROAD TO WAR

To loosely paraphrase the Chinese proverb, it can be said that the road to war, like the road to the IJA's invincible years, began with a single bridge.

The bridge was the seventeenth-century stone Lugou bridge, known in the West as the "Marco Polo Bridge," because the Venetian explorer had written of a predecessor bridge in the same location in the thirteenth century. Spanning the Yongding River about a dozen miles southwest of the center of Beijing, it was a major thoroughfare connecting the former (until 1912) and future (after 1949) capital of China with the south of the country. In 1902, after the Boxer Rebellion, the Japanese had been allowed to occupy the area and to post troops at rail junctions.

On the night of July 7, 1937, Japanese troops had just wrapped up nighttime maneuvers when shots were fired from a Chinese position nearby.

By 1937, open warfare between Japan and China was being perceived as probable, and with 20–20 hindsight, inevitable. On one hand, there was Fumimaro Konoe's doctrine of *Hakko ichiu*, which explicitly asserted that China should lie submissively beneath Japan's roof. On the other hand, Chiang Kai-shek and his Kuomintang

Republic of China government were emboldened by having received a great deal of support in terms of both weapons and training from Germany, Japan's future ally, and the Soviet Union, Japan's perpetual antagonist. At home, Chiang had finally – if temporarily – patched up his differences with the Communists, who were the biggest internal threat to Kuomintang rule.

"Peace is achieved," Zhou Enlai said in an interview cited by John Toland. He continued,

> There is now no fighting between us. We have the opportunity to participate in the actual preparations for the defensive war against Japan. As to the problem of achieving democracy, this aim has only begun to be realized... One must consider the anti-Japanese war preparations and democracy like the two wheels of a rickshaw, for example. That is to say, the preparation for the anti-Japanese war comes first, and following it, the movement for democracy – which can push the former forward.

On the night of July 7, 1937, when the shots rang out, officers on both sides intervened to calm things down, but just as this seemed to have worked, there were more shots, and a rapid escalation of gunfire on both sides. That which might have been allowed to de-escalate into a continued uneasy ceasefire was allowed to mushroom out of control.

In numerous previous incidents, starting with the 1931 Mukden Incident, the politicians in Tokyo had gone head to head with the generals to restore calm. But Fumimaro Konoe was not like his compromising predecessors. Both he and Chiang Kai-shek ordered more troops into the area. Cannons and machine guns were brought to bear and the situation devolved into a firefight that continued for several days, and led to a Japanese offensive which captured Beijing within a month.

The 1937 Marco Polo Bridge Incident marked the beginning of the Second Sino-Japanese War – though in Japan this war has always been called "the China Incident" – which would continue until World War II, and thereafter as part of that conflict until 1945.

Through all those years, especially in 1937, the China Incident was a lopsided affair, in which the Japanese consistently held battlefield superiority, but in which the very geographic scale of China prevented total victory.

Japanese strategy, however, called for occupation, not of China's land mass, but its coastline, its ports, and its major cities. Shanghai, both a major port and China's largest city (with 1.5 million people) was attacked on August 13.

Within the next several days, the Imperial General Headquarters in Tokyo signaled that the China Incident would be a major war, formally activating specific area commands for operations within China. These included the Shanghai Expeditionary Army (Shanahi Haken Gun), and the North China Area Army (Kita Shina Homen Gun), an army group that would ultimately contain three full field armies. In the years before 1941, the war in China would provide a large proportion of the IJA officer corps with its baptism of fire.

On November 7, with the battle of Shanghai coming to a climax and continued operations planned, Japan formed the Central China Area Army by augmenting the Shanghai Expeditionary Army with the IJA 10th Army. Chiang Kai-shek, his armies routed and his government continually on the run, retreated to Chungking (now Chongqing).

The Japanese occupied Canton (now Guanzhou) in October, and by the end of November Shanghai had been fully occupied after weeks of bloody, house-to-house fighting. By the end of December, the Japanese Central China Area Army had captured Nanking, the globally recognized capital of the Republic of China. Thereafter, there ensued a massacre of civilians, lasting many weeks, which has been called "the Rape of Nanking." Around a quarter of a million people – the exact number will never be known – were murdered by large numbers of undisciplined IJA troops.

This orgy of violence, expressly forbidden by IJA orders, ran contrary to the image of discipline and professionalism which the IJA had long attempted to nurture. An example of the extremes of *gekokujo* run amok, this appalling behavior would rear its head again and again before 1945.

Widely reported by Western journalists at the time, the Rape of Nanking turned Western public opinion – even in Nazi Germany – against Japan, and caused shockwaves of fear throughout East Asia. It was time to question the benevolence of the "Asia for Asiatics" rhetoric.

"There was no buffer zone in their thinking between the transcendental and the empirical – between the chrysanthemum and the sword," writes John Toland, who lived in Japan after the war, learned the language, married a Japanese woman, and attempted to interpret the motives of those in the Japanese armed forces who became so incomprehensibly brutal.

> Within the Japanese, metaphysical intuition and animalistic, instinctive urges lay side by side. Thus philosophy was brutalized and brutality was philosophized. The assassinations and other bloody acts committed by the rebels [of the 1936 revolt] were inspired by idealism; and the [IJA] soldiers who sailed to China [in 1937] to save the Orient for the Orient ended by slaughtering thousands of fellow Orientals in Nanking.

Indeed, Nanking was another milepost on the road to World War II because Japanese aggression in China would result later in the United States turning the economic screws on Japan, which was growing desperate for natural resources. Ironically, the metals and petrochemicals which the Japanese sought were needed to support their growing land war in China.

In 1940, with the Japanese now firmly and comfortably in control of China's important cities and ports, Japan moved to consolidate and legitimize its conquest by installing and recognizing a "Reorganized National Government of China," as a rival to Chiang Kai-shek's own Republic of China government. After all, it was the Japanese, not Chiang, who controlled China's major population centers, from Shanghai to Hankow to Guanzhou to Beijing, as well as most of northeast China. To rule its own version of the Republic of China as its head of state, Japan picked Wang Jingwei, a former Kuomintang ally of Chiang who had decided to side with the invaders.

Lieutenant General Hideki Tojo, chief of staff of the Kwantung Army in 1937, was never directly involved in the China Incident. His next posting after the Kwantung Army had been back to Imperial General Headquarters as inspector general of the Imperial Japanese Army Air Force (IJAAF), a job for which he was arguably unsuited, given that he was a ground warfare man, not an airman. In retrospect, this brief posting can be seen as an exercise in broadening the experience of a promising officer as he moved up through the command hierarchy.

Major General Tomoyuki Yamashita, meanwhile, went to China a year after the China Incident began. When it started in July 1937, Yamashita was in command of 4th Division, which had been a component of the Kwantung Army since February 1937. In November of that year, he was promoted to lieutenant general. On July 15, 1938, a year after the China Incident had begun, Yamashita was assigned to the North China Area Army, headquartered in Beijing, as its chief of staff. With most of the action in Japan's new war taking place within the jurisdiction of the Central China Area Army, the activities which consumed Yamashita's new command involved mainly counterinsurgency operations against Chinese resistors to Japanese rule who ran the gamut from the most ardent Nationalists to the most zealous Communists.

Though serving as the chief of an army group was a significant position within the IJA, Yamashita yearned to be where the action was. In retrospect, it is hard to imagine why a man would have wanted to be associated with Nanking, but at the time, Nanking was the front line in the *Hakko ichiu* holy war aimed at imposing the new order of *Shintaisei* upon the Chinese – whether or not they knew that they wanted it.

He confided to Lieutenant General Shigeru Sawada, an old friend from the Kainan military school,

> When I was posted to Korea ... I felt I had been given a tactful promotion
> but that in fact my career was over. Even when I was given my first
> fighting command in North China, I still felt I had no future in the

Army, so I was always in the front line where the bullets flew thickest. I sought only a place to die.

It was a window into the soul of a man who had apparently been battling depression all his life, and who believed his career was over.

Yamashita and Tojo had both moved on from the Kwantung Army, a force that was preoccupied with its northern frontier. As the focus of IJA operations turned south in 1937, that northern frontier was about to come alive with an ongoing conflict with roots that ran back to the turn of the century.

The intensity of the competition for territory in the Far East which had led to the Russo-Japanese War three decades earlier had not diminished after the Russian Empire of the Tsars was superseded by the Soviet Union. Indeed, border conflicts had been an ongoing reality along the border between Japan's puppet Manchukuo, and the Soviet puppet, Mongolia. This is why new army groups were created for the 1937 war with China while the Kwantung Army stayed put in Manchuria as a deterrent to Soviet ambitions.

In the first decade after the declaration of the Soviet Union in 1922, relations with Japan had been relatively congenial, but they deteriorated after 1932, manifested by more than 400 border skirmishes, mainly based on discrepancies over admittedly indistinct borders, over the next four years. The situation naturally worsened when Japan joined with Nazi Germany in the Anti-Comintern Pact of 1936.

The most serious incident to date began on July 29, 1938 when Japanese troops penetrated disputed, Soviet-occupied, territory near Lake Khasan about 80 miles southwest of Vladivostok. Japanese intelligence had erroneously reported the unpreparedness of the Soviet Far East Army, and the latter achieved a decisive victory. Within two weeks, the Japanese withdrew, asking for a ceasefire.

Overshadowing Lake Khasan, the biggest conflict between the two Far East neighbors since the Russo-Japanese War took place on a river called Khalkhyn Gol near the intersection of the borders of Mongolia, Manchukuo, and the Soviet Union. Known to the Soviets as the battle of

Khalkhyn Gol, and to the Japanese as the Nomonhan Incident, after a nearby village, this full-scale border war began on May 11, 1939 with a skirmish between Mongolian and Manchukuo cavalry, and wound down on the last day of August with a decisive Soviet defeat of the Japanese.

An undeclared war that was overshadowed by what was to come in World War II and by what was then happening in China, the Nomonhan Incident is frequently omitted from the history books. Nevertheless, it was an important tactical precursor to World War II in the use of massed tank formations, and extensive tactical airpower operations. It cost each side – by their own estimates – around 9,000 deaths, although alternative estimates run into five figures for Japanese losses.

The contest resulted in the total defeat of the Japanese 6th Army, and a victory by Soviet General (later Marshal) Georgi Zhukov, who was later the victorious leader of Soviet forces in World War II. The only military man to have been awarded the Hero of the Soviet Union decoration four times, Zhukov earned his first at Khalkhyn Gol.

Japan's resounding defeat made a big impression on the Chinese, who had been consistently beaten by the IJA for two years. Weaknesses in the IJA had now been revealed. At home, the defeat brought down the government of Prime Minister Kiichiro Hiranuma, who had come to office in January 1939 when Fumimaro Konoe stepped down from the first of an eventual three terms.

The defeat of the much heralded Kwantung Army also made a big impression on the IJA and the Imperial General Headquarters. It was a wake up call that resulted in the end of the Kwantung Army as a virtually autonomous component of the IJA. As had happened closer to home in the wake of the 1936 Revolt, tighter command controls were imposed, and attempts were made to bring the simmering culture of *gekokujo* into line.

It was none too soon for the Chrysanthemum Empire and its army to get their house into order. Earth-shattering events were on the western horizon.

Even as Zhukov was delivering his final punishment to the Kwantung Army, his bosses in the Kremlin were signing their non-aggression pact with Adolf Hitler. On September 1, 1939, Hitler's legions swarmed into Poland from the west, marking the start of World War II. On September 17, with the Japanese having formally ceased firing on the Khalkhyn Gol front, Soviet armies streamed into Poland from the east to occupy what they had been awarded in the secret protocols to their non-aggression pact.

Stalin turned his attention away from the Far East for the next five years, the bloodiest of the twentieth century. However, on the Manchukuo border, the Japanese never forgot Khalkhyn Gol. The IJA maintained hundreds of thousands of troops on quiet alert through all those five long years, even as their troops pursued other goals which had yet to be articulated during that Manchurian summer in 1939.

CHAPTER 4

THE WORLD AT WAR

Lieutenant General Hideki Tojo, the outspoken military officer with a penchant for politics, finally began his second career as a politician on July 22, 1940. As Japan's new minister of war, he did not even have to hang up his IJA uniform.

The humiliation at Khalkhyn Gol had put the final nail in the coffin of any remaining pretense of civilian government in Japan. The administration of Prime Minister Kiichiro Hiranuma collapsed in August 1939, and he was succeeded by a revolving door of military men. Neither General Nobuyuki Abe nor Admiral Mitsumasa Yonai remained longer than six months. By the summer of 1940, there was a groundswell of support, mainly from IJA hardliners, for the return of Fumimaro Konoe, who was then serving as chairman of the emperor's privy council.

Beyond the narrow world of internal Japanese and IJA politics, one of the biggest issues of that summer had to do with Nazi Germany – its incredible string of astounding military victories in the first ten months of World War II, and the question of whether Japan should formally ally itself with Hitler's victorious Third Reich.

With the passage of time, we know that Japan did do so – and indeed how the alliance played out over the course of the war. As such, it is hard to image that it was not a foregone conclusion, however in the summer of 1940, it could have gone either way. Both Abe and Yonai had opposed such an alliance, citing Germany's non-aggression pact with the Soviet Union, Japan's archenemy. In fact, Yonai favored stronger ties with the United States and the United Kingdom. However, the momentum of global events in the summer of 1940 had taken on a life of its own.

With the defeat of Denmark, Norway, Holland, and Belgium, then France, one of Europe's preeminent powers – in about two months – Germany controlled virtually all of Europe from the Arctic Circle to the Pyrenees, and through its relationship with Fascist Italy and Fascist Spain, it had *de facto* control of most of the Mediterranean shoreline. The stunning successes of the victorious Wehrmacht had won many fans among Japanese militarists. Japan, they reasoned, should back a winner.

On July 22, one month after France inked its armistice with Germany, Hitler danced his famous victory jig at Compiègne. That same day, Mitsumasa Yonai handed the reins of power to Fumimaro Konoe. Two of the new prime minister's first acts were to summon Lieutenant General Hideki Tojo to his side as minister of war, and to appoint Yosuke Matsuoka as his new foreign minister. This man had been the man who had literally marched Japan out of the League of Nations in 1933. A loquacious orator, Matsuoka had a unique understanding of the West which derived from his having spent many of his early years in the United States, where he had graduated from the University of Oregon. Matsuoka was also an old friend of Tojo's, having got to know him while they were both posted to Manchukuo. Both appointments, Tojo and Matsuoka, were particularly symbolic at an important turning point in the lead-up to Japan's involvement in World War II.

Three months later, on September 27, the decision to ally Japan with the Third Reich was made and cast in stone. Konoe's man in Berlin, Saburo Kurusu, sat down with Count Galeazzo Ciono, Mussolini's foreign minister, and Adolf Hitler himself, to sign the Tripartite Pact that created the Rome–Berlin–Tokyo Axis. Through this, the people who had essentially conquered Europe gave Japan a green light to establish "a new order in Greater East Asia."

National Socialist Germany and Imperial Japan had a great deal in common. Both were militarily and economically powerful, and both had avaricious territorial ambitions. The Japanese vision of the Far East was like the German vision of Europe. Each saw itself as the father figure, or big brother, in a family of nations which would be centrally controlled by itself.

Through 1940, Germany and Japan were still in the opening phase of empire building. It was clear to them, and to the rest of the world, that their empires were still works in progress, but thus far, the work had gone well for them. As in the Far East, Japan had taken Manchuria from China and remade it as Manchukuo, so Germany had incorporated places from Alsace to the Sudetenland, and all of Austria, into Germany itself.

As a politician, Fumimaro Konoe had a great deal in common with Adolf Hitler. Both were welcomed by popular opinion as they provided strong, decisive action after long periods of fragmented politics and economic stagnation. Both spoke of past national greatness, and promised to restore former glory. Both saw a future home for his people in other peoples' lands. So too did both Hitler and Konoe swear that their respective nations had the right, and indeed the duty, to be the dominant power, the big brother, on their respective continents. As within Adolf Hitler's vision of a Greater German Reich, the leaders of Imperial Japan very much considered themselves as culturally, and even racially, superior within their sphere of influence.

———

Meanwhile, as Tojo assumed his new role as minister of war, he immediately brought his old colleague, Tomoyuki Yamashita, home from China to assume Tojo's previous post as inspector general of the IJAAF. Like Tojo, Yamashita was a land army man, not an aviator.

"I have no knowledge of aviation," Yamashita admitted affably in an interview at the War Ministry after he formally accepted the job. "As Air Force Inspector, I feel like a duck among eagles, so please treat me as gently as possible." Someone asked him about Germany's Luftwaffe, which had played such an important role in the recent blitzkrieg victories. Knowing that the official Tojo line was to cater to the Germans, Yamashita complimented their air force.

"It has made a great success in the blitzkrieg because the German people have many great scientists," Yamashita told the assembled media. "An air force is like a clock. The fingers move smoothly across the dial, but behind it is a complicated mechanism, a mass of scientific knowledge. In my job as head of the Japanese [Army] Air Force, I intend to take care not only of the watch face but of the more important works behind it." The smoothly moving IJA airmen would well serve their counterparts on the ground in the coming war.

In December, after the ink had dried on the Tripartite Pact, it was time for a high-level military delegation from Japan to call on the leaders of the Third Reich. Their mission was a practical one, essentially to find out how, in terms of weapons and tactics, the Germans had accomplished what they had. To lead this delegation, Tojo picked Yamashita. We may never know whether this was because of a special trust and confidence that Tojo had in a man whom he had long known, or an excuse to keep a potential rival out of Tokyo.

Yamashita's party, numbering about 40 and consisting mainly of military men – from both the IJA and IJN – with technical expertise rather than political ambitions, traveled west across the Soviet Union, which was, at the time, still on non-belligerent terms with the Axis.

Hitler greeted his new allies with pomp and circumstance, marching bands and streets bedecked with banners which blazed with swastikas or rising suns. The Führer greeted Yamashita personally and cordially at the Reich Chancellory. Afterward, Yamashita told the media what he assumed he was expected to tell them, quipping that "I feel that Hitler's mind is spiritual, transcending material plans. The Führer told me that he has been attracted to Japan since boyhood and has promised to instruct Germans to bind themselves eternally to the Japanese spirit."

Hitler probably had in fact said something to that effect, and Yamashita dutifully joined his host in pretending that it was true. To his staff, however, Yamashita admitted that he found Hitler to be "an unimpressive little man [who] may be a great orator on a platform, with his gestures and flamboyant way of speaking, but standing behind his desk listening, he seems much more like a clerk."

Luftwaffe chief Hermann Göring took Yamashita on a tour of occupied France, in which they visited the air bases along the English Channel coast from which the Luftwaffe was still waging its air war against the Royal Air Force (RAF). As he watched Göring's Messerschmitts dueling with RAF Spitfires, Yamashita realized that the Luftwaffe had already lost the Battle of Britain and that he was witnessing a stalemate – the high-water mark of the celebrated blitzkrieg.

In Berlin, Hitler and Göring told Yamashita and his entourage that they were anxious to have Japan join the war against Britain, and – under the assumption that eventual American involvement was inevitable – the United States as well. According to Yamashita's diary, as quoted by John Deane Potter, he told the Führer that:

My country is still fighting in China, and we must finish that war as soon as possible. We are also afraid that Russia may attack us in Manchuria. This is no time for us to declare war on other countries. The main aim for which we have come to your country is to inspect your armed forces and see how we can improve our own defenses.

In March 1941, while Yamashita was still touring sites of military interest in Germany, Foreign Minister Yosuke Matsuoka arrived in Berlin for his own round of meetings with Hitler, and to toast the Tripartite Pact. As in their conversations with Yamashita, Hitler and Göring were not shy about bringing up the subject of the Japanese capturing Singapore from the British. It took no more than a cursory glance at a map of Southeast Asia to understand the strategic importance of the island bastion, but such a campaign did not yet figure in Japanese strategic planning. As Yamashita had been, Matsuoka was as evasive as possible on the topic.

However, Matsuoka found his opposite number, Foreign Minister Joachim von Ribbentrop, to be candidly outspoken on another topic of mutual interest. When Matsuoka told him that Japan, like Germany, intended to sign a non-aggression pact with the Soviet Union, Ribbentrop bluntly told him "Just remember, the USSR never gives anything for nothing."

A week later, Matsuoka had signed this deal, was being wined and dined at the Kremlin, and was toasting Stalin personally. The next day, Stalin personally saw Matsuoka off at the train station with a bear hug and a happy prediction that "There is nothing to fear in Europe now that there is a Japan–Soviet neutrality pact."

Stalin saw the pact as a guarantee that Hitler would not attack the Soviet Union. Matsuoka saw the pact as a means of causing the United States to think twice about challenging Japan's territorial ambitions. Matsuoka even fantasized about following up with a summit conference with the Americans at which he could deal from a position strengthened by his pact with Stalin.

As Matsuoka headed home, Yamashita remained, pursuing his efforts to learn what he could of Germany's military-industrial secrets. In his diary, he wrote that:

> [Hitler's] promise to show all [Germany's advanced technology] was meaningless. There were several secret pieces of information which he did not want us to know about. Whenever I tried to persuade Hitler or the German General Staff to show us certain things, like radar, about which we had a rudimentary knowledge, the conversation always turned tactfully to something else.

However, as Potter explains, Yamashita and

> his air adviser, General Harada, got "lost" on a journey of inspection and, with his experts, made for the secret factory in the forest. When the Japanese drove up, no one questioned them. It was assumed that the visit was official, and the German war factories had been ordered to

throw themselves open to the Japanese generals. Harada was shown everything in the place; his experts took vital notes and carefully scrutinized every piece of apparatus. They came away with the secret of radar.

Potter also notes that Yamashita made a personal visit to the Austrian capital, and that "his staff were amused to notice that he kept a little bottle of hair dye which he used – occasionally, particularly before his trip to Vienna." Here, he met with his old friend Kitty, with whom he had been intimate a dozen years earlier.

Including a side trip to call on Mussolini in Rome, Yamashita and the others remained in Hitler's Europe for six months. They might have remained even longer, had they not received an urgent summons back to Berlin from the Führer himself. It was the middle of June 1941, and Yamashita was told, with utmost secrecy, that if he and his people were going to return to Japan by rail via the Trans-Siberian railway, as they had come, they should be off right away. Yamashita's men took the advice, although the IJN delegation remained in Berlin.

On June 22, even as the Japanese generals were crossing the frontier into Manchukuo, Hitler launched Operation *Barbarossa*, and his mighty Wehrmacht took on the Soviet Union. The admirals were compelled to travel to Argentina aboard a cramped German U-Boat before catching a passenger ship back to Japan.

CHAPTER 5

TWO BUILDING BLOCKS FALL INTO PLACE

The first jewels to be placed in the crown of Japan's vision of all Southeast Asia beneath the single roof of Imperial Japan were added almost painlessly.

When a Japanese strategic planner looked along the Southern Road toward the southeast corner of continental Asia, and to the tens of thousands of islands that lay between China and Australia, he would have seen a map awash with the last great vestiges of nineteenth-century colonialism east of British India.

There were the Americans in the Philippines, the French in Indochina (comprising Vietnam, Laos, and Cambodia) the British in Malaya, Burma, and Singapore; and the Netherlands in those roughly 17,500 islands that constituted the Dutch East Indies. Among all these constituencies, there was a single, lone, independent country – the Kingdom of Thailand, known officially as Siam until 1939.

Meanwhile, of the four colonial powers dominating the rest of Southeast Asia and adjacent islands, two had been defeated and occupied by the Germans in the spring of 1940. However, France and the Netherlands each possessed a distinctly different status.

The Netherlands had been occupied, but had refused to accept defeat. Queen Wilhelmina escaped to London, where she formed a government in exile and allied it with the United Kingdom, and later also with the United States. With the queen's government still functional, albeit in exile, the Dutch East Indies – with a land area more than 50 times that of the Netherlands – as well as Dutch military assets there, remained outside Axis control.

The Royal Netherlands Navy (Koninklijk Marine) fleet in the Indies was unaffected by the defeat in Europe. The Royal Netherlands East Indies Army (Koninklijk Nederlands Indisch Leger, KNIL) and the Military Aviation of the Royal Netherlands East Indies Army (Militaire Luchtvaart van het Koninklijk Nederlands-Indisch Leger, ML-KNIL) also remained intact and ready to face the Japanese.

Meanwhile, one had a choice of two Frances. Charles DeGaulle and his ragtag band had gone to London to form a government in exile. However, DeGaulle's "Free French" were "France" in name only, and France itself was no longer free. They had their place in the world as a beaten nation. Conquered and subdued by the Third Reich, 60 percent of its land area – including Paris – was under German military occupation. The Third Republic, formed to govern France after the fall of Napoleon III 70 years earlier, had collapsed. In its place, a new entity called the French State was established in the resort town of Vichy in July 1940 to rule the 40 percent of France not occupied. To lead this shadow of former glory, France picked 84-year-old Marshal Henri Philippe Pétain, a World War I hero who had served for a month as France's last prime minister before the armistice.

Vichy France was allowed by Germany to retain nominal control of the prewar French Empire, though French actions and activities throughout the world were now subject to German foreign policy approval.

The jewels in the French colonial crown were in North Africa, especially Algeria. These, and other French possessions and mandates in Africa and the Middle East, received a great deal more attention from the pre- and post-armistice French governments than did distant Indochina, which was half a world away – despite the fact that Indochina was rich in tin, tungsten, rubber, and rice.

One of the first actions undertaken by the Vichy government with regard to Indochina was to replace the existing governor general, General Georges Catroux of the French Army, with Vice Admiral Jean Decoux, the commander of French naval forces in the region. While both men instinctively opposed the humiliating armistice imposed on France by the Germans, Decoux was willing to swear his allegiance to Vichy. Catroux stayed on for a time, but later left Indochina to join Charles DeGaulle's Free French, while Decoux remained to face the Japanese.

Toward the end of June 1940, the new governor general was visited by military delegations from both Japan and the United Kingdom, both of which arrived with demands. The Japanese were concerned about supplies reaching China by way of a railroad that ran from the Vietnamese port of Haiphong to Kunming in China. The British were concerned about the French fleet falling into German or Japanese hands, and insisted that French warships be surrendered to the Royal Navy (RN). Decoux, asked to deliver his meager fleet to Singapore, stalled. Meanwhile, the bulk of the French Navy had taken refuge in the harbor at Mers-el-Kehbir in Algeria, and did not budge. On July 3, the RN attacked, destroying most of the ships and killing more than 1,200 French sailors and poisoning relations with its former French ally. This certainly soured Decoux's willingness to work with the British.

Decoux's biggest concern, though, was not France's former ally, but the Japanese. The signing of the Tripartite Pact, giving Japan a green light to establish "a new order in Greater East Asia," was still nearly three months away, but France's newfound status as a defeated vassal of Germany was interpreted by the Japanese as an open door through which to demand concessions, including the basing of troops and aircraft in Vietnam as part of the ongoing campaign against China.

When Decoux refused, Japan responded with intimidation, making it no secret that it was organizing an invasion force, using Hainan Island as the staging base. In the United States, where opposition to Japanese militarism was a key plank of foreign policy, there was an outcry against the bullying of the French in Indochina. The US Congress moved quickly, passing the Export Control Act on July 5. At the time, the United States was the world's largest oil producer, and a major source for Japan, who possessed domestic sources of coal, but not petroleum. A sizable proportion of Japanese petroleum imports came from the still-neutral Americans. The new law curtailed such shipments and greatly limited the export of other goods, including metals and aircraft ports.

Nevertheless, Japan kept up the pressure. Decoux stalled, working with the French ambassador in Tokyo, who in turn was negotiating with Foreign Minister Yosuke Matsuoka. Finally, on September 22, on the eve of the Tripartite Pact signing ceremony, a deal was reached whereby Japan would respect the internal affairs of Indochina if granted limited access to it for the purposes of waging the war against China.

However, the Japanese ignored the details, and the IJA 5th Division under Lieutenant General Akihito Nakamura, operating out of southern China, immediately invaded Vietnam to seize the railroads. They were met by a brigade comprised of colonial and French Foreign Legion troops at a place called Lang Son, which would be the point where the Vietnamese were to stop a Chinese invasion nearly four decades later in 1979. The French held out only until September 25, after which the Japanese had a clear road all the way to Hanoi.

The following day, the Japanese invasion force that had been organized earlier as an intimidation ploy, came ashore south of Haiphong. Supported by naval airpower flying from the carrier *Hiryu* (Flying Dragon), which was later part of the Pearl Harbor attack force, the Japanese landed troops and tanks and swiftly secured Haiphong and Hanoi. Within 48 hours, the great French air base at Gia Lam, constructed only four years earlier, was being readied for operations by Japanese aircraft. Parenthetically, Gia Lam would be a key operational base for Vietnamese MiG fighters during the Vietnam War three decades later.

Meanwhile, Thailand's long history of independence had not been free of the occasional conflict with Britain and France as they built and maintained their neighboring empires. During the later nineteenth century, during the reign of King Rama V, also called "Chulalongkorn the Great," Thailand had fought a long-running war with France over parts of what are now Laos and Cambodia.

Though Thailand still possessed a figurehead monarch, it was ruled by Field Marshal Plaek Phibunsongkhram (also transliterated as Pibulsonggram), who occupied the seat of prime minister. Known generally as "Pibul" or "Phibun," he was a fan of totalitarian governments such as Hitler's Germany, and he had turned Thailand into one of Japan's best friends – "ally" would be too strong a word – in the Far East. Under Phibun, Thailand had recognized Japan's puppet government in Manchukuo, and had begun equipping its armed forces with Japanese-built ships and aircraft.

Following the Fall of France, Phibun was ready to seize the opportunity to take back what his country had lost. A virtual dictator since he had masterminded the 1932 coup d'état that curbed the power of the absolute monarchy of King Rama VII (aka Prajadhipok), Phibun had fended off revolts and threats to his rule through the years. He felt his army to be up to the task of taking on an overseas detachment of the army that had capitulated to the Germans in the space of a few weeks, and had surrendered a major city and a major port to the Japanese after a few days.

France was plunged into its second war of 1940 with a series of minor skirmishes in October, shortly after the Japanese had occupied the Hanoi–Haiphong area. The fighting escalated, with the two sides trading air raids. Much to the chagrin of French fighter pilots, the crews of the Royal Thai Air Force bomber fleet, which included Japanese-built Mitsubishi Ki-21s and Ki-30s, acquitted themselves very well in strikes against Vientiane and Phnom Penh.

In a major offensive in January 1941, the Royal Thai Army managed to recapture most of their objectives in Laos, and to make serious inroads against the French in Cambodia. The French were defeated in the climactic land battle on January 16, 1941, in the vicinity of Yang Dang Khum and Phum Preav, although French Foreign Legion artillery prevented the Thai forces from pursuing the retreating French troops.

The following day, however, the French won a significant naval victory in the battle of Ko Chang, off the coast of Thailand, near the Cambodian border. Admiral Jean Decoux had ordered the light cruiser *La Motte-Piquet* and several smaller gunboats to sail from Cam Ranh Bay, north of Saigon, to attack Thai ports near the Cambodian border. The flotilla was opposed by the Japanese-built coastal defense ship, HTMS *Thonburi*, as well as a pair of Thai torpedo boats. When the battle ended, both torpedo boats had been sunk, the *Thonburi* was dead in the water, and the French ships were still seaworthy.

France won the battle of Ko Chang, but lost the war. Less than a week later after the naval victory, Japan intervened to impose a ceasefire, which compelled France to leave Thailand in control of what it had captured, and left Prime Minister Phibun owing the Japanese a favor.

CHAPTER 6

TAKING THE SOUTHERN ROAD

During the first half of 1941, while General Tomoyuki Yamashita was away, enjoying – or enduring – the hospitality of the Third Reich, great changes had been occurring in Japan. As Yamashita had been visiting the Luftwaffe bases in France – and the mysterious Kitty in Vienna – Colonel Masanobu Tsuji had been at Hainan preparing for the Nanshinron contingency, and Hideki Tojo was consolidating his power in Tokyo in a way that would culminate in his being named as prime minister on October 18, 1941.

Outside the rarified air within the Imperial Palace, Tojo was already the most powerful man in Japan well before being named to succeed Prime Minister Fumimaro Konoe. Indeed, Konoe, once considered one of Japan's most hawkish political leaders, had been falling out of touch with the march of events.

Although the emperor had yet to sign off on the idea, Japan was preparing for war against the United States and the United Kingdom, something which both Konoe and Foreign Minister Yosuke Matsuoka were willing to accept, but which they deeply dreaded.

In the summer of 1941, both the Northern Road and the Southern Road were still options, despite all of the momentum which propelled Japan southward. At a meeting with Emperor Hirohito on July 2, the Southern Road plan, a document entitled *Outline of National Policies in View of Present Developments*, was presented for discussion. It began with plans to pressure the Vichy French to allow full access to Indochina for Japanese troops. Konoe expressed his reservations, as did Matsuoka, who explained that he doubted Japan could accomplish this goal in Indochina diplomatically. Yoshimichi Hara, the president of the Privy Council, went so far as to point out that Germany's invasion of the Soviet Union ten days earlier, which seemed to be massively successful, presented Japan with a golden opportunity to take the Northern Road, attacking the Soviets as they were being hammered into submission by the Wehrmacht.

Matsuoka had signed a non-aggression pact with Stalin, and Konoe still yearned for a similar deal with the Americans. In November 1940, he had sent Kichisaburo Nomura, a former IJN admiral, to Washington as the Japanese ambassador with orders to negotiate a neutrality treaty. He even spoke privately about setting up a face-to-face meeting with President Franklin Roosevelt. There were back channel contacts and rumors, but Nomura made no substantial headway with Secretary of State Cordell Hull.

The Roosevelt Administration, strongly supportive of Chiang Kai-shek and his Nationalist Chinese Government, was increasing economic sanctions on the Japanese. Against the backdrop of ongoing Japanese atrocities in China – beginning with the infamous Rape of Nanking in 1937 – American public opinion was more strongly against Japan than Germany. In the early part of 1941, Americans were divided between isolationists and interventionists, with the latter wishing to actively support Britain against Germany, and/or China against Japan. There was virtually no support for the Axis – especially after *Barbarossa*.

With the Export Control Act and other measures, the Americans were tightening the screws of economic sanctions against Japan. In Japan, the momentum was slipping from the hands of diplomats, into those of the military, and the winds of that momentum blew south.

Even before Vichy France was presented with an ultimatum about Indochina, Yosuke Matsuoka got cold feet. His apprehension about pulling the United States into the war was verging on panic. Tojo demanded that Konoe sack him, and this was taken up at a cabinet meeting on July 16 that Matsuoka did not attend. The vote was unanimous. Matsuoka was replaced by Admiral Teijiro Toyoda, who issued the ultimatum to Vichy, giving them a deadline of July 24 to allow Japanese troops unfettered access to all of Indochina, and the full use of naval and military facilities.

Matsuoka was wrong about diplomacy and Vichy. Much to everyone's surprise, the French readily agreed to the demands. In Europe, Vichy had other pressing concerns, and in Indochina itself, Governor General Jean Decoux was facing a growing challenge from Communist-inspired insurgents called the Viet Minh (Vietnam Independence League), who chose 1941 to begin their insurgency campaign against French rule.

Meanwhile in Washington, DC, Roosevelt and Hull were livid, considering Japan's "invitation" into Indochina to be an invasion – and a Vichy–German-sponsored invasion at that. Unbeknown to the Japanese, the American cryptanalysis program code-named "Magic" had begun breaking into some Japanese diplomatic – but not military – communications in 1940, and the American military leadership did have something of an idea of what was behind Japanese actions.

On July 26, Roosevelt signed Executive Order 8832, "freezing Japanese assets in the United States in the same manner in which assets of various European countries were frozen on June 14, 1941." The countries affected by the order in June included Albania, Andorra, Austria, Czechoslovakia, Danzig, Finland, Germany, Italy, Liechtenstein, Poland, Portugal, San Marino, Spain, Sweden, Switzerland, and the Soviet Union. Earlier orders, dating back to April 8, 1940, had frozen the assets of Axis and Axis-occupied countries including Belgium, Bulgaria, Denmark, Estonia, France, Greece, Hungary, Latvia, Lithuania, Luxembourg, the Netherlands, Norway, Romania, and Yugoslavia.

As the text of Executive Order 8832 read, "this measure, in effect, brings all financial and import and export trade transactions in which

Japanese interests are involved under the control of the Government, and imposes criminal penalties for violation of the Order."

Trade between the United States and Japan, curtailed by the Export Control Act, came abruptly to a halt. The *New York Times* called it "the most drastic blow short of war."

Just *how* drastic was already apparent to Japanese military planners. The order essentially cut off Japan's petroleum supply, and made the Southern Road inevitable. The Dutch East Indies were then the fourth largest oil exporter after the United States, Iran, and Romania, none of which were now accessible to Japan. Controlling the oil fields of the Indies was essential both to Japan's war machine and to its domestic economy.

In his memoirs, Masanobu Tsuji cites a study that had been recently published, concluding that

> lack of liquid fuel would be fatal to Japan. In 1941 the Army and Navy had in storage roughly 1,170,000 kiloliters of aviation petrol [about 240 million gallons], and about 4,400,000 kiloliters of ordinary petrol [about 970 million gallons] … Allowing for maintenance of fifty Army Divisions and the full strength of the Air Force, it would be impossible to carry on war against the Soviet Union for more than a year as liquid fuel supplies would be exhausted within that time.

Indochina, which had seemed to have slipped so easily beneath the big *Hakko ichiu* roof of Japanese domination, was the key that had opened the Southern Road. For the sake of its own prosperity, Japan now desperately needed to bring the rubber plantations, mines, and oil fields of Southeast Asia under the roof of the Greater East Asia Co-Prosperity Sphere.

The Southern Road strategy, long considered in contingency planning, now began to take focus as the primary operational plan. The immediate objective was to capture Malaya and the Dutch East Indies, which contained the raw materials which were so desperately needed – and to seize Singapore, which was the keystone of British naval strategy in the Far East.

Indeed, all operations throughout Southeast Asia, especially in the Dutch East Indies, would be difficult, or even impossible, so long as the British maintained a secure base of operations at Singapore. Knowing this, the British had spent heavily in a decade-long building program aimed at transforming the 274-square-mile island into an impregnable fortress, armed and supplied so as to hold out indefinitely against any attack.

Simultaneously, the Japanese would need to neutralize the ability of the Americans to operate in the Far East, by capturing Wake Island, Guam, and the Philippines. Operations in the Pacific islands, which became so much of a focus in the actions in the coming war, and in our collective memory of the war, were considered as a buffer to protect shipping lanes between Japan and its intended conquests in Southeast Asia.

As Louis Morton writes in Chapter IV of his history of the Philippines campaign,

> the area marked for conquest formed a vast triangle, whose east arm stretched from the Kuril Islands on the north, through Wake, to the Marshall Islands. The base of the triangle was formed by a line connecting the Marshall Islands, the Bismarck Archipelago, Java, and Sumatra. The western arm extended from Malaya and southern Burma through Indochina, and thence along the China coast. The acquisition of the island-studded area would give to Japan control of the resources of southeast Asia and satisfy the national objectives in going to war. Perhaps later, if all went well, the area of conquest could be extended.

To accomplish all of this, Tojo and his fellow Southern Road proponents needed to form one more vitally essential military coalition. As Japan had allied itself with Germany, Tojo had forged an alliance for the IJA that was far more important. By 1940, strategic differences within the IJA were largely a thing of the past. However, the IJA would need to formalize a level of cooperation with its sister service – and for decades, a rival service – the IJN. It was a cooperation driven by practical necessity and the nature of the terrain. On the Northern Road, in China, Manchuria, and Siberia's doorstep, Japanese field armies fought entire campaigns hundreds of miles from the sea on land-locked battlefields. On the Southern Road, the campaign would hinge on amphibious operations at virtually every turn, and be fought on islands and on peninsulas without adequate roads. The IJA was the essential instrument of conquest, but it needed the IJN to transport it to nearly every battlefield, and provide naval gunfire as artillery support. As we shall see, this practical collaboration worked well in the early campaigns, but the institutional rivalry simmered just beneath the surface, occasionally boiling over, and was too deeply ingrained in IJA and IJN culture ever to be resolved.

Army–Navy rivalries existed within the armed forces of most countries, and still do. However, in Imperial Japan, it was an antagonism that verged on hostility. Each side jealously guarded its own turf, considering cooperation to be a show of weakness. They each maintained their own supply system, their own respective air forces, and their own intelligence apparatus.

The IJN also maintained its own land army, roughly analogous to the US Marine Corps (USMC), which is technically a component of the US Navy. In the case of the IJN, it was the Special Naval Landing Forces (Kaigun Tokubetsu Rikusentai), which were created in 1928. Though their activities ashore were greatly overshadowed by the IJA, they had nevertheless played an important role in operations against Chinese coastal cities, and during IJN actions on Chinese rivers, during the 1930s.

The Americans deliberately created a formal Joint Chiefs of Staff to streamline cooperation. This encouraged liaison at the highest levels and greatly improved relations between the Army and the Navy. By contrast, the Japanese services cooperated only when absolutely necessary, and with few exceptions, remained inherantly distrustful of one another throughout the war.

As in the IJA, the IJN was dominated by officers who believed in the projection of Japanese power throughout the Far East, but like the earlier rebel factions within the IJA, the naval officers were strongly opposed to

Japanese expansion in China, and tying down forces in Manchukuo. Like the Southern Road advocates within the IJA, and the Greater East Asia Co-Prosperity Sphere advocates in the Japanese government, they understood that Japan's future lay not in northeast Asia, but in Southeast Asia, with its great oil fields and other strategic natural resources.

Japan's naval officers understood that the key to Southeast Asia was not only controlling the sea lanes within Southeast Asia, though this was vital, but in controlling the Pacific Ocean. When it came to dominance in the Pacific, they knew that this would put the IJN head to head with the USN. As everyone knew, a key prerequisite to the Southern Road strategy was neutralizing the American ability to intervene in Southeast Asia, by fatally crippling the USN's Pacific Fleet. Only the IJN could do this.

Though they did so cautiously, aware of the potential power of the United States, the IJN had been preparing for a Pacific war ever since the Washington Naval Treaty had expired in 1936. The IJN had been the third largest navy in the world since the 1920s (after those of Britain and America) and now it was growing fast. Among the large number of warships that were pouring from Japanese shipyards while the IJA was preoccupied with China and Mongolia were new, larger and better battleships and new aircraft carriers. Among the former were the Yamato class, the largest in the world, the first of which would be commissioned in December 1941. Among the latter were the *Shukaku* (Flying Crane) and *Zuikaku* (Fortunate Crane), the most modern carriers in the world, which were launched in August and September 1941, respectively.

For years, Japanese naval strategy in the Pacific – like the naval strategy of most nations – had been dominated philosophically by the theories presented by the great naval strategist Alfred Thayer Mahan in his seminal work, *The Influence of Sea Power Upon History, 1660–1783*, published in 1890. Mahan looked at naval strategy in terms of decisive surface battles – as had been the case in naval warfare for centuries from the battle of Salamis in 480 BC to the IJN's own great victory at Tsushima in 1905. Japanese naval theorists had long prepared for such a decisive battle, the *Kantai kessen*, to take place in the Western Pacific, with the IJN having lured the USN across the ocean.

However, by 1940, another naval theorist – Admiral Isoroku Yamamoto – had come to the fore, one who advocated going deep, into the enemy's sphere of influence, and fighting the decisive battle while on the offensive, rather fighting it on the defensive close to home. Yamamoto, who had become the commander-in-chief of the IJN Combined Fleet in 1939, was an unlikely man to occupy such a crucial position in Japan's military hierarchy, given his long-running and contentious rivalry with Hideki Tojo, now consolidating his power at the uppermost levels of the Japanese government. Both men had been born in 1888, both had chosen military careers early on, and had risen quickly through the ranks. Both had served abroad during the 1920s, Tojo in Germany, and Yamamoto in the United States, where he attended Harvard, served as a naval attaché in Washington, and learned to speak English fluently. However, Tojo and Yamamoto had been at odds over Japanese strategic goals throughout their parallel careers, with Yamamoto being a seriously outspoken critic of both the Japanese incursion into China and of the Tripartite Pact.

Though he had deep reservations about a war with the United States, Yamamoto was the architect of implementing such a war forcefully and resolutely. Once convinced of the necessity of going to war with the Americans, Yamamoto was also able to bring Admiral Osami Nagano, chief of staff of the IJN – and a Pacific war skeptic – around to this way of thinking.

A strong advocate of naval airpower, Yamamoto's plan was for a daring and decisive blow against the USN nearly 4,000 miles across the Pacific, at their own analog to Singapore, the great naval base at Pearl Harbor in Hawaii.

In a meeting described by John Toland, which took place at the Imperial Palace on July 31, 1941, Admiral Nagano had cautioned Hirohito about the petroleum situation. Citing figures that were somewhat more encouraging than those in the report mentioned by Tsuji, he explained that Japan's current oil and gasoline reserves would last for 24 months, or 18 months under wartime conditions. The Dutch East Indies were essential.

"Under such circumstances, we had better take the initiative," Nagano told the monarch, echoing Yamamoto's strategic plan. He then added, "We will win."

"Will you win a great victory?" Hirohito asked. "Like the Battle of Tsushima?"

"I am sorry," the admiral admitted. "But that will not be possible."

"Then," Hirohito replied, "the war will be a desperate one."

Though the window for diplomacy was nearly closed by the summer of 1941, Konoe was eager to have Nomura continue his negotiations in Washington, still holding out hope that Japan could get what it needed in Asia without a war with the United States. Nomura met with Hull, but Roosevelt was unavailable. About a week after signing Executive Order 8832, he slipped out of Washington to meet secretly with British Prime Minister Winston Churchill off the coast of Newfoundland. A USN flotilla rendezvoused with the British on August 9. Churchill arrived aboard the HMS *Prince of Wales* – which had been part of the task force which had run down and sunk the German battleship *Bismarck* a few weeks before.

The following day, the two leaders began the talks which led to the Atlantic Charter, a document which contrasted the aspirations of democracies with those of totalitarian powers. Germany was on everyone's mind, but the two men also discussed Japan, Indochina, the Southern Road, and the likelihood of war in Southeast Asia.

As Churchill and Roosevelt had their discussions aboard the *Prince of Wales*, with the American battleship USS *Arizona* anchored nearby, nobody present could have predicted that in four months, over the space of just three days, these two formidable battleships would both be sunk – by Japanese airpower.

As Roosevelt began preparing himself psychologically for war, Prime Minister Fumimaro Konoe still held out hope for peace. Time was running out. At a meeting at the Imperial Palace on September 6, Tojo and IJA Chief of Staff Hajime Sugiyama had proposed, and Hirohito had agreed, that if diplomacy had not resolved the impasse by mid-October, Japan should move ahead with preparations for the long-anticipated war against the United States and the United Kingdom. John Toland mentions October 10 as the deadline. Postwar debriefings of Hideki Tojo have the date as October 15.

In any case, diplomacy failed to make any progress, and on October 16, Konoe submitted his resignation. Two days later, Hideki Tojo, Japan's Minister of War, was summoned to the palace by Hirohito and asked to accept a second portfolio as Prime Minister of Japan.

CHAPTER 7

FINAL PREPARATIONS

"For some time I have been patiently waiting for you to come along," Colonel Takushiro Hattori said with a wry smile when Masanobu Tsuji presented his credentials at Imperial General Headquarters on July 14, 1941, three weeks after conducting the amphibious landing exercises on Hainan. Hattori, who headed the Operations section of the General Staff, indicated that something big was in the offing, and that Tsuji was to be part of it.

The IJA was gearing up for a major war outside China, but at that time few men, and only those at the very top, knew whether the service would be taking the Northern Road, Hokushinron, or Nanshinron, toward the south. Tsuji was one of only a handful who knew the details of the extensive contingency planning for Nanshinron, and he knew that an invasion fleet was being readied for the occupation of Indochina – but he did not know for sure whether this was just a sideshow, the taking of an opportunity presented by the weakness of pitiful Vichy France, or a harbinger of major operations on the Southern Road.

As he did not yet know of the Southern Road decision, Tsuji was not privy to the gnashing of teeth and worries about war with the United States that were being expressed by many, from Nagano and Yamamoto to Prime Minister Konoe. As Tsuji writes, the rank and file IJA officers had few concerns about the United States.

Our candid ideas at the time were that the Americans, being merchants, would not continue for long with an unprofitable war, whereas we ourselves if we fought only the Anglo-Saxon nations could carry on a protracted war, that after we had achieved some great victories in the south, the Republic of China would be willing to conclude an unconditional peace treaty based on the principles of an East Asia Co-Prosperity League; that Russia would break away from her western allies; and that after conclusion of peace with China it would be possible for us to move a million troops from that country to Manchuria, which would be sufficient to deter Russia from any further adventure in that direction or to deal with any attack which might develop there.

This expansive and optimistic strategic reasoning is what one would expect from a cocky and confident colonel, and Tsuji was the archetype of such an officer.

He felt himself qualified to follow either road. If Hattori had been "patiently waiting" for Tsuji to go north, his experience in fighting the Russians in 1939 would count in his favor. If it was to the south, his diligent work with Number 82 Section, which had culminated in his successful Hainan operations, glowed from the pages of his résumé.

He was ready for either assignment, but he was earnest in his preference. He had little enthusiasm for a renewed conflict with the Soviet Union, when the Southern Road led to the resources that were needed not only by his country, but to sustain the IJA itself. As Tsuji would soon learn, Hitler's having chosen his own ominous "Eastern Road" would help put Imperial Japan on the Southern Road.

Operation *Barbarossa* and ensuing events would guarantee that there would be no immediate danger from the Soviet armies. Though the IJA would maintain the Kwantung Army with several field armies in Manchukuo throughout the coming war – just in case – there would be little for them to do until the final week of that war.

Tsuji's questions about which road were answered when he was ushered into a meeting at the very pinnacle of the stark, stone Western-style War

Department building. IJA Chief of Staff Hajime Sugiyama was there, and so too was his boss, Minister of War Hideki Tojo.

Perfunctory bows having taken place, Sugiyama asked for a briefing on the Hainan maneuvers, listened with interest, and then reiterated the mileposts on the Southern Road which would soon be military objectives. He then posed a question he had asked before.

"What is your estimate of the rate at which the operations can progress?"

"If we commence on Meiji Setsu [November 3, Meiji's birthday], we will be able to capture Manila by the New Year," Tsuji replied. "Singapore by Kigensetsu [National Foundation Day, February 11], Java on Army Commemoration Day [March 10] and Rangoon on the Emperor's birthday [April 29]." In his memoirs of the 1942 campaign. Tsuji correctly bragged that "this estimate proved close to the results subsequently achieved."

"How do you believe the war against Britain and America will end?" Tojo asked, having listened impassively while others spoke. As Tsuji recalls, the consensus was "We hope the war will be brought to a conclusion as rapidly as possible by co-ordination of political and military strategy." He adds that "all present predicted that a protracted war might end unfavorably."

———————

Within two weeks of this meeting, on June 26, the Southern Road decision became a fait accompli by way of the freezing of Japanese assets by the Americans, but the October deadline had not yet been set, and Konoe was still putting his energy into a diplomatic work-around.

Tsuji recalls that it was in early September, around the time of the Imperial Palace meeting, that preparations began in earnest. Unofficially until September 25, he was given an assignment as the staff officer in charge of operations and planning for the Malayan Peninsula operations, which would culminate with the efforts to capture "impregnable" Singapore.

The joint plan of operations was formulated during October and presented to Emperor Hirohito on November 2. Hirohito asked whether there was still a diplomatic alternative – the negotiations between Nomura and the Americans would continue until December, though mainly as a ploy – and he was told there was not.

At a formal meeting with the council three days later, the generals and admirals came to the palace to go over the plan in detail. Operations in Malaya, the Philippines, and the Dutch East Indies were explained, and it was noted that 200,000 troops and 600 aircraft were available for operations, although this was just a small proportion of the number that were then committed to either China or Manchukuo.

Present at this meeting was General Tomoyuki Yamashita, who had been urgently summoned back to Tokyo from Manchukuo. After his return from Europe in June, he had taken a short seaside vacation with his family before being sent on assignment to the Kwantung Army. In his diary, he grumbled that he had been exiled by Tojo to get him out of Tokyo during the critical summer of 1941, and because there was some talk that Yamashita might have been in line for Tojo's job as Minister of War. In any case, Tojo now had another job for his old colleague, this being as commander of the 25th Army, the unit which would be assigned to the vitally important Malaya–Singapore operation.

Time was of the essence for a number of reasons. Naturally, there was the petroleum reserves situation, but also the fact that Britain was starting to reinforce Malaya and Singapore, as were the Americans sending more assets to the Philippines. And there was the weather. To avoid both the monsoons and the hottest part of the year, it was considered imperative to begin operations in the tropics in December. It had been decided that offensives against all major objectives – Malaya, the Dutch East Indies, the Philippines, and Pearl Harbor – would begin simultaneously and without warning. The specific date, referred to as "X-Day," would be set as December 8 (December 7 across the international dateline at Pearl Harbor). This would be transmitted to field commanders at the end of November.

As the November 5 meeting was taking place, Saburo Kurusu, the special envoy who had signed the Tripartite Pact on behalf of Japan, was sent to Washington to join Nomura in the pointless negotiations now intended merely to distract the Americans. Kurusu lived until 1954, always maintaining that he had no idea that Japan was preparing for war.

On November 6, Yamashita formally accepted command of the 25th Army, which included the 2nd Imperial Guards Division under the command of Lieutenant General Takuma Nishimura, the 5th Division under Lieutenant General Takuro Matsui, and the 18th Division under Lieutenant General Renya Mutaguchi. The 25th was also assigned the 3rd Tank Brigade, which was equipped with large numbers of Type 95 light tanks. Armed with 37mm guns, these tanks were designed to support infantry assaults and had proven very useful in Manchuria and China.

Also on November 6, the IJA created the Southern Expeditionary Army Group, as an umbrella organization for all Southeast Asia operations. It was placed under the command of a former minister of war, General Count Hisaichi Terauchi, whose headquarters was established in Saigon, French Indochina. Later a field marshal, Terauchi was the man who had stepped in as the IJA's hand-picked minister of war after the attempted coup on February 26, 1936. His command would include the four field armies that would be responsible for the remarkable series of victories in the coming months which would make the IJA appear to the rest of the world as invincible.

In addition to Yamashita's 25th, these field armies, also activated early in November 1941, were the 14th Army under Lieutenant General Masaharu Homma, created for the Philippines campaign; the 15th Army under Lieutenant General Shojiro Iida, for operations in Burma; and the 16th Army under Lieutenant General Hitoshi Imamura, for the campaign in the Dutch East Indies.

Colonel Masanobu Tsuji was assigned to the 25th Army as Yamashita's chief of staff for plans and operations, a role in which he had been functioning for about six weeks. By now, Tsuji was in Saigon, from where he had already flown as an observer on two aerial reconnaissance missions over the Malay Peninsula in late October. This, as well as earlier tours of Malaya by Japanese "tourists" was essential, given that the Japanese did not even possess a large-scale map of the Malay Peninsula!

In his memoirs, Tsuji notes that the personnel strength of the 25th Army was approximately 60,000 or half that of the total British force in Malaya and Singapore, and that the British also outnumbered the Japanese two to one in artillery. On the other hand, he reckoned that the IJAAF had 459 aircraft available, along with 158 IJN aircraft, while the British had fewer than 300. The IJN was committing a cruiser and about ten destroyers to the operation, while the RN had a force of a similar size that had recently been reinforced by the battleship HMS *Prince of Wales* and the battle cruiser HMS *Repulse*.

Conventional wisdom for the Malaya campaign held that after an initial landing, the beachhead should be secured, and that troops and supplies should be built up here over a period of time before offensive operations were begun. Tsuji disagreed, proposing that a sufficient force should be landed in order to begin the offensive immediately.

It was intended that the invasion force should land on the east coast, cross the peninsula, and drive south toward Singapore on the west coast, where the British had constructed an efficient modern highway paralleling the main rail line between Bangkok and Singapore. Tsuji felt that speed was essential, in part because he wanted the 25th Army to get across the Perak River before the British had a chance to blow up the bridges. If this happened, he feared that it would delay the 25th Army by a month, giving the British more time to prepare for the attack on Singapore. Though he did not mention it in so many words, Tsuji was planning a blitzkrieg.

As he studied the tactical situation, Tsuji observed the big British air bases in the northern Malay Peninsula, at Alor Star (now Alor Setar) on the west coast, and Khota Bharu on the east, and realized that in order to neutralize British air support, capturing these would have to be one of the first tasks after the landings. Tsuji developed a plan that called for simultaneous landings of the 18th Division near Khota Bharu, and the 5th Division farther north, up the coast at Singora (now called Songkhla) and Patani. One inconvenient complication in making landfall at the latter locations was that these cities are in Thailand.

In fact, the Southern Army's master plan called for numerous incursions into Thai territory. Indeed, Shojiro Iida's entire 15th Army was intended to pass through Thailand from Indochina, both overland and through landings from the sea south of Bangkok, in order to attack Burma. To avoid tipping their hand, the Japanese deliberately did not provide an advance briefing for Thailand's mercurial Prime Minister Plaek Phibunsongkhram. Instead, they crossed their fingers and hoped that he would remember that Japan had done him a favor earlier in the year by compelling the French to make severe territorial concessions.

When encountering Thai defenders, the invading Japanese troops were told to employ the "Asia for Asiatics" rhetoric of the Greater East Asia Co-Prosperity Sphere. They were to identify themselves as friends who came in peace, and to urge the Thai troops to join them in their war against the British.

Postponing the diplomatic contact with Thailand, the IJA sat down to negotiate the cooperation of the IJN in providing the shipping that was necessary to transport most of two divisions to Singora, Patani, and Khota Bharu. At a meeting held in Saigon on November 15, with Tsuji, Yamashita, and Count Terauchi representing the IJA, Vice Admiral Jisaburo Ozawa, commander of the Japanese Southern Expeditionary Fleet, and of naval operations in the South China Sea, surprised the soldiers by readily agreeing that "I shall do everything possible that is desired by the [IJA] forces."

This was to include transporting the invasion force from Hainan and supporting them with naval gunfire and naval airpower, as well as transporting subsequent waves of 25th Army troops who would be landed during December.

The Philippines, like the Dutch East Indies, constituted an archipelago of islands (7,107 and 17,500 respectively), but operations for General Masaharu Homma's 14th Army in the Philippines could be focused primarily on the island of Luzon, home to most of the Philippines population, all the major cities and more than a third of the land area.

Of the four objectives set out for the Southern Expeditionary Army, the Dutch East Indies presented the most complex logistical and strategic challenge. Whatever the difficulties of terrain, both Burma and Malaya are contiguous land masses, with Singapore an island that is less than a mile off Malaya's southern tip.

While Homma could focus on one main island, the Dutch East Indies included five major islands. Three of them, Sumatra, Java, and Celebes (now Sulawesi), were entirely part of the Dutch colony. Borneo, which was mostly Dutch, had four small British protectorates – Sarawak, Brunei, Labuan, and British North Borneo – across the northwest side. Finally, there was New Guinea, which was divided roughly in half between Dutch and Australian administration.

To give a sense of size, the Dutch East Indies extended more than 3,000 miles from east to west, and more than 1,200 miles north to south. To give a sense of scale, New Guinea and Borneo are the world's second and third largest islands (after Greenland), and the total land area of the Dutch East Indies was more than 50 times that of the European mother country. The Dutch East Indies were also the most populous entity in Southeast Asia, with 60 million people, ten times the number in Malaya, and more than three times the population of Thailand and Indochina combined. There were more people in the Dutch East Indies than there were in either France or the United Kingdom.

————

If cooperation between the IJA and the IJN was important to the Malaya and Philippines operations, it would be essential in the Dutch East Indies. Indeed, the IJA and the IJN "land army," the Special Naval Landing Forces, divided the operations in Borneo, with the IJA being assigned the British part, and the IJN the Dutch part.

Of the five major islands, Borneo was the primary objective because of the great oil fields that were located in both the British north and on the Dutch west side. While Japanese air attacks were planned against numerous targets throughout the Dutch East Indies, only Borneo was to be the object of ground operations during 1941, and these were planned against the north, with operations in the east scheduled for January 1942.

Of all the targets of Japanese action in Southeast Asia, Borneo, because of its petroleum, had by far the highest practical value as an objective. Ironically, it was the most lightly defended by both the British and the Dutch. Japanese strategic planners took this into account. While multiple divisions were assigned to other objectives, the plans for Borneo involved reinforced regiments.

The force chosen for the northern Borneo campaign was not drawn from Lieutenant General Hitoshi Imamura's 16th Army, which had the overall Dutch East Indies assignment, but mainly from the 18th Division, which was part of Yamashita's 25th Army command. The specific unit was the 35th Infantry Brigade, commanded by Major General Kiyotake Kawaguchi, and therefore known as the Kawaguchi Detachment.

The core of this brigade was the 124th Infantry Regiment, with engineers and support units, as well as the 33rd Field Artillery Battalion of the Kwantung Army, attached to it. Kawaguchi would operate under the direct command of Hisaichi Terauchi's Southern Expeditionary Army, and ship out after the other invasion fleets in order to make his landing in northern Borneo on December 16, six days after X-Day.

For Dutch Borneo, where operations were not scheduled to begin until January 1942, the assigned unit was the brigade-equivalent 56th Infantry Group, drawn from the 56th Division, the rest of which was assigned to Burma operations. Commanded by Major General Shizuo Sakaguchi, the 56th Infantry Group had as its core unit the 146th Infantry Regiment.

During the final days of November and the first week of December, the threat of war still seemed remote and unreal among the defenders. Indeed, in all the places toward which the four field armies of the Southern Army sailed, minds were indifferent to the Japanese threat. In

Manila, they were thinking of Christmas. In Singapore, the Gibraltar of the East, the impregnable bastion of British might, Lieutenant General Arthur Ernest Percival, the commander of the British garrison, was confident that any Japanese invasion of the Malay Peninsula would be stopped in its tracks. He wasn't even thinking about defending Singapore. That was ridiculous, because his island was impregnable. Kenneth Attiwill, who was there at the time, writes that "complacency ruled the island – solid, more impenetrable than the Malayan jungle. It was a compound of easy living, wishful thinking, misinformation, ignorance, and deceptive appearance."

At Pearl Harbor, toward which Yamamoto's IJN battle fleet sailed, the fleet was in, the palm trees swayed gently, the surf crashed, and a relaxing Sunday morning awaited the sailors of the USN Pacific Fleet.

PART II
BANZAI BLITZKRIEG

CHAPTER 8

DECEMBER 8, 1941

The six IJN aircraft carriers *Akagi*, *Kaga*, *Soryu*, *Hiryu*, *Shokaku*, and *Zuikaku* reached a point about 200 miles north of Pearl Harbor and prepared to launch a strike force of nearly 400 aircraft. It was the cusp of dawn on December 7 in Hawaii, and across the international dateline, in Singapore and Singora, it was just past midnight on December 8. Colonel Masanobu Tsuji, aboard the troop transport *Kashii Maru*, spotted the Singora lighthouse through his binoculars.

Japan was about to enter World War II. Her intended foes, who were not oblivious, could not have imagined the suddenness and determination with which numerous, well-coordinated hammers were about to strike. Their complacency bordered on arrogance.

On December 3, Air Chief Marshal Sir Henry Robert Moore Brooke-Popham, Commander-in-Chief of the British Far East Command, responsible for defense matters in Singapore, Malaya, Burma, and Hong Kong, had observed at a press conference that "there are clear signs that Japan does not know which way to turn. Tojo is scratching his head. There are no signs that Japan is going to attack anyone."

As Kenneth Attiwill reminds us, Brooke-Popham's greatest worry had been fighter aircraft, but he was satisfied with the Brewster Buffalo.

"We can get on all right with Buffaloes out here," he said, "but they haven't got the speed for England. Let England have the super-Spitfires and hyper-Tornadoes. Buffaloes are quite good enough for Malaya."

By the end of the year, Brooke-Popham was out of the picture, replaced by General (later Field Marshal) Archibald Percival Wavell, who headed the British India Command, as well as the Joint American–British–Dutch–Australian (ABDA) Command, which superseded the British Far East Command on January 15, 1942, and which ceased to exist two months later.

Attiwill, for whom that December day was a first-hand experience, writes that the day before had been

a time for relaxation. The week's exertions had ended and there was the weekend peace to be enjoyed before work was resumed. There were long, cool drinks to combat the heat; cricket, golf, tennis, yachting, swimming, or bridge for entertainment, according to personal taste and means. There were dinners and dances at luxury hotels, or conversation at club or home over whisky and cocktails and iced beer. It was the customary life of the white man in the tropics.

Life was like that on Sunday, December 7, 1941, in Singapore. The city on its island, suspended like an emerald below the scimitar blade of the Malayan peninsula, was wrapped in its blanket of security. The streets, their shops and bazaars gay with holly and mistletoe and Christmas toys, were thronged with people – Europeans and Chinese, Malays and Indians, civilians and soldiers, especially soldiers. There were British and Australian, Moslem and Sikh, Gurkha and Malay. There were airmen from Great Britain, Australia and New Zealand, and the Netherlands East Indies. There were European and Asiatic members of the Volunteer Forces. At dances and in the crowded cinemas, three-quarters of the audiences were in uniform. They were a great comfort to the civilians.

At 3:30 am on December 8, Fighter Control Operations in Singapore detected a formation of unidentified aircraft headed south toward the fortified island. They phoned the civilian air raid protection service, but there was no answer. There was nobody in the office at that hour, and before long, the first Japanese bombs were falling.

————————

As yet undetected from shore, the troops aboard Tsuji's ship and the *Ryujo Maru* began climbing into the landing boats. The seas were rough, it was dark, and the whole experience was unnerving, but they were anxious to get onto dry land after their four-day trip from Hainan. In all, the invasion force included seven transports supported by the cruiser *Kashii* and six destroyers. General Takuro Matsui's 5th Division, along with General Yamashita's 25th Army headquarters, would land here at Singora and Patani, while General Renya Mutaguchi's 18th Division landed at Kota Bharu.

The flotilla had been spotted by two RAF patrol planes, one a Catalina that was shot down before its crew could report in, and one a Hudson, whose crew did make a report – but no alarm was raised because the British Empire was not yet at war with the Chrysanthemum Empire.

The invasion force dragged their motor boats ashore and inspected the Thai defensive positions, which were not occupied. There were three Thai infantry battalions in the Singora–Patani area, the 5th, 41st, and 42nd, but they were not guarding the shoreline.

Tsuji made his way to the Japanese Consulate. The consul had been supposed to arrange for vehicles and talk the local Thai police out of opposing the Japanese landing, but he hadn't got the message because the man in charge of deciphering the message had burned the key without memorizing it. Tsuji and his party met resistance at the Singora Police Station, and made several attempts using white flags to get close enough to parley with the Thai police. Eventually, the station was surrendered and it served briefly as Yamashita's field headquarters.

The Japanese managed to capture some nearby Thai airfields without resistance, but soon came under fire from Thai artillery. The shooting continued until around noon, when a Thai officer came forward to tell the invaders that Prime Minister Phibun had learned of the situation and had ordered that resistance be "suspended for the time being."

Preoccupied with the secrecy cloaking the invasion, the Japanese had waited until the last minute to fill Phibun in on their plans to violate his territory. The news came clumsily in the form of an ultimatum delivered at nearly midnight on December 7, just a couple of hours before the 5th Division came ashore in southern Thailand.

The demand was simple: if the IJA were not allowed to pass through Thailand at will, they would fight their way through. As it evolved, the incursion into Thailand by the main body of General Shojiro Iida's 15th Army was relatively uneventful although they did encounter sporadic resistance as they approached Bangkok. Elsewhere, however, there were serious clashes, as Thai forces met Japanese landings south of Bangkok with stiff resistance. At Prachuap Khirikhan, for example, the Japanese admitted to losing 115 troops in a shootout with provincial police, who held them at bay until the ceasefire was ordered.

The ceasefire might have come sooner, but Phibun was indisposed, and could not be located by his government until late on the morning of December 8, as his cabinet was debating whether to resist or surrender. He was insulted that he was not given prior notification, but what could he do?

He had been courted by the British about allying with them, but they were hundreds of miles away, and the Japanese 15th Army was outside the window. Phibun knew he could put up a fight. He had a modest, but modern air force, and a well-trained army numbering more than 25,000 men, with twice that many in reserve – and he had used this force to defeat the French a year earlier. On the other hand, he was an admirer of the Axis powers, and he both respected and feared Japan. He agreed to a ceasefire at noon, and ordered Thai troops to stand down. A week later, on December 14, Phibun signed a secret agreement to contribute troops to the Japanese operations in Malaya and Burma. One week after that, Thailand and Japan agreed to a formal alliance.

Tsuji notes that after the noon ceasefire on December 8, the Thai civilians welcomed the Japanese troops with plates of food. Tsuji didn't linger long. He attached himself to a small spearhead force of about 300 troops, supported by three tanks and a field gun, that was being led by Lieutenant Colonel Shizuo Saeki. He urged the troops to get moving quickly on the road toward the border with Malaya. Tsuji writes in his memoirs:

> it was essential for us to break through the frontier without loss of time. This task was given to the troops at the head of the 5th Division, who were already moving along the road to the west. I followed them as fast as possible, and en route picked up three medium tanks which were waiting by the roadside for reinforcements. Together we made rapid progress. Farther along the road I collected a number of soldiers and a field gun – the artillery was being landed with difficulty and had not yet received orders to advance – but I took the gun and its escort forward with me because of the danger that the enemy troops might counterattack, in which case it would have been important to meet them as soon as possible with the greatest strength available to prevent their attack reaching our beachhead. As staff officer in charge of operations I did not wait for orders, but substituting for the commander-in-chief, in the interests of the whole Army, I promptly speeded up the advance of every unit.

As Saeki's small force moved out, they learned that a British mechanized force was also moving north to meet them. Shortly before midnight, the Japanese reached the border at Ban Sadao and discovered that the British troops had dug in there to ambush them. As the field gun returned fire, Saeki sent his men into the rubber plantations that paralleled the highway, with orders to outflank the British. After an hour-long firefight, the British retreated down the road and the Japanese advanced. In a blood-stained armored car Masanobu Tsuji discovered a large-scale map with the defensive positions around the Malayan cities of Jitra and Changlun penciled in.

Tsuji writes that he proudly took this prize to General Yamashita, who was organizing the main force back at the Singora and Patani beachheads, although in John Deane Potter's account, based on Yamashita's diary, the first detailed maps did not come into Japanese hands for six weeks.

Though the 5th Division had come ashore successfully, and had penetrated as far as the Malay border, Yamashita had learned that the 18th Division, landing at Kota Bharu, had met stiff resistance from British Indian troops in fortified positions, and had been attacked by British Hudson bombers. The Japanese had broken through, but it had cost them the entire day and more casualties than Yamashita would have liked.

In the Philippines, in the early hours of December 8, USMC Lieutenant Colonel William Clement was the duty officer at the Asiatic Fleet headquarters in the Marsman Building in Manila, when the radio operator rushed into his office.

"Air Raid on Pearl Harbor. This is no drill."

Clement looked at the clock. It was 2:30 am local time.

The message was in the hands of Admiral Thomas Hart, the fleet commander, before the minute hand reached the top of the hour. Before another 30 minutes had passed, the message had reached the penthouse apartment at the Manila Hotel that was the residence of General Douglas MacArthur, commander of US Army Forces in the Far East (USAFFE). Both Hart and MacArthur notified all their subordinate commanders that a state of war existed with Japan.

The man charged with the defense of the Philippine Commonwealth, MacArthur had been the US Army Chief of Staff from 1930 until his retirement in 1935. He had then been invited by Philippines President Manuel Quezon to build the Philippine Army (with the rank of field marshal), but in July 1941 he had been recalled to active duty by President Franklin Roosevelt and named as Commander USAFFE, with headquarters in Manila.

In defense of the Philippines, MacArthur had assigned eight Philippine Army divisions to Luzon, and three to the other islands as the

Visayan–Mindanao Force. Four of those on the main island constituted the North Luzon Force, commanded by Major General Jonathan Wainwright, which was expected to take the brunt of any Japanese invasion. US Army units under MacArthur's command included the Philippine Division (later the 12th Infantry Division), the 26th Cavalry Regiment (Philippine Scouts), and several field artillery units as well as coastal artillery to defend the harbors.

The US Army Air Forces' Far East Air Forces (USAAF FEAF), commanded by Major General Lewis Brereton and headquartered at Clark Field, north of Manila, had around 100 reasonably modern fighter aircraft and 35 B-17 Flying Fortress bombers, with more on the way. At Clark, the epicenter of US airpower in the Western Pacific, they had already learned of the Pearl Harbor attack from commercial broadcasts, and they were on high alert. Plans had previously been discussed about using the B-17s based there for a preemptive strike against Japanese air bases on Taiwan, 500 miles to the north, but such a mission was not executed.

Meanwhile, however, both IJNAF and IJAAF bombers were already en route from Taiwan, headed for the Philippines. Fearing an attack on Clark, the two squadrons of B-17 bombers were ordered to take off without bombs as a protective measure. Meanwhile, in case the bombers were headed for Manila, fighters were launched from Clark and from Nichols Field, nearer Manila, to intercept them.

It turned out that the bombers were actually targeting locations in northern Luzon, including the mountain resort of Baguio, which was the summer residence of President Quezon. The American aircraft returned to base by 11:30 am to be refueled. At this same moment, however, another wave of Japanese bombers was headed south. This second wave was actually intending to attack the targets that had been feared for the first.

Shortly after noon, the refueling at Clark was being completed, and the B-17s were lined up neatly on the runway as Japanese bombers and fighters came over. As the bombs began to fall, the air raid siren sounded. The base was bombed and strafed for about an hour, and when it was over, hangars and other facilities had been destroyed, fuel supplies were ablaze, and half of the B-17s were totally destroyed. Similar attacks were ongoing at other places across Luzon, including Nichols Field. When it was over, the FEAF had lost 18 B-17s, 53 P-40 fighters, and around 30 aircraft of other types.

―――――――――――

As the Philippine Commonwealth was coming under the attack, the Japanese were also stretching their military muscle against Guam, 1,600 miles across the Pacific to the east. A Spanish colony since the sixteenth century, Guam had been part of the territory that was lost to the Americans in 1898, along with the Philippines. By 1941, Guam was being used as a refueling stop for the Pan American Airways flying boat service to the Philippines. There was no significant American military here until late in 1941, when a small contingent of about 150 Marines arrived to support fewer than 300 USN personnel.

Guam lay as an isolated outpost at the center of a vast swath of the Pacific spanning 40 degrees of the earth's circumference that included the Marshall, Caroline, and Mariana archipelagos which had been mandated to Japan as League of Nations trust territories in 1920, when Germany was stripped of its overseas territorial possessions after World War I. By the late 1930s, a strong IJN and IJA presence had been established on these relatively tiny islands. At Truk (now Chuuk), the IJN built its largest and best fortified naval base outside Japan itself.

Saipan, 130 miles north of Guam in the Marianas, was part of the Japanese mandate. Japan undertook an accelerated colonization, and within two decades, the Japanese outnumbered the native Chamorro people nine to one. As with many of the other islands, Japan also militarized Saipan as part of its Pacific defense strategy, building fortifications and establishing a substantial IJN and IJA presence.

At daybreak on December 8, a Japanese armada was already steaming south from Saipan to Guam. Aboard was the South Seas Detachment, a brigade-sized IJA force which had been formed earlier in 1941 under the command structure of the IJN South Seas Force (based on the 4th Fleet) for offensive operations in the Pacific islands. Commanded by Major General Tomitaro Horii, the detachment was centered on the 144th Infantry Regiment, and other units detached from the 55th Division.

At 8:27 am, a Japanese aircraft from Saipan strafed the military facilities and damaged the minesweeper USS *Penguin*, the largest naval vessel in the harbor, but was shot down itself. Further air attacks were followed by Horii's amphibious landing in the predawn hours of December 10. The South Seas Detachment put 400 men ashore north of the main city of Agana to attack the marine barracks, and 5,500 at other points around the island. Governor George McMillan surrendered Guam to Horii, after less than two hours of fighting, at 6:00 am, and the Japanese ran up the flag of the rising sun.

Wake Island, 1,500 miles east of Guam and 2,300 miles west of Pearl Harbor, had, like Guam, been an American possession since 1898. An atoll with an area of less than 3 square miles, Wake was important to the outside world only for its airport, which was used as a Pan American refueling base, and for a small contingent of USMC aircraft. To the Japanese, it was a "must have" strategic point which lay between its mandated territories and Pearl Harbor. For the South Seas Detachment, it was the next target after Guam.

December 8 saw IJNAF air attacks against Wake launched from Kwajalein that were aimed at destroying the dozen USMC F4F Wildcat fighters based on the island. An attempt at an amphibious invasion on December 11 was thwarted by a contingent of fewer than 500 Marines under Major James Devereux, who managed to sink two IJN destroyers. A substantial rescue mission, including three heavy cruisers and ten destroyers, departed Pearl Harbor, but they were ordered to turn about on December 22 when reports came in that a Japanese fleet including two battleships and two aircraft carriers was in the area.

The South Seas Detachment, now reinforced and supported by the carriers *Hiryu* and *Soryu*, achieved a successful landing on Wake at about 2:30 am the following day. The outnumbered Marines fought through the day, but were defeated by afternoon. Many of the captured personnel were shipped to Japan and elsewhere. The Japanese kept 98 POWs on the island as a work detail, but they were all murdered in 1943.

On December 8, as the Americans were feeling the heat of Japanese bombs in the Philippines, and the British the same in Malaya and Singapore, elements of the IJA 23rd Army invaded the British Crown Colony of Hong Kong.

One of the coastal concessions that the European powers had been granted by the Qing Dynasty in the nineteenth century, Hong Kong Island had been occupied by Britain since 1841, and had been ceded "in perpetuity." In 1898, in order to expand the colony, Sir Claude MacDonald, Britain's ambassador to the Qing throne, had negotiated a deal to expand the colony through adding the mainland city of Kowloon, as well as more than 300 square miles of mainland that came to be known as the "New Territories." MacDonald picked 99 years as the lease term because it seemed at the time that this was "as good as forever." And so it seemed to the British expatriates who came and went through the coming decades – until 1997. As in Singapore, it was an island of urbane tranquility on a troubled continent, where golf, tennis, and cocktails at exclusive private clubs were part of an established way of life.

By December 1941, the Hong Kong garrison, commanded by Major General Christopher Maltby, numbered around 14,000 British, Canadian, and Indian troops, backed by the Hong Kong Volunteer Defence Corps. The RAF component, based at Kai Tak Airport near Kowloon, possessed a mere handful of mainly obsolete aircraft. The largest ships of a small RN contingent had been ordered to withdraw to Singapore.

Opposing this was a force of more than 50,000 Japanese troops, under Lieutenant General Takashi Sakai, who commanded the 23rd Army, a component of the China Expeditionary Army which was based in Canton (now Guangdong) province. The invasion force was comprised mainly of the veteran 38th Division augmented by support troops. The division was commanded by Major General Takeo Ito, who had been with the unit since it had first gone into combat at the beginning of the war in China. Ito's troops launched a two-pronged assault into the New Territories at about 8:30 am, much later than the first Japanese attacks elsewhere that morning.

Later on December 8, American pilots flying for the China National Aviation Corporation undertook to evacuate civilians from Kai Tak Airport. Flying in and out between Japanese bombing raids, they carried refugees to cities under Nationalist control, including Chungking (now Chongqing), the capital of Nationalist China, which was nearly 700 miles away.

The following day, Chiang Kai-shek would order a relief column under General Yu Hanmou to march toward Hong Kong.

———

By the end of the day that Japan entered World War II, the USN Pacific Fleet had been crippled beyond what could have been imagined a day earlier. Four of eight battleships had been sunk, and the other four put out of commission. Nearly a dozen other ships were damaged or sunk, and at Pearl Harbor the nearly 200 aircraft destroyed included B-17 heavy bombers that were, ironically, en route to the garrison in the Philippines. In the Philippines, the USAAF FEAF had lost half of its total strength in a few hours. The Japanese had lost fewer than ten aircraft. Further air raids on December 9 added to the American losses.

———

In Southeast Asia, Thailand surrendered in less than a day. In the offensive against Malaya, Japanese forces had crossed the beachheads, penetrated beyond the Malay border, and had access to every air base in Thailand.

The next day, as he went to Congress to ask for the declaration of war, President Franklin Roosevelt said that it had been a day that would "live in infamy." It was also a day that stunned the world for the audacity of the Japanese war machine, and for the unbelievable successes that had been scored all across Asia.

CHAPTER 9

THE FIRST WEEK

By the second day after the invasion of Thailand and northern Malaya, Japanese troops were already moving south. However, the British had an ace in the hole in the form of the battleship HMS *Prince of Wales* and the battle cruiser HMS *Repulse*. The mightiest warships in Southeast Asia had just arrived in Singapore. In the small hours of December 10, accompanied by several destroyers, the great vessels put to sea to attack the Japanese invasion fleet, to pound and pummel the enemy ships with the same 14-inch guns that had sunk the *Bismarck*. Coincidentally, they were part of a flotilla operating under the code letter "Z," the same letter that had been assigned to the task force that Yamamoto had sent to attack Pearl Harbor.

Off the coast of Malaya east of Kuantan, Force Z was intercepted by IJN bombers armed with bombs and torpedoes, and attacked in four waves. The *Prince of Wales* was fatally damaged in the second attack, but the *Repulse* survived largely unscathed until the fourth. She sank at 12:33 pm, and the *Prince of Wales* followed her down less than an hour later. Their loss was a severe blow to British naval power in Southeast Asia, and a worse blow to British morale.

Within three days, both IJA and IJN aircraft were operating from captured air bases in Malaya. The RAF bases, which included Alor Star as well as Kota Bharu, were much better constructed than those in Thailand, and had been abandoned so fast that fuel remained in storage and bombs were still in the bomb dumps. Attempts by RAF bombers and retreating British artillerymen to undo this oversight were only partially successful.

Soon the bases were swarming with Japanese bombers which could now operate against British targets in Malaya and Singapore from bases that were 600 miles closer than when the bombers had been based in Saigon a few days earlier. In his diary, Tomoyuki Yamashita wrote "in spite of heavy fighting, my troops are in good spirits and are successful. The IJN should be proud of them."

In Singapore, General Percival admitted that the enemy had landed, but insisted there were "rather less than a Japanese division." In fact, there was the better part of two divisions, plus the tanks. A third, the Imperial Guards Division, had crossed into Thailand with the 15th Army and would soon be coming south to join the 25th Army. Meanwhile, the 56th Division, under Lieutenant General Masao Watanabe, was not assigned to the 25th Army, but was held in reserve in Saigon in case Yamashita needed it. Having decided that he did not, Yamashita released it in mid-January. In his memoirs, Winston Churchill mentions the Japanese having five divisions in Malaya, but there were never more than three, and the 18th Division was deliberately kept below full strength for much of the operation for logistical reasons.

In Malaya, the battlefield was a narrow one. Because most of the peninsula is impenetrable jungle, the battle was confined to a narrow corridor comprised of rubber plantations that extended only a short distance into the jungle from the main highway. It was a battlefield utterly unsuited for mechanized warfare, except for the slender ribbon of highway, which was ideal for operations by the tanks which Yamashita had insisted on adding to his force.

For the defenders, it was a matter of building short defensive lines across this corridor. The first major line was established between Changlun and Jitra by the British 11th Indian Infantry Division under Major General David Murray-Lyon. The Japanese, with the tanks commanded by Shizuo Saeki in the vanguard, pushed through hastily prepared defensive positions and closed in on the main body of the 11th Division at Jitra late on December 11. The defensive line here was reinforced by the natural barrier of the Jitra River.

The Japanese advance was held here overnight, but late on December 12, Murray-Lyon ordered a withdrawal farther south, below the Bata River. Unfortunately, not all of his troops got the message, and some remained to face the Japanese as the rest of the 11th Division withdrew.

Percival attempted to implement Operation *Matador*, a plan to occupy part of Thailand in the event of war, but the Japanese had already beaten him to the punch. British troops defending northern Malaya were too few for anything but holding actions and the Japanese moved a great deal faster than the defenders had expected.

Just as Yamashita was able to quickly turn the superb RAF bases against the British, so too did he use the excellent British-built highway system to his advantage. He had made a command decision to bring relatively few motor vehicles aboard the crowded transport ships. Instead, he stocked the holds with bicycles.

This mode of transportation became an icon of Yamashita's campaign, and of Japanese operations across Southeast Asia. The spearhead of Yamashita's force could move much more quickly on bikes than they could on foot. The bicycle troops were not, in most cases, deterred by bridges which were blown up by the British to slow the Japanese advance.

In summarizing the situation, Masanobu Tsuji writes that

the main reasons for the phenomenal speed of the onslaught in the Malayan campaign were the special attention given to the equipping and training of infantry formations, and the great achievements of the Engineer Corps ... A division was equipped with roughly five hundred motor vehicles and six thousand bicycles. The training to accustom troops to these new conditions did not exceed a period of more than one or two months immediately before the outbreak of hostilities.

In planning his invasion force, Yamashita had put a premium on lightness and mobility. As he brought more bikes than trucks, he brought more man-portable mortars than heavy artillery. He saved his precious bulky item cargo space for his tanks. The British, meanwhile, had plenty of trucks and artillery, but no usable modern tanks. They did have armored cars and Universal (also called "Bren") Gun Carriers, lightly armed and armored vehicles that were no match for the Japanese Type 95 light tanks with their 37mm guns.

Ironically, so many British trucks were abandoned in the early withdrawals that some Japanese units were equipped almost entirely with captured motor vehicles, and fueled by the substantial fuel stocks which were also abandoned in the retreat.

As for the damaged bridges, an important component of the training that Masanobu Tsuji had arranged for the troops during the Hainan exercises had involved bridge-building training for the engineer troops who now accompanied the 25th Army. Because an important element of the Malayan economy had been the lumber industry, the Japanese engineers were able to scrounge lumber, and beams of substantial size from sawmills along the way. Tsuji recalls:

In Malaya, almost without exception, bridges were demolished in front of our advancing troops. When all motor transport was loaded with officers, men and equipment, it would have reduced their speed to walking pace if they had had to wait for the advance of the infantry and the repair of bridges, and it would have taken over a year to break through eleven hundred kilometers [nearly 900 miles]. With the infantry on bicycles, however, there was no traffic congestion or delay. Wherever bridges were destroyed the infantry continued their advance, wading across the rivers carrying their bicycles on their shoulders, or crossing on log bridges held up on the shoulders of engineers standing in the stream. It was thus possible to maintain a hot pursuit of the enemy along the asphalt roads without giving them any time to rest or reorganize.

In response to Winston Churchill's assertion that the Japanese Army had made secret preparations in each Malay district for stockpiling of bicycles, Tsuji scoffs,

> I have to say that these are not the facts of the case. The truth is that Japanese-manufactured bicycles, because of their cheapness, had become one of the chief exports from Japan to the whole of Southeast Asia, where they were widely purchased by the inhabitants. For this reason replacements and spare parts were easily available everywhere throughout Malaya.

———

The first landings by the IJA in the Philippines took place during the first week of the war, although they were merely preparatory operations in expectation of the long-anticipated main invasion that would come at the end of the month. Batan Island (not to be confused with the Bataan Peninsula), halfway between Taiwan and the Philippines, was captured on December 8, and in northern Luzon, landings were made at Aparri and Vigan. Two days later, a detachment under Major General Naoki Kimura, staging out of Palau, landed at Legaspi, at the southeast tip of Luzon. While the main drive on Manila would come from the north, this beachhead would provide possible access for a second thrust on the capital.

Meanwhile, on December 20, Major General Shizuo Sakaguchi's Detachment, the centerpiece of which was the 146th Infantry Regiment, would land at Davao, on the southernmost Philippine island of Mindanao. This landing, and one that took place four days later on remote Jolo Island, were not part of the Philippines operation, but were aimed at securing staging bases for activities in the Dutch East Indies.

In the Hong Kong campaign, the outnumbered and overstretched defenders had conceded much of the New Territories by the second day after the invasion, withdrawing into a smaller area which included the city of Kowloon and Kai Tak Airport, around which there was perceived to be a shorter and more easily defended perimeter line. This line was held only briefly, as General Christopher Maltby, the garrison commander, began ordering units to withdraw across Victoria Harbour to Hong Kong Island for a last stand.

The last unit on the mainland, a British Indian regiment under Lieutenant Colonel R. Cadogan-Rawlinson, was evacuated on December 13. General Takashi Sakai, the 23rd Army commander, who also commanded the overall IJA Hong Kong operation, demanded that Hong Kong Island surrender, but he was rebuffed by Hong Kong's governor, Sir Mark Aitchison Young. According to Philip Snow, in his book *The Fall of Hong Kong*, Young had been told by Winston Churchill personally that "every part of [Hong Kong] Island must be fought over and the enemy resisted with the utmost stubbornness. Every day that you are able to maintain your resistance you help the Allied cause all over the world."

Two days later Sakai's artillery began a sustained barrage of Hong Kong, with the first Japanese invasion craft touching the shores on December 18, as General Maltby created separate brigades to defend the east and west side of the island. Fighting was fierce, but the Japanese swiftly got the upper hand. By December 20, they had achieved separate encirclements of Maltby's two brigades and began cutting their water supplies. The Hong Kong relief column promised by Chiang Kai-shek never arrived.

CHAPTER 10

HOMMA IN THE PHILIPPINES

In the predawn darkness of December 22, 1941, Japanese transport ships in Luzon's Lingayen Gulf began to disgorge their contents into small boats in rough and choppy waters. As had been the case with Tomoyuki Yamashita's 25th Army disembarkation two weeks earlier, the seas were not cooperating with Masaharu Homma's 14th Army. Some of the transports had overshot their specified positions, and his troops would be out of alignment when they went ashore. Born on Sado Island in the Sea of Japan, Homma was used to the sea, and he understood it as an unforgiving environment in which to work. His teeth were clenched as he peered into the inky darkness at things not going according to plan.

A 1907 graduate of the IJA Academy, he had been a military attaché in the United Kingdom for eight years, had become fluent in English, and had actually seen service with the British Expeditionary Force in France during World War I. Since then, he had toured Germany, shaken hands with Adolf Hitler, and commanded the 27th Division during the war in China.

The 14th Army, which went ashore at Lingayen over the course of 48 hours, was centered on the 48th Division, commanded by Lieutenant

General Yuitsu Tsuchihashi (translated in US Army sources, notably by Louis Morton, as Yuichi Tsuchibashi). They were, in turn, supported by the 8th Field Artillery Regiment, with 105mm guns and the 22nd Field Artillery with 75mm guns, as well as two units with 150mm guns, the 9th Independent Field Artillery Battalion and the 1st Field Artillery Regiment. Between them, the 4th and 7th Tank Regiments brought nearly 100 tanks.

While Homma took the main part of the 14th Army ashore on December 22 at Lingayen Gulf, about 120 miles north of Manila, the 16th Division under Lieutenant General Susumu Morioka would go ashore at Lamon Bay, about the same distance southeast of the capital, two days later.

The plan was that after initial operations, the 48th Division would ship out to the Dutch East Indies and be replaced by the smaller and less combat-capable 65th Brigade, under Lieutenant General Akira Nara, which was intended mainly as an occupation force.

The Lingayen landing took place on the east shore of the gulf across a roughly 15-mile beachhead between the towns of Bauang and Agoo. The city of Baguio was in the mountains about 20 miles directly inland from the beachhead. Favoring Homma's troops was that Highway 3, a paved road that went all the way to Manila, ran parallel to the beachhead, connecting all of the landing sites.

A landing at Lingayen Gulf was an ideal choice. The high seas notwithstanding, it was a bay, not open ocean, and there were no major terrain features between it and Manila. Though some distance would have to be covered in the march toward Manila, there were paved roads running generally parallel to the rivers in the area, minimizing the number of bridges that would have to be secured or rebuilt.

Opposition was minimal. A landing here was not unexpected by Homma's foe, General Douglas MacArthur, who had previously discussed plans for an aggressive defense, but the landings were met only by small arms fire. There were two Philippine Army divisions of General Jonathan Wainwright's North Luzon Force in the area, but only one had artillery, and it was anticipating an attack on the south shore of the gulf. MacArthur had said that he would meet the invaders on the beaches, and Homma worried about such a thing, but a vigorous defense was not mounted.

Thus Homma's troops were able to get ashore and expand their beachhead north to San Fernando Point. To the south, however, their advance from the beachhead inland to Rosario was held up by the US Army's 26th Cavalry Regiment, still a horseback cavalry outfit, commanded by Brigadier General Clinton Pierce.

Meanwhile, the 16th and 20th Regiments of Susumu Morioka's 16th Division had landed across a 20-mile beachhead on shallow Lamon Bay at 1:30 am on December 24 in calm seas. They too, met minimal opposition. The units of the South Luzon Force under Major General George Parker were scattered and in the process of changing positions. Those in the vicinity of Lamon Bay had no artillery.

Homma came ashore himself at Lingayen on December 24 to set up his 14th Army headquarters and to observe preparations for the attack southward through Luzon's central valley toward Manila. Spearheaded by the 7th Tank Regiment, they began moving south at 5:00 am, but two hours later, they met and were halted by the 26th Cavalry. The ensuing firefight was costly for both sides, but the Scouts managed to hold up the Japanese until mid-afternoon before withdrawing south of the Agno River. General Wainwright, a former cavalryman himself, arrived to see this action and commented that it was a "true cavalry delaying action, fit to make a man's heart sing. Pierce that day upheld the best traditions of the cavalry service."

Almost as quickly as it had begun, however, the battle of northern Luzon was over in the mind of Douglas MacArthur. He had already begun implementing plans for a strategic withdrawal into the rugged, 500-square-mile Bataan Peninsula north of Manila Bay.

The theory, which had been articulated in the prewar War Plan Orange (WPO-3), was that the terrain was defensible, and MacArthur's forces could hold out there until reinforcements arrived from the United States – as expected. However, while those on the ground in the Philippines assumed that help was on the way, the US Army War Plans Division was on the verge of making a firm decision to write off the defenders. A rescue mission, they decided from the comfort of their Washington offices, would be too costly and time consuming at a time when resources should be devoted to the war with Germany.

In a message to Chief of Staff General George Marshall, on December 22, MacArthur indicated that he might have to make his move to Luzon rather quickly because his command numbered less than 50,000 men on Luzon, and that the "Japanese disembarking from the 70 to 80 transports in Lingayen Gulf had a strength of 80,000 to 100,000 men." In fact, like Percival in Malaya, he was overestimating by a substantial factor. The total strength of the 14th Army invasion force was 43,110.

In a meeting with President Manuel Quezon, as well as their respective aides, Colonel Manuel Nieto and Lieutenant Colonel Sidney Huff, related in Quezon's book, *The Good Fight*, MacArthur told the president that he was "preparing for the worst in case the Japanese should land in great force at different places," at which time, he would concentrate his army on Bataan, move his headquarters, the High Commissioner's office, and the Commonwealth Government to Corregidor and declare Manila an open city.

"Do you mean, General," asked Quezon, "that tomorrow you will declare Manila an open city and that some time during the day we shall have to go to Corregidor?"

"No," MacArthur said, he didn't think it would be necessary quite that soon.

Quezon recalled being "startled" by MacArthur's sudden pessimism.

Nevertheless, MacArthur decreed that WPO-3 was in effect and ordered that the shipment of supply stockpiles to Bataan should begin.

To oppose the 14th Army offensive that was coming south toward Manila, the USAFFE implemented the North Luzon Force Plan, which called for a series of delaying actions that would take place at specific places surveyed before the war under the scenario that an enemy landing would take place at Lingayen Gulf. There would be five defensive lines separated by a distance of one night's march. Each one was associated with a specific defensible terrain feature, such as a river, hill, or swamp. The first defensive line, called D-1, lay in the flats about 15 miles south of Lingayen, and had already been breached by December 24.

D-2, the second defensive line, ran parallel to the Agno River, the only major river in the area that ran across, rather that parallel to, the broad valley between Lingayen and Manila. The American and Filipino troops began digging here on Christmas Eve, hoping for the best.

At that same moment, President Quezon and his family, along with High Commissioner Francis Sayre and other Philippine Commonwealth officials boarded the interisland steamer *Mayan*, and left Manila for the relative safety of Corregidor, the heavily fortified island in the center of Manila Bay.

CHAPTER 11

BLACK CHRISTMAS

During the first week of World War II in the Far East, the IJA had made amazing progress in every one of the campaigns they had begun. They had met resistance, they had been slowed, they had been forced to pay dearly for ground, but these were isolated instances. In no place were the defenders able to successfully reverse the tide of victory. Adjectives such as "surprised" and "stunned" were the best that could be used to describe those who faced the IJA.

During the second half of December, insufficient preparation and overconfident strategic predictions on the part of the Allies left the IJA in command of the initiative everywhere.

In Malaya, Tomoyuki Yamashita's 25th Army controlled everything north of the Perak River, nearly a third of Malaya's west coast, within a fortnight, while the 18th Division, which had landed at Kota Bharu on December 8, was working its way down the less heavily populated or defended east coast, where progress was limited mainly by the rugged terrain and lack of decent roads. Because of lack of transport and the difficult roads, the full strength of the 18th was not landed until the eve of the assault on Singapore at the end of January.

The Japanese victories, which appeared so easily achieved, buoyed the spirits of the attackers and demoralized the defenders. The victory at

Jitra on December 12 was a case in point.

As Masanobu Tsuji writes in his memoirs, "the much bragged about Jitra Line, which was to have been defended by a division for three months, was penetrated in about fifteen hours by barely five hundred men."

By moving more quickly – by a factor of months – than the British anticipated, the Japanese were also able to capture and make use of abundant supply dumps before they could be moved. Tsuji mentions shells "piled up like mountains, as were also gasoline, provisions, ammunition, and so on ... Our officers and men who since embarkation had been living on dry bread and salt ... found tobacco, cakes, and tinned foods piled up chuckfull in a storehouse in the rubber plantation."

The Japanese, who belittled the British and Indians as rich in supplies, but deficient in fighting spirit, came to refer to these numerous caches as "Churchill supplies." Tsuji writes that, as the offensive progressed, the Japanese were able to rely on the Churchill supplies for all of their gasoline requirements.

Major General David Murray-Lyon of the 11th Indian Infantry Division, who ordered the Jitra withdrawal, was relieved of command on December 23. On December 15, in a wireless transmission, Winston Churchill himself cautioned Percival to "Beware lest troops required for ultimate defence of Singapore Island and Fortress are not used up or cut off in Malay Peninsula. Nothing compares in importance with the fortress."

Within Singapore, life appeared as normal, with restaurants functioning as usual despite rationing. Indeed, the ration of things such as meat and butter was triple the ration in Britain itself. Nevertheless, preparations were already quietly underway to evacuate women and children to India "temporarily."

Yamashita's bicycle brigades and bridge-building engineers were again moving south toward Singapore at a rapid pace. The engineers were also able to repair damage that had been done to the railroad running along the west coast, and supplies were running in captured rolling stock. General Takuma Nishimura's Imperial Guards Division arrived by rail from Bangkok to join the 5th Division.

Penang Island, containing the largest British colonial presence north of Singapore, was evacuated of Europeans and abandoned on December 17 – much to the chagrin of the local population who had been loyal to the British, and now felt abandoned. The IJN quickly took over the former RN base at Penang, and used it as home to the IJN 6th Fleet's 8th Submarine Squadron. The German Kriegsmarine also set up a major facility here at Penang, commanded by Captain Wilhelm Dommes, for the basing of the Gruppe Monsun (Monsoon Group) U-Boats operating in the Indian and Pacific Oceans.

Many Japanese troops, all of whom had been briefed to treat the Southeast Asians as "little brothers" beneath the roof of the Greater East Asia Co-Prosperity Sphere, did not behave in a brotherly way toward the Malay people. Theft and cruelty were rampant. Even Yamashita complained about this, writing in his diary that "I want my troops to behave with dignity, but most of them do not seem to have the ability to do so. This is very important now that Japan is taking her place in the world. These men must be educated up to their new role in foreign countries."

––––––––––––––––

The Japanese also dominated the skies with excellent air superiority fighters. The IJAAF Nakajima Ki-43 Hayabusa (Peregrine Falcon) and the IJNAF Mitsubishi A6M "Zero" were vastly superior to the Brewster Buffalo, which was standard equipment for the RAF and Royal Australian Air Force (RAAF) fighter squadrons. Already outnumbered, and at less than half their authorized strength, Allied bombers were far less effective than their Japanese counterparts. Inferior equipment had been relegated to the Far East earlier in the year with the understanding that it was too obsolescent to stand up to the Luftwaffe. Those aircraft not considered obsolescent were frankly obsolete. It was another case of grossly underestimating Japanese capabilities.

Barely three weeks had passed since RAF Air Chief Marshal Sir Henry Brooke-Popham had quipped that England could keep their "super-Spitfires and hyper-Tornadoes. Buffaloes are quite good enough for Malaya." They absolutely were not.

Reinforcements were promised, and on Christmas Day Bristol Blenheim bombers arrived from Britain – but only seven of them. It was another case of too little, too late. However, the British had other concerns at that moment, notably the effort to block Germany's Afrika Korps from reaching the Suez Canal.

Early in January, the RAF received 52 Hawker Hurricanes to aid in the air war over Malaya, and in the air defense of the Singapore Island, which was now frequently the target of Japanese bombing raids. One of the RAF's most advanced fighter aircraft, Hurricanes had proven themselves against the Luftwaffe in the Battle of Britain in 1940, and were vastly superior to the obsolete Brewster Buffaloes. However, much to their chagrin, the RAF found them to be barely a match for the Japanese Zeros and Oscars, which were lighter and capable of outmaneuvering the Hurricanes.

By Christmas, the Japanese 25th Army, its bicycles, its tanks, and its captured Churchill supplies, had reached the Perak River, a natural barrier roughly half way from the invasion beaches to Singapore. Fortunately for Yamashita and his men, the river was not one that the British chose to exploit as a defensive line aside from destroying the bridges.

Because the Perak was too broad and too deep to ford, many of the motor boats that had been used in the landings at Singora were brought forward and used to ferry the combat troops across. On December 26, the 5th Division crossed near Blanja, and the Imperial Guards Division crossed upriver at Ipoh virtually unopposed. Once across, they secured the southern shore for the engineers who would rebuild the bridges in order to permit the tanks and supply convoys to cross.

Masanobu Tsuji reports that when Yamashita was told by the engineer in charge that it would take three weeks to rebuild the bridges, he quipped, "Dear me, Major General, it can be done in a week." As Yamashita sat down at the 25th Army command post near Taiping, overlooking the river, to impatiently monitor their progress, the engineers pressed infantry troops into service as laborers, and the job was done in a week.

———

Tsuji reports that while the 25th Army was on the Perak River, they received good news from Hong Kong. By Christmas Day, General Takashi Sakai's 23rd Army troops had reduced resistance within the island to isolated pockets. Deciding that further fighting was useless, the governor, Sir Mark Aitchison Young, went to Sakai's headquarters at the prestigious Peninsula Hong Kong Hotel to surrender the Crown Colony.

Numerous well-documented massacres of civilians, medical personnel, and POWs by Japanese troops took place in Hong Kong that day, followed by a reign of terror against the civilian population that lasted for some time. These earned the day of surrender the sobriquet of "Black Christmas," which was long remembered in Hong Kong.

The yuletide occupation of Hong Kong left only one of the numerous nineteenth-century European enclaves on the Chinese coast. The Portuguese colony of Macau, 40 miles south of Hong Kong, was not attacked by the Japanese because Portugal had declared itself neutral in the war. Indeed, Macau actually flourished during the early years of World War II as the only neutral port in the Far East.

Portugal's other colony in the Far East, Eastern Timor, had been "invaded" by a joint Dutch and Australian force, operating from Dutch Western Timor on December 17. Neutral Portugal complained loudly to Australia and the exiled Dutch government, but the island of Timor was occupied in its entirety by the Japanese two months later.

Defenseless and cut off from communication with their mother country, the Portuguese in Macau put up nervously with Japanese troops coming and going at will – as did the French in Indochina – but the two sides never came to blows.

———

Across the South China Sea from the Malay Peninsula, the British protectorates across northern Borneo felt the boots of the Japanese invader on December 16. These were an interesting group of potentates.

General Tomoyuki Yamashita stunned the world with his swift and efficient conquest of Malaya and Singapore, for which he became known as the "Tiger of Malaya." He commanded the IJA 25th Army. (NARA)

General Hideki Tojo became the face of Japanese militarism and expansionism. During much of World War II, he was the most powerful man in Asia short of Emperor Hirohito, serving simultaneously as Japan's prime minister, minister of war, and later also as chief of the IJA General Staff. (Author's collection)

General Masaharu Homma commanded the IJA 14th Army in the Philippines. He captured Manila in about a week, but it took him five months to completely defeat American and Filipino troops. (Author's collection)

General Hitoshi Imamura commanded the IJA 16th Army in its conquest of the Dutch East Indies. He wound up swimming ashore when his transport ship was hit by friendly fire on the first night of the invasion of Java. (Author's collection)

Prince Fumimaro Konoe, who served three terms as Japan's prewar prime minister, was a leading exponent of the idea that there should be a new order in the Far East with Japan as its center. (Author's collection)

Colonel Masanobu Tsuji was the planning officer for the 25th Army during the Malaya–Singapore campaign, and later served in other operations. Though described as a tactical genius by some, many IJA officers also considered him a madman. (Author's collection)

Yamashita's 25th Army met only sporadic resistance when it captured Kuala Lumpur, the administrative center of British Malaya, in January 1942. (Author's collection)

Japanese troops celebrate the conquest of the Bataan Peninsula in the Philippines in April 1942. (NARA)

Imperial Japanese Army troops marching into action in 1942. (NARA)

Australian antitank gunners take out a Japanese tank on the road through the Malay Peninsula north of Singapore in January 1942. (NARA)

The view from central Singapore as the naval petroleum storage facilities burn and the Japanese advance, February 1942. (NARA)

British troops surrender to the Imperial Japanese Army in Singapore, February 1942. (Author's collection)

Victorious troops of Yamashita's 25th Army march into Singapore, February 1942. (Author's collection)

Imperial Japanese Army infantry troops eat breakfast, poured from buckets of Miso soup. In the field, conditions would be less formal than in a barracks mess hall. (NARA)

Dutch workers dig out a railway car that was hit in a Japanese air raid near Surabaya on the island of Java in February 1942. (NARA)

This prewar illustration shows the Netherlands holding its most precious jewel, the Dutch East Indies. For the Japanese, the great petroleum reserves of Borneo were a coveted gem. (Author's collection)

The signature secret weapon for the Imperial Japanese Army, especially in the Malaya and Java campaigns, was the lowly bicycle. Seen here is a prewar Japanese bicycle factory. (Author's collection)

General Masaharu Homma comes ashore at Lingayen Gulf in northern Luzon to begin his conquest of the Philippines, December 1941. (NARA)

They were not technically British colonies, but "protectorates," all of whom depended upon the British for their protection and to run their foreign affairs. British North Borneo was administered by a chartered company of the same name. Labuan, just off shore, had been managed in this way, but in 1941, it was administered directly by the British from Singapore. Brunei was a sultanate, and therefore an autonomous entity, although it was under British protection, and the resident British administrator wielded more practical administrative power than the sultan.

Sarawak, meanwhile, was a kingdom ruled since 1841 by the British-born Brooke family, who were called the "White Rajahs." Looking for protection from pirates and other regional powers, the Brookes were interested in a protectorate relationship with Britain, but the British were content to simply recognize them as an independent country. Oil, and its importance, had yet to be discovered, and the British were not interested. A footnote to the story is that on the eve of the American Civil War, James Brooke, the first Rajah, had offered to give Sarawak to the United States as a colony. Abraham Lincoln declined. In 1888, the United Kingdom finally granted protectorate status. In 1941, the sitting White Rajah was Charles Vyner Brooke. December found him in Australia, where he remained until after the war.

Gradually, as the industrial revolution progressed, and the importance of oil entered the global consciousness, the outside world became interested in Borneo. Oil exploration on the 287,000-square-mile island dates back to the nineteenth century, first in the Dutch part of the island, and in the north by 1899. The first wells in Brunei were drilled near Brunei Town (now Bandar Seri Begawan) around that time, and at Miri in Sarawak in 1910. With the notable exception of the British Malayan Petroleum Company, most of the early prospectors and freelance drillers across Borneo were bought out by the Anglo-Dutch Royal Dutch Shell group before World War II. Royal Dutch Shell had been formed in 1907 through a merger of the Royal Dutch Petroleum Company (Koninklijke Nederlandsche Petroleum Maatschappij) and the United Kingdom's Shell Transport and Trading Company Limited. In turn, Shell had built a refinery at Lutong, near Miri, in 1914. Further major discoveries had been made near Seria in Brunei in 1929.

———————

Having met with Count Terauchi on Hainan, Major General Kiyotake Kawaguchi rejoined his 35th Infantry Brigade, who had shipped out of Cam Ranh Bay north of Saigon aboard ten transport ships, escorted by an IJN escort under Rear Admiral Shintaro Hashimoto, a task force which included the cruiser *Yura*, four destroyers, and a sub-chaser. It was an imposing force, considering that northern Borneo was virtually undefended.

Air Chief Marshal Brooke-Popham had chosen to post just one battalion plus a 6-inch gun battery, unsupported by air or naval assets, in northern Borneo. As Britain depended heavily on Indian troops for defending remote locations, the battalion was drawn from the 15th Punjab Regiment. Given the area's importance as an oil producer, he should have done more. In fact, he had *lessened* the defensive obligations of the 1888 protectorate agreement. There had been a small RAF contingent at Kuching, but this had been pulled back to Singapore several months earlier. An RN presence had been withdrawn in 1940. Brooke-Popham's orders in case of a Japanese attack were simply to burn, not defend, the petroleum industry infrastructure.

Coincidentally, the White Rajah seems to have understood the importance of airpower better than Brooke-Popham, who was an RAF officer. In the months leading up to December, it was he who had ordered airfields to be constructed at key locations throughout Sarawak for the use of the RAF. He possessed no combat aircraft to base on them. The Rajah had, however, assembled a small army of local tribesmen into a unit which he called the "Sarawak Rangers," a force which was actually larger than the contingent which Brooke-Popham had assigned to protect northern Borneo. The defenders, Punjabis as well as rangers, were under the unified command of Lieutenant Colonel C.M. Lane as the Sarawak Force (SARFOR).

Given the Japanese strategic understanding of the petroleum situation, it is little wonder that the landing sites for Kawaguchi's troops were at Miri in Sarawak, and Seria in Brunei.

The invasion on December 16, undetected ashore until the Japanese ships appeared on the horizon, was almost anticlimactic and virtually unopposed, except by the 6-inch guns and a single company of Punjabis. Unlike the situation of the initial 25th Army landings on the Malay Peninsula, the Borneo landings took place in relatively calm seas. Being on the flats near the coast, both oilfields were seized almost immediately, and the refinery at Lutong was captured by the end of the day.

Anticipating Brooke-Popham's order to destroy the drilling and refining facilities, Kawaguchi had arrived prepared. He brought with him four field well drilling companies of the Oil Drilling Section of the Kwantung Army's 21st Field Ordnance Depot. The petroleum infrastructure was torched on December 8 at the first notice of the Japanese attacks from Malaya to Pearl Harbor, but the Japanese engineers were capable of repairing and restoring the drilling and refining equipment that had been damaged.

Overhead, the only air support for the defenders, and as it turned out the most effective counterstrikes, would come from the Dutch, operating out of bases far to the south in Dutch Borneo. The first came three days after the invasion, on December 19; two Dutch Dornier Do 24 flying boats roared into the skies heretofore unpopulated by Allied airpower, damaging one of the troop transports and sinking the destroyer *Shinonome*.

On December 22, having achieved their immediate objectives, the Japanese resumed their offensive. As Japanese bombers struck the nearest Dutch air base, at Singkawang, a short distance west of the Sarawak border, Kawaguchi's detachment moved toward Kuching (aka Sarawak City), which was the headquarters of the only official military defense of northern Borneo. The attack might have gone as smoothly as the initial operations on December 16, had it not been for the Dutch.

On the evening of December 23, as the Japanese troop ships approached Kuching, two submarines from the Koninklijk Marine Divisie Onderseeboten III (Royal Netherlands Navy Submarine Division

III) successfully struck the invasion fleet. In a rapid succession of attacks on the convoy beginning at 10:40 pm, the submarine *K XIV* sank two Japanese troop ships and left a third dead in the water. Shortly after midnight, the submarine *K XVI* attacked and sank the Japanese destroyer *Sagiri*. However, on Christmas Day, the *K XVI* was attacked and sunk by the Japanese submarine *I 66*.

In the meantime, the Japanese convoy succeeded in launching its amphibious attack against Kuching. Despite bombing attacks by Dutch B-10 bombers, the Japanese succeeded in capturing all their objectives over the next 36 hours, securing both its airstrips by sundown on December 25.

Next, the Japanese moved across the border, defeating Dutch forces and capturing Singkawang and its airfields by December 29, as Colonel Lane's remaining SARFOR troops, as well as the Dutch defenders on the ground, withdrew into the jungle.

The mopping up and securing of the remainder of northern Borneo began on New Year's Eve, with an attack on Jesselton (now Kota Kinabalu) in Brunei, followed by landings on Labuan Island on January 3, 1942. The final Japanese amphibious operation began as Japanese ships assembled off Sandakan, the administrative center for British North Borneo, on January 18. As Dr James Taylor, a surgeon in Sandakan, later recalled, Brooke-Popham had earlier assured the residents that the waters offshore were too shallow for an amphibious landing. To this, Taylor observes, "he was an old fogey and the Japanese came ashore in little [shallow draft] boats anyway."

The following morning as these boats landed, Governor Charles Robert Smith officially surrendered the last British protectorate to General Kawaguchi. The only major resistance in this final push had come at Jesselton, where a small constabulary force had held out for nine days. By this time, the Japanese assault against Dutch Borneo was already underway.

Across the South China Sea in Manila, the Christmas decorations that had gone up under happier circumstance before December 8, still glittered in homes and shop windows, but the air was filled with nervous electricity and the stench of a million gallons of fuel oil that was being burned to keep it from being used by the Japanese. A week earlier, people spoke of "if" the Japanese came. Now, it was "when."

The NBC radio correspondent Bert Silen proclaimed, especially to listeners listening in via short wave in the United States, "Let it be known that our Christmas Eve was the darkest and gloomiest I ever hope to spend."

Colonel (then Major) Carlos Romulo writes in his book *I Saw the Fall of the Philippines* that "no girls in slacks and shorts were bicycling along the water front … the Yacht Club, the night clubs and hotels … all looked like funeral parlors."

Up on the D-2 Defensive Line, 30 miles inland from Lingayen Gulf, soldiers faced the IJA 14th Army, who launched a renewed offensive at 2:00 am on Christmas Day. The 91st Division and the 26th Cavalry, spread thinly along the Ago River, had been ordered to hold the line until the following day. After bitter fighting, Lieutenant Colonel Kuro Kitamura's 48th Reconnaissance Regiment managed to fight their way across the river about 7:00 pm on the evening of December 25, and the Americans and Filipinos fell back from D-2 the following day.

In Manila, President Quezon had relocated to Corregidor on Christmas Eve, and on Christmas Day General MacArthur's USAFFE opened for business at its new headquarters on the island. On December 26, with the USAFFE officially transferred to Corregidor, Manila was proclaimed by its municipal fathers to be an "open city," meaning that it would not resist an invasion in the hope that it would be merely occupied, and not attacked. The proclamation was trumpeted by the media, banners were put up and the blackout, in effect for two weeks, ended.

The scene was surreal.

"It was a beautiful moonlit night," Colonel James Collier of the USAFFE Operations Staff wrote in his diary of crossing Manila Bay to Corregidor on Christmas Eve aboard the steamer *Don Esteban*. "The cheerful, peaceful murmuring of the rippling waves from the cutting prow of the ship belied the havoc of war."

PART III

RISING SUN OVER ASIA

CHAPTER 12

A NEW YEAR IN MALAYA

"On this first day of the new year, I breathe the air of the South," Tomoyuki Yamashita wrote in his diary as the pivotal year of 1942 opened on an IJA in motion across Southeast Asia. "I was up at 5 am and it was already hot. I must put away recollections of the past. My duty is half done, although success is still a problem. The future of my country is now as safe as if we were based on a great mountain. However, I would like to achieve my plan without killing too many of the enemy."

Writing of the Japanese tactical plan in the Malay Peninsula as 1942 began, Masanobu Tsuji could have been speaking of the Japanese strategic perspective on the entire operation from Sumatra to Luzon when he observed that "the 5th Division pushed southward as fast as possible in order to give the enemy no time to develop new defensive positions."

However, on New Year's Eve, it was Tsuji who was scrambling for a defensive position. As the bridge work on the Perak River was ongoing, the spearhead of Japanese 5th Division infantry troops, specifically Major General Saubro Kawamura's 9th Brigade, including the 41st Infantry Regiment, continued cycling southward on the highway. They had penetrated another 40 miles southward toward the capital of British Malaya at Kuala Lumpur, and had reached a point north of the city of Kampar by December 30. Tsuji and a couple of aides had "requisitioned" an automobile in Ipoh and had decided to drive south "to share a glass of wine with the troops in the line to celebrate the New Year on the battlefield."

As they approached Kampar, they came under fire from British artillery in the surrounding hills. The 11th Indian Infantry Division, temporarily commanded by Major General Archie Paris (of the 12th Indian Infantry Brigade), had chosen Kampar to erect the sort of defensive barrier the defenders should probably have established on the Perak. Tsuji arrived just as the battle was being joined, and apparently he left shortly thereafter, as Kawamura's troops undertook a bloody fixed battle that halted the Japanese advance for four days.

At exactly the same time that the battle of Kampar was taking place, Tsuji's boss, General Tomoyuki Yamashita, the commander of the 25th Army, was implementing a daring tactical move with which his planning officer, Tsuji, fervently disagreed. Indeed, it would result in a brief tantrum of *gekokujo* from Tsuji that threatened to mar the amazing precision and achievement of the operation thus far.

Yamashita's plan – brilliant in retrospect as are all unorthodox plans that succeed – was to circle behind the British defenses. This plan, conceived before the battle of Kampar, was to outflank Archie Paris's 11th Division line, which ran for roughly 30 miles, from Kampar to Telok Anson (now Teluk Intan), where the meandering Perak River flows into the Straits of Malacca. Using the motorized landing boats from the Singora landings that had been brought up for the Perak River crossing, as well as others captured along the way, Yamashita would land 1,500 men, mainly from the 5th Division's 11th Regiment, behind the enemy's lines, south of the mouth of the Perak.

Tsuji complained that he was sure the men would be intercepted by British air or naval assets, and not only the men, but vessels necessary for the eventual landings on Singapore's fortress island, would be lost. In his memoirs, Tsuji writes dramatically that as he watched the regimental commander walk away to undertake the operation, "I could see the shadow of death on his back."

The contingent put to sea late on December 30 from Lumut, and landed on January 4 near Sungkai. While en route, they were strafed once, but only once, by British aircraft. Realizing that they were sitting ducks for a determined air attack, they expected to be finished off at any moment, but the British never returned. The "shadow of death" that Tsuji had seen was merely an apparition. Yamashita's plan worked.

In the meantime, Kawamura's spearhead, reinforced by replacements rushing south from the Perak River crossing, were able to claw their way through the 11th Indian Division positions in Kampar and the surrounding hills. The 11th suffered severe casualties in the battle, but Japanese 5th Army's 41st Infantry Regiment, which bore the brunt of the unexpectedly difficult fight, had to be withdrawn from combat to regroup.

Despite the damage inflicted to the Japanese at Kampar, this battle had been conceived as a delaying action, not as a counterattack, and in the aftermath, the British executed a further withdrawal, this time to the town of Slim River (now Sungai Slim), near the river of the same name. Meanwhile, any small measure of satisfaction that might have been gained from the successful holding action was offset for the British by the discovery of Japanese troops in their rear along the coast. This only served to hasten the withdrawal and add to the confusion.

The 11th Indian Division defensive position began 4 miles north of Slim River at Trolak, because farther south, the dense jungle gives way to open terrain, which is less easily defended. The total distance from Trolak to the road and rail bridges across the Slim River was about 16 miles.

The 5th Division spearhead, now Colonel Tadao Ando's 42rd Infantry Regiment, reached Trolak on January 5, and exchanged fire with the defenders. The following day, a detachment of more than a dozen tanks under the command of Major Toyosaku Shimada caught up to the 42nd. While Ando favored a flanking operation through the jungle, Shimada insisted that his tanks would get bogged down in this terrain, and successfully argued for their use in a frontal attack along the highway.

This assault began under cover of darkness at about 3:30 am on January 7 with Shimada's tanks leading the way. However, when the first three tanks were taken out by antitank defenses, the attack stalled because the thick forest crowded the edges of the road and there was no way for the following tanks to immediately bypass the burning tanks. This left a traffic jam which, like the Japanese troops at sea a few days earlier, left the Japanese as sitting ducks for an air or artillery attack. However, as in the case of the contingent in the boats, luck was with the Japanese, and an attack never came.

At first light, Shimada's men were able to find a bypass road though the jungle, and by 6:00 am they and the 42nd Regiment infantry had managed to break through the first enemy defensive position. From here on, the vanguard of Shimada's force, tanks under the command of Lieutenant Sadanobu Watanabe, executed a dash through British defenses that would have been worthy both of the axiom of a hot knife through butter, and of praise from the most audacious of the Panzer unit commanders of the Wehrmacht.

The next strong point, in and around the town of Trolak, was manned by the 2nd Battalion of the British Army's Argyll and Sutherland Highlanders Regiment (ASHR), a recently arrived unit which had been trained specifically for jungle warfare and attached to the 11th Indian Division. They were caught largely by surprise, having not yet prepared their defensive positions. Watanabe's tanks managed to break through quickly, splitting the Highlander force, and penetrating the positions of the 28th Gurkha Brigade, while inflicting heavy casualties among the defenders.

This done, Watanabe raced the retreating enemy toward the road and rail bridges across the Slim River, which lay several miles ahead. Indeed, having cut through lines of combat troops, guns blazing, the tanks dashed straight through rear echelon and headquarters units as the British officers stood by slack-jawed.

By mid-morning, Watanabe had slashed through the 11th Indian Division headquarters and had reached the Slim River highway bridge before the British engineers could destroy it. Indeed, much of the 11th Division force was still north of the bridge.

At this point, Watanabe dismounted and dramatically cut the wires leading to the demolition charges with his samurai sword. In his memoirs, Masanobu Tsuji writes that when the 42nd Regiment infantry arrived to secure the bridge, Watanabe led ten tanks and a contingent of infantry across the bridge and secured three additional bridges across other streams in rapid succession. The British resisted at the next bridge, and Watanabe, though now wounded, was able to capture this one as well before halting for the day.

In his book *Singapore Burning*, Colin Smith quotes Lieutenant Colonel Arthur Harrison, a British artillery commander who was at the battle, as paying a respectful comment to Watanabe. "Heedless of danger and of their isolation they had shattered the [11th Indian Division]," Harrison admits. "They had captured the Slim Bridge by their reckless and gallant determination."

Lieutenant Colonel Ian Stewart, commanding the 12th Indian Brigade, meanwhile, accepted the blame for having not destroyed the line of tanks at the beginning of the battle when it might have made a huge difference in the outcome. As he wrote to the British Army's official historian after the war, "I am rightly criticized for ... not using the Field Artillery in an anti-tank role ... It is no excuse, but I had never taken part in an exercise embodying a coordinated anti-tank defence or this type of attack. The use of tanks on a road at night was a surprise." "Surprise" had been the purpose of the night attack, and this gamble, which might have failed, worked splendidly for the vanguard of Yamashita 25th Army.

If the time it took his engineers to rebuild the Perak River bridge is an indication, capturing the Slim River bridges intact shaved a week off Yamashita's timetable. Meanwhile, the battle of Slim River devastated the 11th Indian Division. Its 12th and 28th Brigades were so badly mauled that they were practically erased, as was the 2nd Argylls. As many as 500 men were killed, and more than 3,000 were captured. Of those who were unable to retreat southward along the main road, a few managed to escape into the jungle. Some were captured and others simply disappeared. One man was found alive, still living off the land, in 1949.

As the morale of the IJA soared with every victory, that of the Allied defenders plummeted. Kenneth Attiwill later wrote:

brooding above all, adding weakness to morale as well as to military efficiency, lies the jungle itself – a terrifying morass of tangled vegetation, steamy heat, nerve-racking noises and the discomfort of insects; mosquitoes by the myriad, moths, beetles, insects of all kinds, biting, buzzing, irritating and debilitating. Rubber, too, with its gloom, dampness and sound-deadening effect breeds a feeling of isolation. The enemy may be anywhere – everywhere – in front or behind to left or to right. Noise is difficult to pinpoint; men appear and disappear like wraiths. Rumor begins to spread. In the monsoonal season there is the added handicap of torrential rain, hissing down incessantly upon the greenery, dripping dankly on heads and bodies, humid, sweaty, destructive.

Speaking of himself, Attiwill went on to say that:

it was like this for the young and inexperienced troops who took up their places for the first defensive battle of the Malayan campaign, a battle which was noteworthy for two reasons – it was Britain's first defeat in the jungle; it was the pattern of future defeat in all the attempted defensive actions down the Malayan peninsula.

Masanobu Tsuji recalls debriefing an unnamed British brigade commander who was among the large army of prisoners that had been captured, asking, "Why did your men raise their hands so quickly?"

"For what reason did you attack only on the front where we had not prepared to meet you?" replied the British officer. "When we defend the coast, you come from the dense jungle. When we defend the land, you come from the sea. Is it not war for enemies to face each other? This is not war. There will be no other way than retreat, I assure you."

As Tsuji comments, "this criticism was characteristic of the British attitude throughout the whole period of operations, and was common to every front."

The stunning British defeat at the Slim River and the equally surprising Japanese amphibious landings along the coast were met with great consternation by the British. The initial outflanking maneuver along the coast had worked so well that Yamashita conducted more of these using troops of General Takuma Nishimura's Imperial Guards Division.

On January 22, having learned of this turn of events, Winston Churchill penned a scathing memo to the First Sea Lord, Admiral Dudley Pound, complaining that:

> we have been absolutely outmanoeuvred and apparently outfought on the west coast of Malaya by an enemy who has no warship in the neighbourhood. Consequently our forces are made to retire from successive positions, precious time is gained by the enemy, and a general state of insecurity engendered in our fighting troops. The shortcomings are only too evident. Why were the enemy allowed to obtain all these craft? We apparently have none or very few, although these were waters we, until recently, controlled… This command of the western shores of Malaya by the Japanese without the possession of a single ship of war must be reckoned as one of the most astonishing British lapses recorded in naval history.

As the Imperial Guards Division leapfrogged down the Malacca Coast, the 5th Division continued south on the main highway where the next major milepost was Kuala Lumpur, the capital and, with a population of 80,000, the largest city in British Malaya. It was an objective long on symbolism, but short on defense. Arriving on January 11, the Japanese troops were met with only sporadic gunfire, and swept through the city easily. The British Army had abandoned the city.

The RAF base at Kuala Lumpur was occupied and prepared for Japanese aircraft operations. All of the government buildings were taken over and made ready for the subsequent Japanese occupation administration, and the infamous, Victorian-era Pudu Prison was transformed into a POW holding facility. The prison complex, designed by the British to include a caning area on the grounds, went on to be used by the Japanese as a torture chamber.

In the railyard at Kuala Lumpur, the Japanese found more than a dozen entire trains which had simply been abandoned because the single-track main line between there and Singapore was so heavily clogged with southbound traffic. In one car, they discovered stacks of boxes of highly detailed maps of Singapore, which had just been printed in Kuala Lumpur and were awaiting shipment to Percival's garrison. For Yamashita, it was an incredible gift.

———

The disasters of early January resulted in a rethinking of British strategy and a decision to regroup south of Kuala Lumpur, and stop the Japanese advance at a place barely 70 miles north of Singapore where the broad Muar River and its swampy flood plain were nearly a mile wide. For this action, Wavell and Percival pulled the badly beaten 11th Indian Division out of the fray entirely, replacing it with the Australian 8th Infantry Division under the command of Major General Gordon Bennett.

When World War II had begun in September 1939, Australian Prime Minister Robert Menzies had decided to augment Australia's small peacetime militia by mobilizing the 2nd Australian Imperial Force (AIF). As with the 1st AIF, which had been formed in World War I, the primary mission was in support of Great Britain, to which Australia was tied as a member of the British Empire. The 2nd AIF was comprised ultimately of four infantry divisions (6th through 9th) and the 1st Armoured Division. However, all but the 8th Division and the 1st Armoured had been deployed to help the British fight the German Afrika Korps in North Africa. The 8th Division, less the 23rd Brigade, was sent to help the British defend Malaya.

The British and Australians constructed their stand on the Muar River around two strongpoints, both part of an amalgam of units known as Westforce. A smaller contingent, known as Eastforce, was assigned the task of slowing the progress of the Japanese 18th Division on the opposite side of the Malay Peninsula.

The westernmost components of Westforce included elements of the 53rd Infantry Brigade of the British Army, and the fresh, but not fully trained 45th Indian Brigade. They faced the Japanese Imperial Guards Division at the mouth of the Muar River, overlooking the Johor Strait, south of the Straits of Malacca at the city of Muar.

The inland component of Westforce faced the Japanese 5th Division along the main highway near the town of Gemas. The units involved included elements of the 8th Indian Brigade and the 27th Australian Brigade, a component of the 8th Australian Division.

Churchill had ordered that the 5th Army should be ambushed, and the ambush site chosen was the Gemenchah (or Gemensah) Bridge, which crossed the small Kelemah River, north of the main crossing of the Muar River. The unit picked to execute the ambush was the Australian 2/30th Battalion under Lieutenant Colonel Frederick "Black Jack" Gelleghan.

At about 4:00 pm on December 14, the first bicycles of the 5th Division arrived and were allowed to pass. As the motorized vehicles and tanks arrived and began crossing the bridge, 2/30th Battalion's Company B detonated explosives under the bridge and began raking the bicycle troops with machine gun fire. The Japanese troops, exposed on the road with their rifles tied to their handle bars, suffered heavy losses. The Japanese managed to cut the Australian field telephone line so they could not call for artillery support, but Japanese artillery fell along the road, inadvertently hitting the Japanese troops.

All but a handful of the Company B men managed to slip away to join the remainder of their battalion on the road between Gemas and Tampin. The following day, after Japanese airpower raked the Australians in and around Gemas, and Japanese engineers repaired the Gemenchah Bridge, the 5th Division resumed its offensive.

The Australians of 2/30th Battalion met them with antitank guns, inflicting a disproportional level of damage before withdrawing. The "Diggers" as the Australian troops had referred to themselves since before World War I, had made a good account of themselves in a difficult campaign in which the momentum was against them.

Hearing of the successes of his troops, General Bennett, who was in Singapore, bragged to the media that his men had stopped the Japanese and would soon be pushing them back. Perhaps, if only for a moment, he actually believed his own hyperbole.

On the coast at the mouth of the Muar River, it was the opposite story. The Japanese Imperial Guards arrived late on January 15, and as there was no bridge, they commandeered ferries and sampans, and attempted to cross the following morning. Turned back by Australian artillery, the Japanese moved upstream and crossed successfully at the city of Muar.

Here, the Japanese artillery barrage fortuitously caught the headquarters of the 45th Indian Infantry Brigade, injuring its commander, Brigadier Henry Duncan, while killing or injuring his staff officers, and the battalion commanders. Ill-prepared to begin with, the 45th was now largely leaderless and easy prey for the Japanese, who outflanked and nearly destroyed it. The few survivors fell into a headlong retreat toward the town of Bakri about a dozen miles to the south.

Also on January 16, the heroic Australian 2/30th Battalion successfully withdrew from their increasingly untenable position on the highway at Gemas. They had fought bravely, and they had cost Yamashita's 25th Army around 1,000 casualties, but had delayed his offensive by only two days.

On January 17, Brigadier Duncan was ordered to pull together what remained of his brigade and recapture Muar. However, the battered troops were attacked before they could get underway, and found themselves back on the defensive.

By this time, the Imperial Guards had barged their tanks across the Muar River, and the following morning they used them to assault the position in Bakri held by the 45th Brigade, and now supported by the Australian 2/29th Battalion.

Taking a page from the playbook of Sadanobu Watanabe in the Slim River battle, the commander of the Imperial Guards spearhead tank detachment, Captain Shiegeo Gotanda, rushed the entrenched troops without infantry support. This had worked for Watanabe because he had been slicing through unprepared troops caught suddenly in unprepared positions. Gotanda was attacking troops who had been preparing all night to resist his attack. As a result, all of Gotanda's tanks were knocked out by Australian antitank gunners.

Having suffered an unanticipated setback on January 18, Tomoyuki Yamashita ordered the Imperial Guards to undertake an encirclement of the 45th at Bakri, as well as of elements of the British 53rd Brigade farther south at Yong Ping, who were to cover the withdrawal of the 45th. This movement also included another seaborne assault, with the fleet of landing boats delivering a sizable contingent behind the lines of the defenders.

After some skirmishing against the 53rd on January 19, Nishimura closed the jaws of the beartrap of encirclement on January 20, albeit after the 45th had begun its withdrawal. Many of the troops managed to slip through the net, although Brigadier Duncan, who had recovered from the concussion suffered in the Muar bombardment, was killed leading a fixed bayonet counterattack.

Now led by Lieutenant Colonel Charles Anderson, the battered 45th headed south toward Batu Pahat, where a last stand took shape at the Batu Pahat Bridge. By now, it was a retreat under fire, as the Japanese were nipping at their heels and harassing them from the air and with ambushes. On January 22, realizing that they could not escape as a unit, Anderson ordered his survivors to disperse into the jungle, leaving the wounded behind at the mercy of the Japanese. According to historian Colin Smith, the 45th Brigade and the supporting Australians had begun the week with 4,000 men, but only about 900 managed to make it through to British lines north of Singapore. John Deane Potter puts the respective figures at 4,500 and 850.

The wounded, and the medics with them, were taken to Parit Sulong, confined as prisoners, and later murdered under orders from Takuma Nishimura. Based on the eyewitness account of Australian Lieutenant Ben Hackney, one of two men who managed to crawl away, Colin Smith writes that:

> Some of the prisoners were let out of the bungalow to find their captors waiting for them with water and cigarettes which they held just out of

reach while a party of Japanese war correspondents took pictures of the captives, about to receive them. When the correspondents had gone, the water was poured away, the cigarettes pocketed and the men bundled back inside … While most of the Australians, the majority roped together like a chain gang, were first shot, some of the Japanese officers decided it was time the samurai swords they carried – often family heirlooms – tasted blood, and practiced their skills on the Indians.

So much for the "Asia for Asiatics" doctrine.

The Japanese had paid a high price for their crossings of the Muar River at Gemas and the stubborn resistance between Bakri and Batu Pahat, but by the last week of January they were within 40 miles of the Johor Strait separating Malaya from Singapore.

Meanwhile, the 18th Division, moving down the east coast of the Peninsula, had met a British Eastforce roadblock after capturing the city of Endau on January 21. In the meantime, the men and materiel intended to bring the 18th up to full strength were en route from Cam Ranh Bay in Vietnam, escorted by the IJN cruiser *Sendai*, with six destroyers and five minesweepers.

In January 26, as the reinforcements were being landed at Endau, the invasion fleet was intercepted by two destroyers, HMS *Thanet* and HMAS *Vampire*, as well as two waves of British and Australian bombers, all dispatched from Singapore. In the ensuing battle, no ships were lost to air attack, but both of the Japanese transports were damaged by gunfire from the two Allied destroyers. In turn, the Japanese destroyers sunk the *Thanet*, but the Australian destroyer escaped. Once ashore, the Japanese troops found that the order had already been given for Eastforce to disengage and withdraw toward Singapore.

Though the Japanese momentum was no longer threatened on the ground, the RAF now intervened with renewed vigor, encouraged by the recent arrival of an additional 48 Hawker Hurricanes. Because the airfields on Singapore Island were under constant attack, and many of the first batch delivered on January 3 had been destroyed on the ground, these fighter planes were delivered by the aircraft carrier HMS *Indomitable* to airfields near Palembang on Sumatra in the Dutch East Indies. While the Hurricanes had been shown to do no better than to hold their own against the Japanese fighters, at least they could do that, and it boosted British morale to see Hurricanes involved in air-to-ground strafing missions against Japanese ground troops. However, the ground war in Malaya was all but over, and these were another installment in the checklist of measures that were too little, too late.

By January 31, the three Japanese divisions were converging on Johor Bharu, the capital of the Sultanate of Johor, one of the British client states in Malaya. Here, General Yamashita was met cordially by Sultan Ibrahim II, one of the world's richest men and a long-time friend of Britain, who had made a personal gift of £250,000 sterling to King George VI when he visited the United Kingdom in 1939.

Ibrahim was also no fool. He had had seven weeks to get used to the idea of Japan as a victorious presence in the land and, if only for self preservation, he readily accepted that the Japanese, not the British, were the new colonial masters of Malaya. Masanobu Tsuji reports that the first time he saw Ibrahim's palace, called Istana Bukit Serene, high on a hill overlooking the Johor Strait, it was flying a Japanese flag.

The sultan was later named as a consultant to the Japanese occupation, and his palace became Yamashita's headquarters for the invasion of Singapore. Indeed, from the tower at Ibrahim's residence, the Japanese general could look out and see Singapore Island spread out before him like a map.

In the space of 54 days from the initial landings, the three divisions of the Japanese 25th Army had traveled nearly 700 miles under fire, despite often problematic terrain, and had conquered British Malaya, a task which many prognosticators on both sides believed would take 12 to 18 months. In his report to Tokyo, penned in the comfortable surroundings of the sultan's palace, Yamashita reckoned that his army had taken 8,000 prisoners, killed 5,000 enemy troops in battle, captured 280 vehicles and rebuilt more than 250 bridges. Yamashita's men had defeated a force which outnumbered them two to one.

Like many postwar historians, Tsuji cites the lowly bicycle as the single most important weapon in the campaign:

> The British Army formations were almost completely equipped with motor cars and trucks, and whenever we were able to steal a march on them and seize bridges in front of them, or destroy their vehicles by shell fire or aeroplane bombing, their soldiers had to abandon their cars and trucks and continue their retreat on foot. Even the long-legged Englishmen could not escape our troops on bicycles. This was the reason why they were continually driven off the road into the jungle, where, with their retreat cut off, they were forced to surrender. Thanks to Britain's dear money, spent on the excellent paved roads, and to the cheap Japanese bicycles, the assault on Malaya was easy.

CHAPTER 13

A NEW YEAR IN THE PHILIPPINES

Masaharu Homma's 14th Army had also brought bicycles to the Philippines, where American money had also provided excellent paved roads – Highways 3, 5, and 13, which funneled down through a broad valley from the invasion beaches to Manila. In the capital, people were scrambling in droves to escape.

"The roads back into the hills were black with people striving to reach their native villages," writes Clark Lee of the evacuation of Manila in his book *They Call it Pacific*. There were paved roads on the evacuation routes too, and good railways on Luzon as well. "The few trains still running into the provinces were literally jammed to the car tops."

"To the native population of Manila, it seemed like the end of the world," writes Charles Van Landingham in his article, "I Saw Manila Die," published in the *Saturday Evening Post* on September 26, 1942.

"In the brief period of seven days, from Christmas Eve to the year's end, there had been a radical change in the situation in northern Luzon," writes Louis Morton in the official history of the campaign. "The Japanese, who on 24 December had just secured their beachhead, now threatened Manila and the road net into Bataan. The enemy had broken out of his initial lodgment and was now moving rapidly in two columns down the broad central plain of Luzon."

The inexperienced and lightly equipped Philippine Army divisions, the 11th, 21st, and 91st, bore the brunt of the Japanese assault, and endured the confusion of the staged withdrawals under fire that were part of the Luzon defensive strategy. The US Army's 26th Cavalry Regiment had twice held the IJA 48th Division for extended periods of time, inflicting heavy casualties, but they had suffered greatly themselves, and General Jonathan Wainwright, commanding the North Luzon Force, had been forced to pull them out of action to regroup.

Having pulled back to their D-2 Defensive Line at the Agno River at Christmas, the North Luzon Force reached D-3, between Santa Ignacia and San Jose, on December 27, as Homma had halted at the Agno to bring up the preponderance of his artillery and armor from the beachhead.

Hammered by the Japanese with renewed ferocity, the three Philippine Army divisions, acting independently, each straggled back to D-4, between San Miguel and Cabanatuan between December 28 and 30. At the same time, Homma was sending his 4th and 7th Tank Regiments wide to the east in attempt to outflank the defenders.

By New Year's Eve, with the tanks on their right flank, the North Luzon Force had withdrawn roughly 50 miles from D-1, to the last Defensive Line, D-5, where the 11th and 21st Divisions had dug in at Bamban and on the north side of Mount Arayat. The 91st Division on the North Luzon right flank, however, took the main hit from the 48th Division coming south on Highway 5, and from the two tank regiments, and was pushed well south of the line.

On the opposite end of D-5, troops at Fort Stotsenburg were busy shipping the post's stores, including 8,000 pounds of fresh beef and 100,000 containers of dry rations, to Bataan. Lieutenant Colonel Wallace Durst, the base quartermaster, reported that he burned 300,000 gallons of gasoline and saved about 50,000 gallons by shipping it out in every available container and filling the tanks of every available vehicle.

While two divisions held the left end of D-5 as planned, the 91st was pushed back nearly 20 miles to Baliuag. This put Homma's spearhead barely 40 miles from the edges of Manila, but, more critically, it placed the Japanese barely 10 miles from a vital road junction at Baliuag on the highway between Manila and Bataan. The North Luzon Force tenaciously and successfully fought through most of December 31, supported by Brigadier General James Weaver's Provisional Tank Group, which would be an important unit supporting the actions of the coming weeks.

Meanwhile, Homma had missed an enormous opportunity when he had failed, all week long, to destroy the railroad and highway bridges across the Pampanga River at Calumpit, which were the main conduit of supplies going into Bataan. Japanese bombers were attacking Manila, destroying facilities that would later be necessary to the occupation, but neglected this strategically important target.

The supply situation on Bataan was critical, and Homma might have made it worse. Originally, WPO-3 had called for moving food to sustain 43,000 troops for six months into Bataan when a war broke out. This goal would not be met. On top of this, MacArthur would have 47,500 troops, plus around 32,500 other personnel and 25,000 civilians to feed.

By the end of the last day of 1941, the North Luzon Force withdrew from D-5 to take up positions guarding the Bataan evacuation routes. As Louis Morton writes,

> the first part of the withdrawal had been completed. Although it had been successful, there had been difficult moments. Communications had broken down at times, supply had proved difficult, and some of the bridges had been blown too soon. The defense lines had sometimes been hastily and inadequately manned, or not occupied at all.

To the south, the two regiments of Susumu Morioka's 16th Division, who had landed at Lamon Bay on Christmas Eve, had overcome the more rugged, mountainous terrain in that area, and were nearing the southern edge of Manila by December 31.

Inside Manila, New Year's Eve was greeted with melancholy and resignation. Although Radio Tokyo had acknowledged the open city proclamation on December 26, the Japanese aircraft that had attacked the city occasionally throughout the week did not. A major air strike, involving multiple waves of bombers, had struck on December 27. Both the *Philippines Herald* and *Manila Bulletin* reported that night clubs were open for New Year's Eve, and a dance was held at the Fiesta Pavilion of the Manila Hotel, but the mood was subdued and those party-goers who were on the street dodged piles of garbage that had gone uncollected for days.

On New Year's Day in the capital, they were still waiting for the Japanese, but they had been following the news of their inexorable march ever since Homma's men had broken out of the Lingayen Gulf beachhead on Christmas Eve. The city, which had had a prewar population of 285,000, seemed all but deserted. Those who had not fled, especially the expatriates, stayed home, correctly assuming that internment was coming and that they might not see their homes again for years, if ever.

As the sun came up over the Philippine Commonwealth on the first day of 1942, the objectives of Masaharu Homma's 14th Army appeared to have been substantially completed. Undefended Manila lay between the jaws of a Japanese vise like a nut waiting to be cracked. Homma knew of MacArthur's withdrawal into the Bataan Peninsula, but dismissed the challenges of capturing it as negligible. He had been given two months to capture the Philippines, and he had done so much in just one week. In that time, his troops had captured an area ten times the size of Bataan, and they were geared up with momentum. How hard could it be to pluck that one last plum?

Most of the 14th Army personnel assumed that they would greet the new year by marching into Manila on January 1, but the cautious Homma ordered them to halt with the city in sight. As he explained after the war, "If those divisions went in together from south and north, anything might happen."

At 10:40 am, Lieutenant General Yuitsu Tsuchihashi, the 48th Division commander, contacted Homma, reminding him of the huge fires that had been raging in the vicinity of the port, whose facilities would be needed by the Japanese, and he offered to go in and "to rescue Manila from this conflagration."

At 8:00 pm, from his 14th Army headquarters in Cabanatuan, Homma approved the proposal, but ordered Tsuchihashi to wait until daylight the following morning. General Morioka of the 16th Division was ordered to move out at the same time and occupy the naval yard at Cavite, about 10 miles south of Manila, before entering the city.

It was 5:45 pm on January 2 when Major General Koichi Abe finally led his 48th Division infantry group, the Japanese spearhead, into Manila. The rest followed, flooding into the city to occupy all of the government buildings, and taking over hospitals for Japanese wounded.

As General Morioka writes in his operational report, "the joyful voices of the Japanese residents were overwhelming." Meanwhile, British and American residents were ordered to register as "enemy aliens" and report for internment. Almost 3,000 people were sent to Santo Tomas University, where they would spend the next three years in confinement under increasingly difficult conditions.

Three days later, after the newspapers resumed publication, they carried a proclamation from Homma's Kempeitai military police that:

> anyone who inflicts, or attempts to inflict, an injury upon Japanese soldiers or individuals, shall be shot to death [but] if the assailant, or attempted assailant, cannot be found, we will hold ten influential persons as hostages who live in and about the streets or municipalities where the event happened … the Filipinos should understand our real intentions and should work together with us to maintain public peace and order in the Philippines.

As both sides prepared for the imminent battle of Bataan, MacArthur reorganized his command, redesignating the North Luzon and South Luzon Forces as I Philippine Corps and II Philippine Corps, commanded respectively by General Jonathan Wainwright and General George Parker. The two were of roughly equal size, with 22,500 and 25,000 men, respectively. Fortunately for MacArthur, Homma was operating under the assumption that the total force on Bataan was 25,000. Because the topography of Bataan is centered on a steep central mountain range, the two corps were divided geographically, with I Corps to the west of the mountains, and II Corps in the east, where Bataan's major thoroughfare, Highway 110, ran along the coast. In their rear, around the port of Mariveles, at the tip of Bataan, MacArthur established a Service Command Area, where supplies were stored.

Bataan afforded excellent defensive opportunities. As Colonel Harry Skerry, the North Luzon Force engineer, wrote in his after-action report, "taking it all in all, the rugged terrain of the Bataan Peninsula, covered as it was by a thick jungle, concealed the works of the defender even when the enemy had constant air superiority and air observation."

The Japanese, meanwhile, also reorganized the 14th Army. As previously planned, the 48th Division was pulled out and reassigned to General Hitoshi Imamura's 16th Army for operations in the Dutch East Indies. On the eve of the Bataan campaign, Homma was now losing the largest unit under his command, and the one which had proven to have been the most effective in the Philippines campaign thus far. The veteran 5th Air Group was also being transferred out of 14th Army control.

Fortunately, Homma had accelerated the departure from Taiwan of the 65th Brigade, under Lieutenant General Akira Nara, which had been earmarked to join the 14th Army on January 22 as an occupation force. It was smaller and less capable than the 48th Division, but it was manpower which Homma would need, and it arrived in the Philippines on January 1 with 6,700 officers and men.

The opening skirmishes of the Bataan campaign followed directly after the Japanese breached the USAFFE's D-5 Defensive Line on December 31. Carrying forward with the momentum of the preceding week, the Japanese turned west to converge on Layac, a crossroads town at the neck of the Bataan Peninsula. As the Japanese moved forward, the defenders fought a determined holding action to permit the establishment of the main battle line across the peninsula.

This line lay 15 miles south of Layac, and about 40 highway miles north of Mariveles. It ran from Mauban in the west to the Mabatang–Abucay area in the Highway 110 corridor on the east coast. At its center was 4,222-foot Mount Natib. A secondary, fall-back, or reserve battle line was planned for about 15 miles farther south between Bagac and Orion. Most of the defensive positions were placed along the coastal roads, and there was some concern about protecting the rugged, almost impassible center of the peninsula, but the Japanese would not fully employ this difficult terrain.

By midnight on January 5 the last of the Bataan force had reached Bataan, the last bridge demolition, designed to slow the Japanese advance, had been completed, and the defenders were as ready as they could be. They had three days to catch their breath.

The main battle of Bataan got underway at 3:00 pm on January 9 with a thundering artillery barrage, faulty intelligence regarding the main defensive line, and an unrealistic estimate of the strength and determination of the American and Filipino troops. Each of the five defensive lines south of Lingayen had been breached in about 24 hours, and Homma planned on a repeat of this timetable on Bataan. In retrospect, Homma also erred in assigning Nara's inexperienced 65th Brigade to the initial ground assault. The 16th Division was not committed to the battle until January 18.

According to Louis Morton, a postwar interrogation of Lieutenant General Maeda, Homma's chief of staff, revealed that:

Homma and the majority of the 14th Army staff believed that American resistance on Bataan would be weak and that operations there would be quickly concluded. The plan for the attack, therefore, was conceived of as a pursuit rather than an assault against a strongly fortified position in depth.

Nara's plan called for sending two regiments under Colonel Susumu Takechi against I Corps on the Highway 110 corridor in the east, and Colonel Takeo Imai's 141st Infantry Regiment against I Corps in the west. Both would be supported by mobile artillery.

For about a week, the two sides traded fire, probing efforts, attacks, and counterattacks, without any appreciable changes in position. It was not until late on January 16 that Nara was able to break through the II Corps left flank, which had been weakened in the heavy fighting. He knew that if he could move quickly enough, he could exploit this breakthrough to encircle the American and Filipino troops and pin them against Manila Bay. As it was, the line held.

On January 15, Homma had made the decision to commit elements of the 16th Division to the battle. These centered on the 16th Infantry Group, commanded by Major General Naoki Kimura, who had led the landing at Legaspi on December 10. Known as the Kimura Detachment, this unit included the 20th Infantry Regiment, supported by artillery. It reached the west coast opposite Wainwright's I Corps on January 18, and successfully scored a breakthrough on the American and Filipino right flank inland from Mauban on January 21. After several days of fierce fighting, I Corps was forced to withdraw from the line.

Meanwhile, Parker's II Corps line near Abucay, which had held on January 16, came under pressure from the 65th Brigade, was pushed back, but restored its position through a counterattack on January 22. However, that night, based on the pressure being felt against the entire line, MacArthur ordered a general withdrawal to begin the following day.

Both corps reached their positions in the reserve line on January 24, having held off the Japanese for over two weeks.

The Japanese had not anticipated their tenacity. Despite their having pushed the American and Filipino troops from one line to another, they too had suffered. Nara's 65th Brigade lost about a quarter of its strength, causing him to admit that his unit had "reached the extreme stages of exhaustion."

While the withdrawal to the secondary line was clearly a setback for the American and Filipino troops, it had been done in an orderly fashion, and it would take some time for the Japanese to reach their new position.

Frustrated with the slow pace of the overland campaign, Homma borrowed from Yamashita's successful campaign along Malaya's west coast, by authorizing a bold amphibious flanking maneuver along Bataan's west coast to outflank I Corps and cut it off from its supplies. A force, numbering approximately 2,000 troops of the 2nd Battalion of the Kimura Detachment's 20th Infantry Regiment, was dispatched to execute three landings in the American and Filipino rear, in the Service Command Area near Mariveles.

This maneuver, which would have been called "bold and decisive" if it had worked, met with difficulties almost immediately. The terrain was a jagged coastline studded with rocky points and inlets, all of which were nearly impossible to see in the dark, especially from boats in high seas.

On the night of January 22–23, the first landing party was discovered in the darkness by Lieutenant John Bulkeley's PT-34, and two boats were sunk. The rest of the force landed on Longoskawayan Point near Mariveles, and managed to get ashore to set up defensible positions. Two further landings over the next several days managed to secure beachheads on points farther north, but none of the landing parties was able to move beyond its initial perimeter.

The Japanese troops were attacked from ashore by infantry, tanks, and artillery, and from the sea by the guns of the minesweeper USS *Quail*, but held on in caves and other positions until early February. The last survivors escaped inland on February 12, but were caught and cornered by the 26th Cavalry on February 16. What came to be known as the Battle of the Points was a victory for the defenders, but it only served to show how vulnerable their position at the tip of Bataan really was.

As February began, the reserve line between Bagac and Orion still held, but with one eye on the jungle and the other on their dwindling food stocks, it was hard for the defenders not to grow fatalistic. On the day that they had marched back down the road to the reserve line, Lieutenant Henry Lee of the Philippine Division sat down and wrote a poem entitled "Abucay Withdrawal," in which he writes that ironically:

Bataan was saved for another day
Saved for hunger and wound and heat
For slow exhaustion and grim retreat
For a wasted hope and a sure defeat.

Lee later died in captivity, but his notebook was recovered, and his poems published posthumously in 1947 in the book *Nothing But Praise*.

CHAPTER 14

THE PLOESTI OF THE EAST

In the literature of World War II, much has been written about the reliance of Germany upon the great petroleum center at Ploesti, Romania. Far too little has been written to underscore the fact that Balikpapan, on the eastern shore of Borneo, would become the Ploesti of the Japanese Empire. Balikpapan was the keystone of Japanese strategy in Southeast Asia, and to the future of the Japanese war machine. By the opening days of January 1942, this keystone was within easy reach.

The Japanese conquest of the British protectorates of northern Borneo had been initiated and completed within the final two weeks of December 1941, but this left the unfinished business of Dutch Borneo. It was especially within this area, on the island's east side, that great petrochemical production and refining operations helped to make the Dutch East Indies the world's fourth largest oil producer.

That story began with the discovery of petroleum as a fuel and lubricant for the industrial revolution in the nineteenth century, and the worldwide quest by industrialized countries to find and possess it. This led to the realization, late in the nineteenth century, of the value of the oil seeping out of the ground in Borneo, and in turn, to the creation in

1890 by Jean Baptiste August Kessler and Henri Deterding of an oil company. With an official charter from King William III of the Netherlands, this little company on a distant tropical shore earned itself a distinguished name as the Royal Dutch Petroleum Company (Koninklijke Nederlandsche Petroleum Maatschappij).

As noted in Chapter 11, this firm merged in 1907 with the Shell Transport and Trading Company Limited of the United Kingdom to become Royal Dutch Shell, which went on to become – and to remain to this day – one of the half dozen largest oil companies in the world.

Though Shell had become the dominant player in Dutch Borneo, as well as the British-controlled north, it was by no means the only oil company present. As a small footnote to the petroleum story on the island on the eve of the war, it should be mentioned that one of the active independent producers was the Borneo Petroleum Company, founded in 1929 as a joint Dutch–Japanese venture. By 1941, however, the Dutch were minority players, with controlling interests held by the Japan Petroleum Company and Mitsui Bussan Kaisha, a steamship transportation company that was part of the Mitsui family *zaibatsu*, or conglomerate.

By 1941, the oil industry on the east coast of Dutch Borneo, including both drilling and refining, was centered at two locations. First was Tarakan Island, in the Sesajap River Delta about 250 sea miles south of Sandakan in British North Borneo. Second was Balikpapan, across the equator and about 400 sea miles south of Tarakan. At the time, Balikpapan City had a population of about 30,000, with Tarakan City being about one third this size.

The Japanese battle plan called for Tarakan Island to be invaded on January 10, with Balikpapan assaulted soon after. In preparation, the Japanese flew a number of reconnaissance missions, and had begun flying bombing missions on Christmas Day.

Leading the attack would be the Sakaguchi Detachment, drawn from the IJA 56th Infantry Group of the 56th Division, commanded by Major General Shizuo Sakaguchi, based on the 146th Infantry Regiment, and reinforced by artillery, armored, and engineer units drawn from the division. Whereas the northern Borneo attack had launched from Cam Ranh Bay in Vietnam, the Sakaguchi Detachment sailed from Davao in the Philippines, which they had captured in December as a base of operations for the Dutch Borneo assault.

Also involved in the Dutch Borneo operations was the 2nd Kure Special Naval Landing Force, a battalion-sized contingent of IJN ground troops under Lieutenant Commander Masanari Siga. The inclusion of "Kure" in the designation identified the unit's base as Kure Naval Base. Landing force units were identified by the name of their parent base. In addition to Kure, other Special Naval Landing Forces originated at Maizuru, Sasebo, and Yokosuka.

Used more often in the Dutch East Indies than elsewhere in Southeast Asia, the Special Naval Landing Forces were a naval infantry force roughly equivalent to the US Marine Corps. At the beginning of the war, they were an elite force, but as time progressed, their ranks were filled mainly with poorly trained and poorly disciplined troops brought in randomly from other units.

Tactically, Borneo presented the Japanese with a significantly different terrain situation than they were encountering in Malaya. Both consisted almost entirely of dense, essentially impenetrable and largely uninhabited jungle. However, in Malaya the British had constructed both a highway and a rail system. These were confined to narrow corridors, but they ran from one end to the other without interruption. In Borneo, there were no roads connecting the major cities. All long-distance transportation was by sea. For the invader, there was no opportunity to use tanks, motor vehicles, or that stellar conveyance of the Malay campaign, bicycles. Each of the objectives would require a separate amphibious assault.

However, the defenses in place to fend off these attacks were inadequate at best. As with the British in northern Borneo, the Dutch had left the east side of the island only lightly defended, planning to depend on a scorched earth policy to deny their petroleum resources to the Japanese.

The Royal Netherlands East Indies Army (Koninklijk Nederlands Indisch Leger, KNIL) maintained its 6th Infantry Battalion at Balikpapan, and its 7th Infantry Battalion at Tarakan. These units were each supported by two field artillery batteries, and the ports were defended by coastal artillery batteries, each of which consisted of a pair of 120mm guns and four 75mm guns. The Dutch commanders at the two locations were Lieutenant Colonel Cornelius van den Hoogenband at Balikpapan, and Lieutenant Colonel Simon de Waal at Tarakan.

Bandjarmasin, the Dutch administrative capital for its part of Borneo, located near the southern tip of Borneo along a marshy coastline 210 miles south of Balikpapan, was effectively undefended. Lieutenant Colonel Henry Halkema commanded a contingent of about 500 troops and no artillery, which were all that were assigned to protect a city of around 70,000 people. Like Tarakan and Balikpapan, Bandjarmasin was also a center of petroleum activities, but of less significance than the other two.

Overhead, the mainstay of Netherlands Naval Aviation (Marine Luchtvaartdienst, MLD) were Dornier Do 24 flying boats, while the Military Aviation of the Royal Netherlands East Indies Army (Militaire Luchtvaart van het Koninklijk Nederlands-Indisch Leger, ML-KNIL) was equipped with American-built aircraft, such as Glenn Martin bombers, as well as Curtis Hawk and the Brewster Buffalo single-seat fighters of the type that had proven so inadequate in Malaya.

Most ML-KNIL bases were on Java, but the service had forward-deployed Martin bombers and Buffalo fighters to Balikpapan. However, they were pulled back to Samarinda in northwest Borneo, or to Java and Sumatra in January. Aside from the submarines of its Divisie Onderseeboten III, and a small number of support vessels, the Royal Netherlands Navy had also withdrawn from eastern Borneo.

Meanwhile, the 16 transport vessels carrying the IJA's Sakaguchi Detachment and the Special Naval Landing Force were escorted by the cruiser *Naka*, 11 destroyers, three No.31-class patrol ships (converted from Momi-class destroyers), two seaplane tenders, and a bevy of minesweepers and patrol boats under the command of Rear Admiral Shoji Nishimura.

Seaplane tenders were a usual part of IJN invasion fleets because they were an efficient means of providing air support for observation and strike missions in lieu of aircraft carriers or dependence upon land-based airpower operating from distant bases.

As the invasion fleet arrived off the coast of Tarakan at sunset on January 10, the setting sun glowed red through the towers of smoke which boiled upward from the burning oil rigs. The Dutch had already torched the oil fields.

The assault went forward that night as planned, with the assault troops using the fires to navigate through the smoke and darkness. The first of two waves of IJA troops, commanded by Colonel Kyohei Yamamoto, reached the island around midnight, albeit not at their assigned location, with the IJN landing force coming ashore shortly thereafter.

Tarakan is a large island, comprising 177 square miles, much of it jungle or marshland. The swampy terrain, combined with the smoke and fires, not to mention the darkness, was a recipe for confusion. The attackers encountered pockets of resistance from KNIL troops, mainly ethnic Indonesians, and were compelled to beat off one determined counterattack. Nevertheless, with their superior numbers and superior firepower, Yamamoto's troops were able to battle their way through to the vicinity of the main oilfield by noon on January 11. The IJN landing forces, meanwhile, ran into tough going in the jungle and did not occupy the Tarakan airfield until the following morning. During their advance on the airfield, they were hit by a small number of ML-KNIL bombers flying from Samarinda.

Realizing that his position was untenable, and knowing that his command had essentially been sacrificed to delay the Japanese, Lieutenant Colonel de Waal conveyed an offer to surrender. Yamamoto accepted and advised General Sakaguchi. However, because of the general confusion that then prevailed, and lack of adequate communications, not all of the KNIL forces got the message.

The second wave, or left wing, of the IJA 146th Infantry landed on Tarakan at 3:00 pm on the afternoon of December 11. Their objective was to capture the coastal artillery battery, which was manned by troops who were not yet aware of de Waal's surrender. While they were making their way through deep jungle to reach the guns which dominated the entrance to the harbor at Tarakan City, it was the turn of the IJN not to get the message.

At some point on January 12, a notice, preserved in US Army records, was transmitted to the ships of the invasion fleet which read "Although the enemy has offered to surrender, it is feared that the coastal battery located at the south end of the island is not aware of this and it would be dangerous to proceed to the Tarakan pier, therefore hold up your sailing."

Failing to heed the warning, two minesweepers made for the waters off Tarakan City, entered within range of the coastal guns, came under fire and were sunk. There was much rejoicing in the gun batteries, but deep embarrassment for de Waal, who had already surrendered. He agreed to obtain a surrender of the battery to avoid further bloodshed, but when the artillerymen came down to give themselves up, the Japanese tied them up and threw them into the bay. It is estimated by the Allies that 219 men were drowned.

General Shizuo Sakaguchi came ashore on Tarakan at midday on January 12 to supervise the mopping up operations and to accept de Waal's formal surrender. He remained for 48 hours before embarking with most of his detachment for the next objective, Balikpapan.

He also met with the man who had been the local manager for Borneo Petroleum. He cut a deal by which the Japanese would hire him to supervise the repairs to the badly damaged facilities on Tarakan which he had previously helped to sabotage on behalf of the Dutch colonial authorities. For Sakaguchi, it was an expedient transaction, because the Borneo Petroleum people knew their way around and could get the job done more quickly than Japanese engineers.

The bargaining that had ensued gave the Japanese general an idea. If he could convince the Dutch to surrender Balikpapan intact, the Japanese could be on line with their own production without a lengthy period of reconstruction. It was a long shot, and it delayed his operational timetable, but apparently Sakaguchi felt that it was worth a try.

On January 16, two Dutch and three Japanese officers departed from Tarakan aboard the commandeered Dutch motor vessel *Parsifal*. Four days later, a Dutch Do 24 seaplane spotted the boat at sea, landed, and took the passengers aboard. Having been flown to Balikpapan, they presented Sakaguchi's proposal to Lieutenant Colonel van den Hoogenband, the garrison commander.

Despite the threat that any damage done in Balikpapan would result in the execution of all the Dutch troops captured if the Japanese attacked, van den Hoogenband rejected the ultimatum out of hand. Indeed, he had already ordered the limited demolition of facilities in the port area on January 18. Destruction of wells and other facilities farther inland was not, however, part of this order. Perhaps he still imagined that the Japanese would be somehow defeated and the oil fields should be preserved.

When the three Japanese officers returned to Tarakan on January 23 with the Dutch refusal, Sakaguchi had already initiated a Plan B, and was en route to Balikpapan. As it was obvious to the Dutch at Balikpapan that the Japanese were coming, Sakaguchi understood that the sort of tactical surprise that he had enjoyed at Tarakan on January 10 had been lost. However, an opportunity arose by which he thought he might achieve a modest element of surprise for part of his operation, specifically the capture of Balikpapan's substantial airfield. The idea was to use his main attack as a diversion to draw attention away from a covert operation against the airfield.

During the debriefing of ethnic Indonesian KNIL troops captured at Tarakan, some were turned up who appeared to be sympathetic to the propaganda message of the Greater East Asia Co-Prosperity Sphere. Using two of these men who had lived at Balikpapan as guides, Sakaguchi sent a small surprise attack contingent via canoe to infiltrate the heavily wooded coastline, travel up a jungle river, and capture the Balikpapan airfield. They departed on January 20.

Though spotted at sea by Dutch aircraft, the canoes successfully eluded detection as they made their way inland. Meanwhile, there had been no element of surprise for the convoy. Detected by Dutch reconnaissance aircraft on January 22 as they entered the Makassar Strait separating Borneo from Celebes, they were attacked by nine Martin bombers, escorted by 20 Buffaloes, the following day. One transport ship was sunk, and another was damaged.

Beneath the sea, the Dutch submarine *K XVIII*, part of Divisie Onderseeboten III, which had successfully attacked the Japanese invasion fleet off northern Borneo a month before, was quietly in pursuit. As the convoy approached Balikpapan on January 23, the submarine struck, sinking a Japanese ship. Initially it was believed to have been a destroyer, but subsequent comparisons to Japanese records show the lost ship to have been a transport.

The convoy, which reached the waters off Balikpapan later that day, began landing the invasion troops after nightfall, as was the typical Japanese practice for amphibious operations. By around 9:30 pm, most of the force was ashore, having overcome light opposition. Meanwhile, van den Hoogenband had ordered a withdrawal of his forces from Balikpapan City, but they ran into the Japanese surprise attack contingent coming the other way. Having captured the airfield, they were coming into the city to link up with the main landing force. Caught in a vise, most of the Dutch troops were compelled to surrender. Though the battle for Balikpapan City would continue for another two days, the airport had been secured, and operations were proceeding according to plan.

Offshore, though, it was another matter, for the submarine *K XVIII* continued to stalk the Japanese convoy. As the clock ticked toward midnight, its torpedoes struck, sinking another of the transports. In the small hours of January 24, another Dutch torpedo hit one of the three Japanese patrol ships, damaging it beyond repair.

At this point, Admiral Nishimura angrily ordered the destroyers escorting his transports to hunt and kill the escaping submarine, thus drawing them away from the troop ships. Perhaps the last thing on his mind was a surface attack against his flotilla, but this is exactly what he got.

Upon news of the imminent Japanese assault on Balikpapan, four Clemson-class USN destroyers of Destroyer Division 59, along with the cruisers USS *Marblehead* and USS *Boise*, had earlier been dispatched by the newly formed (January 7) American–British–Dutch–Australian Command (ABDA) to intercept the Japanese. The cruisers had to drop out of the pursuit, but the destroyers, under the command of Commander Paul Hopkins Talbot, continued north toward Balikpapan.

The USS *John D. Ford*, USS *Parrott*, USS *Paul Jones*, and USS *Pope* arrived at around 2:45 am to see the Japanese ships silhouetted against the fires burning ashore. With the Japanese destroyers on their submarine chase, the transports were protected mainly by the two surviving No.31-class patrol ships. Built as destroyers two decades earlier, they had been converted as landing craft carriers for the IJN landing forces, and had had much of their armament, including their torpedo tubes, removed.

The four American destroyers attacked, sailing directly into the formation of Japanese ships, and pounding them for several hours, using both torpedoes and their 4-inch guns. The Americans sank another of the patrol ships, along with four of the troop ships, and damaged two more transports. The toll might have been higher, but the USN was still working out bugs in its Mark 15 torpedoes, which had a tendency to run too deep. With no effective counterfire, the four destroyers escaped with minimal damage.

For the USN, it was the first major surface action of World War II, and the first since the Spanish American War nearly half a century earlier. For the IJN, it marked the climax of 48 hours of the most serious losses to date in the Southeast Asia campaign. However, had the destroyers arrived eight hours earlier, before the invasion troops disembarked from the transports, things would have been much worse for the Sakaguchi Detachment.

With the Allied naval elements having withdrawn, and the mopping up concluded on January 26, quiet descended once again upon Balikpapan. The only sounds of war were those of a few crackling fires amid the petroleum infrastructure near the docks, and gunshots near the old fortress of Klandasan, as around 80 Dutch prisoners were executed.

Sakaguchi had now achieved the goals of his assignment in Borneo. He had crushed the minimal Dutch military force that had stood up to him, and had seized the two great petroleum centers, with the largest, at Balikpapan, in much better shape than Tarakan.

For General Shizuo Sakaguchi, the conquest of Balikpapan on January 26 left only Bandjarmasin at the south end of Borneo, which was important because it was the seat of Dutch power and the only major population center on Borneo that was not yet under Japanese control. The area around Bandjarmasin was strategically important to the Japanese because of the well-constructed airfields, such as those at Martapura and Kotawaringin, which would be important bases for Japanese bombers patrolling and controlling the waterways to the south as operations were undertaken across the rest of the Dutch East Indies.

For this next step, Japanese tactics changed significantly. Largely because Japanese naval power was being assembled for operations in Java and Sumatra, and because the Sakaguchi Detachment had lost most of its transport ships to enemy action, the next step would not be an amphibious operation. Rather, it would be a pincer movement that depended mainly on an overland march across the southern tip of Borneo.

Rather than embarking most of his entire force, as he had done after Tarakan, Sakaguchi established his permanent 56th Infantry Group headquarters at Balikpapan, and sent just one battalion to capture Bandjarmasin. On January 27, a reinforced infantry company under Captain Yoshibumi Okamoto left Balikpapan aboard small boats, intending to follow the coastline all the way to Bandjarmasin.

Four days later, the 3rd Battalion of the 146th Infantry Regiment, commanded by Colonel Kyohei Yamamoto, was landed at Adang Bay, about 100 miles south of Balikpapan. They marched due west carrying nine days' worth of field rations and bicycles, which proved useless on the jungle trails and were discarded. The mountainous terrain proved to be a far greater obstacle than the handful of KNIL troops which they encountered, and many of the Japanese soldiers came down with malaria or other tropical diseases. Nevertheless, the fact that they made it at all was a triumph, and the fact that they made it in fighting form earned acclaim for Yamamoto from those higher up the command hierarchy.

By the end of the first week in February, Okamoto's contingent had come ashore south of Bandjarmasin, and the two prongs of the pincer were closing in on the city. On February 10, the airfield at Martapura was captured, and the Japanese marched without opposition into Bandjarmasin. Most of the Europeans who had been living there had been evacuated to Java earlier in the month. Colonel Halkema, meanwhile, had abandoned the city with his last 75 troops, and had retreated into central Borneo, where he was ordered to undertake the impossible task of defending the airfield at Kotawaringin.

Meanwhile, a number of civilians and KNIL personnel had separated from their units and had managed to escape from southern Borneo in small boats. Some of them managed to reach Java, where the residents were still more in denial, rather than fear, of a possible Japanese invasion of the colony's most populous island.

The IJA, which had soundly defeated a superior British force in Malaya, had now secured Dutch Borneo in the space of just 30 days without a significant land battle. With the latter victory – counterintuitively underreported in the global media of 1942, and largely overlooked in the history books – Japan had secured the petroleum that would fuel its triumphant war machine indefinitely.

CHAPTER 15

INDIES STEPPING STONES

As the oilfields of Borneo – and two weeks later, the oil fields of Sumatra – would fulfill a strategic objective on the Japanese Southern Road, other moves made on the Dutch East Indies chessboard were designed to address tactical concerns. As the Japanese closed in on Java and Sumatra, the Dutch, who had barely defended Borneo, were concentrating their resources, just as General Arthur Ernest Percival intended to do with his British Commonwealth assets in Singapore.

Just as IJA and IJN airpower was keeping pace with Tomoyuki Yamashita's 25th Army on the Malay Peninsula, moving into abandoned RAF bases closer and closer to the front, the tactical plan for the ultimate battle in the Dutch East Indies required a network of airfields on other islands which were closer to Java and Sumatra. One such island was the major Dutch East Indies island of Celebes (now Sulawesi) to the east of Borneo and due south of the Philippines.

Offshore, the Celebes operation was supported by a naval force commanded by Rear Admiral Raizo Tanaka which included the cruiser *Jintsu*, his flagship, ten destroyers, two seaplane tenders, and several minesweepers. An additional covering force under Rear Admiral Takeo

Takagi included the cruisers *Nachi*, *Haguro*, and *Myoko*, and two destroyers. They were all part of the growing IJN presence in the nearly 3 million square miles of Dutch East Indies waters.

The IJN surface fleet in this area was divided generally into two operating groups. The Western Force under Vice Admiral Jisaburo Ozawa, commander of the Japanese Southern Expeditionary Fleet, was tasked with operations in the South China Sea, and had supported the campaign in Malaya and Singapore. The Eastern Force, commanded by Vice Admiral Ibo Takahashi, conducted operations from eastern Borneo, east through Celebes, Ambon, Timor, and eastward to New Guinea.

Operations ashore in Celebes were conducted entirely by the IJN Special Naval Landing Forces, and occurred simultaneously with the IJA and IJN landings on Tarakan. This ground action, which was a brief one that history treats almost as a footnote to the Borneo operations, is notable for including the first Japanese airborne operation in Southeast Asia. The latter was a precursor to tactics that were to be revisited a month later in Sumatra.

Under the command of Captain Kunizo Mori, 2,500 men of the 1st and 2nd Sasebo Special Naval Landing Forces conducted the initial amphibious landings near the northern Celebes cities of Manado (also spelled Menado) and Kema before dawn on January 11, overwhelming the outnumbered KNIL defenders.

Meanwhile, staging out of Davao, 28 transport variants of the Mitsubishi G3M medium bomber carried more than 300 paratroopers from the 1st Yokosuka Special Naval Landing Force to a drop zone behind the invasion beaches. Landing at about 9:30 am on January 11, the paratroopers surprised the Dutch defenders, and began an assault on the airfield at Langoan and the seaplane base at Kakas.

The unexpected attack from above certainly reminded the Dutch troops of the use by the Germans of airborne troops in the conquest of their home country in May 1940. Indeed, Japanese tactical planners in both the IJA and IJN had made note of the successful use of German *Fallschirmjäger*, or paratroopers, as a spearhead during the

Wehrmacht spring offensive of 1940, and had begun training their own airborne troops. Germany's capture of the entire island of Crete, solely by airborne troops, in May 1941, must have been especially noteworthy as the Japanese planners pondered the island-studded map of the Southern Road. In retrospect, it is a wonder that the tactic was not employed on a wider scale.

A second airborne attack by the 1st Yokosuka on January 12 brought additional landing forces to Celebes, and assured the capture of the Langoan airfield. Though some of the Dutch troops managed to hide out in the mountains for about a month, northern Celebes was secured by the middle of the month.

With this, Captain Kunzio Mori's 1st and 2nd Sasebo headed south. Just as Sakaguchi had leapfrogged down the Borneo coast from Tarakan to Balikpapan, Mori embarked from Manado and headed for Kendari, at the southeast corner of Celebes. His Special Naval Landing Forces, aboard six transports, were escorted by a task force commanded by Rear Admiral Kyuji Kubo, which included the cruiser *Nagara*, his flagship, eight destroyers, and support ships. As with the task force that had supported Mori at Manado, Kubo's contingent was part of the IJN Eastern Force.

Mori went ashore under cover of darkness on the night of January 23–24, the same night that Sakaguchi had landed at Balikpapan. Within 24 hours, the defenders had been overcome, and the Japanese were in control of the strategically important airfield at Kendari.

Capturing airfields was a priority second only to the petroleum facilities in the Dutch East Indies, for they brought land-based Japanese fighters and bombers incrementally closer to future battlefields farther south on the Southern Road. The air base at Kendari was destined to be one of the most important. Centrally located within the Dutch East Indies, it would be an important refueling stop. It was also the base of operations for the devastating air attack on Darwin, Australia, which would terrify the land down under three weeks later.

Just as the airfields on Celebes were part of the Sumatra and Java strategy, other Dutch islands far to the east hosted airfields that would be useful in operations against Dutch- and Australian-administered New Guinea, which were scheduled for April. Centrally located between Celebes and New Guinea was 299-square-mile Ambon Island, part of the Molucca (now Maluku) Archipelago, 500 miles east of Celebes, 1,600 miles east of Palembang, and 250 miles west of New Guinea. The strategic importance of Ambon and the substantial, paved airfield at Laha on the island had been lost on neither the Dutch nor the Australians. They had agreed to jointly reinforce the island, but the first contingent of RAAF Hudson bombers had not touched down at Laha until December 7, 1941, less than 24 hours before the general outbreak of hostilities across Southeast Asia and the Pacific.

The Australians also sent troops, but they had few to spare. As we have seen, three of the four infantry divisions which comprised the Australian Imperial Force (AIF) were in North Africa helping the British fight the German Afrika Korps. Most of the 8th Division, except the 23rd Brigade, was helping the British defend Malaya.

The one brigade held back was given the precarious and impossible task of the forward defense of Australia itself. It was divided into what were known as the "Bird Forces," having been given what the Australian Department of Veterans' Affairs historical factsheet colorfully describes as "ominously non-predatory names." Forward defense of Australia meant outposts on islands north of that country and east of Malaya which were astride important sea lanes between Japanese-held territory and Australia. It was Gull Force that was dispatched to Ambon, while Sparrow Force went to Timor, and Lark Force went to New Britain, far to the east.

Each of the Bird Forces was essentially a single battalion, roughly a thousand or fewer infantrymen, reinforced with artillery and support troops. Deployed in 1941 before the full weight of the immense Japanese offensive had been experienced, each was sent to do a job that should have been done by a force a dozen times larger.

Deploying about ten days after Pearl Harbor, the 1,100-man Gull Force, centered on the 2/21st Battalion of the AIF, arrived on Ambon, joining a Dutch garrison on the island that consisted of the poorly trained 2,800-man KNIL Molucca Brigade, commanded by Lieutenant Colonel Joseph Kapitz. Gull Force was initially commanded by Lieutenant Colonel Leonard Roach, but he was replaced on January 16 by Lieutenant Colonel John Scott, who was no stranger to amphibious operations, having participated in the Gallipoli campaign during World War I. Scott arrived to find his new command in pitiful condition, with malaria and other diseases rampant in the equatorial heat, which still swelters in January.

Both USN and Koninklijk Marine flying boats operated out of Ambon, flying patrol missions, as well as frequent evacuations of civilians, but they were pulled out in mid-January, against the backdrop of increasing Japanese air attacks. Air defense of Ambon consisted of a few Brewster Buffaloes, which rose to meet IJN seaplane bombers that began visiting Ambon early in January at the same time as the offensive against northern Borneo.

The Buffaloes held their own for a while, but they were no match for the carrier-based IJN Zeros that first appeared over the island on January 24, the same day as the invasions of Balikpapan and Kendari. For the Ambon operation, the IJN brought in the carriers *Hiryu* and *Soryu*, both of which had been part of Admiral Isoroku Yamamoto's Pearl Harbor strike force. At Ambon, they targeted Dutch and Australian aircraft, compelling Wavell to make the decision to pull out the last of the Allied aircraft to preserve them to fight another day. When the invasion fleet was sighted at dusk on January 30, the Allied ground troops knew they would have to face the enemy with no air cover.

The fact that the IJN had used seaplanes and carrier-based aircraft to conduct operations against Ambon is, in itself, an illustration of why the Japanese needed to have airfields at locations across the sprawling Indies.

The remainder of the naval escort for the ten transport ships of the invasion fleet to which the *Hiryu* and *Soryu* were attached was largely the same contingent that had supported operations against Manado on January 11. Commanded by Rear Admiral Raizo Tanaka, this force was comprised of his flagship, the cruiser *Jintsu*, as well as eight destroyers and support vessels. The same covering force under Rear Admiral Takeo Takagi that had supported Tanaka at Kendari also accompanied him to Ambon.

As in Borneo, the ground operation at Ambon was to be a joint operation between the IJA and the IJN Special Naval Landing Forces. The latter contingent included 820 men from the 1st Kure Special Naval Landing Force, while the IJA contingent of approximately 4,500 men was centered on the 228th Infantry Regiment, one of three regiments in the 38th Division, which had taken part in the conquest of Hong Kong. This joint force was known as the Ito Detachment and commanded by Major General Takeo Ito, who had commanded the entire 38th Division at Hong Kong, and who operated at Ambon under the banner of the division's headquarters.

The first wave of IJA Ito Detachment came ashore during the night of January 30–31, with the IJN landing forces in the north, and the 288th mainly in the south. Ambon is nearly bisected by Ambon Bay, which cuts into the island from the southeast. The southern part contains the major population centers, while Laha airfield was across the bay on the northern part. Most of the defenders were located in these areas, but the initial Japanese landings were on the lightly defended north, and the least-defended area on the south side, well away from coastal guns guarding the entrance to Ambon Bay. Of course, established beachheads can be expanded more easily than landing troops under fire.

During January 31, the Japanese moved rapidly, reaching Australian-defended Laha from the north, and capturing Ambon City in the south by around 4:00 pm.

As the Allies shifted troops to face the landings, they left holes in their lines, which were exploited by the Japanese. A second wave of Ito Detachment troops came ashore at Passo (also written in some accounts as Paso) at the neck of the Laitimor Peninsula, effectively cutting the island in two. At the same time, the Japanese also snipped the telephone line which was the only way that the Allied troops could communicate with one another. The absence of communications isolated the various units and created confusion.

Kapitz ordered his men to continue fighting, which they did. However, shortly after midnight, the Japanese captured Kapitz, who had moved his headquarters close to Passo. For most of February 1, the action involved an Allied withdrawal, away from Passo and Ambon City, toward the southeast tip of the Laitimor Peninsula. These troops, with Colonel Scott still in command, had their backs to the Banda Sea, and realized that their position was essentially hopeless.

As this was ongoing, Admiral Tanaka ordered his minesweepers into Ambon Bay to clear the mines laid by the Koninklijke Marine, before they withdrew from Ambon earlier in January. This was in preparation for landing additional troops inside the bay. However, much to the immense joy of the troops fighting for their lives on the peninsula, one of the minesweepers struck a mine, blew up, and sank. Another was damaged.

Nevertheless, the jubilation that the Allied troops enjoyed at this juncture was certainly qualified by the pounding that was being dished out to them in the form of offshore naval gunfire and air attacks from the air wings aboard the *Hiryu* and *Soryu*. Throughout February 1, the naval bombardment also fell on the Australian and Dutch troops that were still trying to defend the airfield across the bay at Laha. On the morning of February 2, having encircled Laha, the landing troops, under Commander Kunito Hatakeyama, launched a ferocious assault aimed at dislodging the defenders. At around 10:00 am, Major Mark Newbury, commanding the joint force at Laha, decided that any further resistance would waste lives in an impossible situation, and ordered his men to surrender. Scott surrendered the defenders of the Laitimor Peninsula on February 3. About 30 Australian Diggers managed to successfully escape Ambon by canoe.

Newbury's hopes of saving lives by his surrender were darkened when, over the ensuing two weeks, Hatakeyama randomly murdered around 300 prisoners at Laha. Newbury himself was killed on February 6. Scott survived the war as a POW, although most of the troops who surrendered on Ambon died in captivity. In 1946, witnesses and makeshift graves were located, and Hatakeyama was tried, convicted, and executed as a war criminal.

By the time that Ambon fell, Captain Kunzio Mori's 1st and 2nd IJN Sasebo Special Naval Landing Forces had secured Manado in northern Celebes, and Kendari on its southeast corner. This left the airfield at Makassar on the southwest corner, the Celebes field closest to Java. His move on this final Celebes objective was supported by the same naval task force that had backed his landing at Kendari, this being commanded by Rear Admiral Kyuji Kubo, aboard the cruiser *Nagara*, with 11 destroyers – three more than at Kendari – and support ships.

Opposing Mori's landing forces here was a 1,000-man Dutch garrison commanded by Colonel Marinus Vooren. Like so many in the KNIL officer corps, Vooren was born in Java of Dutch parents. He had spent only three of his 53 years in the Netherlands, so the Indies were his homeland. As February began, Vooren was overseeing the evacuation to Java of ethnic European women and children – most of them Indies-born – and waiting for Mori's inevitable arrival. The only reinforcements coming the other way consisted of Lieutenant Colonel Jan Gortmans, who came in from Java to train Indonesian civilians to fight the Japanese as guerrillas.

On February 9, Mori's 8,000-man Special Naval Landing Forces went ashore near the town of Makassar. Recognizing that resistance here was a lost cause, the Dutch withdrew northward into the interior, where the Japanese tanks would be ineffective, Vooren to Tjamba, and Gortmans to Enrekang, places that to this day barely show up on maps. They held out almost until the end of February, but when they found themselves in tactically untenable positions, they each surrendered. Gortmans was beheaded in captivity, but Vooren survived the war and remained in the Indies until 1958, when he retired to the Netherlands.

CHAPTER 16

THE TIGER OF MALAYA STRIKES AT SINGAPORE

It was the afternoon of January 31, 1942 when General Tomoyuki Yamashita, anointed in the Western media as the "Tiger of Malaya," first stood in his soon-to-be command post at the Sultan of Johor's Istana Bukit Serene Palace, and looked out across to the island of Singapore, just a mile away. All conventional wisdom considered it impossible to capture.

As Yamashita scanned his target with field glasses, he also had the benefit of the freshly printed maps of Singapore, captured in Kuala Lumpur less than two weeks before, which showed the island and its defenses in great detail.

That morning, at the crack of dawn, to the mournful sound of a lone bagpiper, the Argyll and Sutherland Highlanders were the last British unit to march out of the Malay jungle and cross the Johor Strait Causeway into Singapore. They had headed north across that causeway in December 1941, numbering 880 strong. After the battle of Slim River, and other actions along the way, their ranks now numbered just 90 men. At 8:15 am, the British engineers blew a 70-foot gap in the causeway. Kenneth Attiwill, who was there, reported hearing one of them say grimly that "that should stop the little bastards."

Singapore Governor Sir Thomas Shenton Thomas had told the island by radio on February 1 that "All we have to do is to hang on grimly and inexorably, and not for long, and the reward will be freedom, happiness and peace for every one of us." As he knew, and as everyone in Malaya except Tomoyuki Yamashita knew, Singapore was impregnable. Or was it?

That evening, Yamashita wrote in his diary:

> The Imperial Guards and the 5th Division continue to advance, pressing hard on all fronts. At 16:47, the troops of the 5th Division advanced to the Johor Strait and are clearing the enemy remnants there. I am now preparing for my plan for Singapore, which I will attack within a week.

In London, Field Marshal Alan Brooke, the Chief of the Imperial General Staff, briefed Winston Churchill and his war cabinet that, after the arrival of reinforcements, General Arthur Percival's Singapore garrison numbered around 100,000, mostly Indian, but including 33,000 British and 17,000 Australians. In fact, Percival had a large military administrative staff and closer to the 85,000 troops in combat units that Percival himself mentions in his memoirs, and most of these were poorly trained. However, when Brooke told his government that "it is doubtful that the Japanese have as many in the whole Malay Peninsula," he was right.

Even with the Japanese 18th Division having been brought up to full strength, Yamashita had only about 30,000 men. Percival was short of ammunition for his artillery, and in planning for a three-month siege, he rationed it to 20 rounds per gun per day. However, Yamashita had even less ammunition, and fewer than two dozen serviceable tanks. His food supplies were running short, and he understood that the inefficient Japanese logistical chain would not be able to materially alter this situation any time soon.

Percival knew nothing of this, and assumed that the 25th Army, which had beaten him so soundly in Malaya, was comprised of more than 100,000 troops who were at least as well supplied as were the British Empire troops. Even in his memoirs, published in 1949, he still insisted that Yamashita had a force of 150,000. In Malaya, Percival had outnumbered Yamashita two to one, but in Singapore, his total numerical advantage was closer to three to one.

Meanwhile, just as Percival overestimated his enemy, Yamashita underestimated the size of the Singapore garrison. He thought Percival had only about 40,000 troops.

Yamashita realized the immensity of the challenge that lay before him. Across the Johor Strait, he faced one of the most thoroughly fortified positions in the world, and one that was surrounded by the moat of the Johor Strait. Across that moat, the Singapore shoreline was swampy muck, through which his landing force would be dragging themselves while exposed to concentrated enemy fire.

Millions upon millions of British national treasure had indeed been invested in the defenses at Singapore, but the formidable batteries of coastal artillery, armed with 15-inch battleship guns, had been constructed only on the south side and the eastern tip of the island, under the theory that any attack against Singapore would come from the sea. Before December 8, 1941, no strategic planner in his right mind would have predicted that an enemy force could ever capture all of Malaya – and certainly not in seven weeks – in order to assault Singapore from the north.

A popular historical myth holds that these guns, located in fixed positions, could not be turned to fire inland. In fact they could be turned – and they were – but most of them were located in places on the island that were farthest from where the invasion and ensuing battles would take place. They were also equipped mainly with armor-piercing ammunition for use against warships, rather than high explosive rounds for use against advancing armies. Because most of Percival's field artillery was of smaller caliber, the ammunition could not be interchanged.

Meanwhile, the British garrison had been stocked with sufficient food supplies to hold out almost indefinitely. However, none of the planning had anticipated that the prewar population of 550,000 would more than double as refugees streamed south out of war-torn Malaya.

To defend the island, Percival organized his forces into two front-line areas. The principal elements within the Northern Area, east of the causeway, were the 11th Indian Division and the British 18th Division, organized as components of III Corps. Within the Western Area, west of the causeway, were the 8th Australian Division, and the 22nd and 27th Australian Brigades. Percival also planned for a Reserve Area in the center of the island, and a Southern Area, concentrated around the city of Singapore, into which he dreaded to imagine withdrawing for a last stand.

Yamashita, who could not afford a three-month siege, much less an indefinite siege, knew that there was no choice but the same swift, decisive tactics that he had employed in Malaya. His plan was to begin with what he hoped would be a demoralizing artillery barrage, a bluff to confirm Percival's fears of unlimited Japanese ammunition supplies. Indeed, the pleas of Yamashita's supply officer to truncate the barrage would fall on deaf ears.

The barrage would be accompanied by a feint toward the northeast part of the island using the Imperial Guards Division, opposite Percival's Northern Area, to capture the island of Ubin Palau in the Johor Strait. The use of the Imperial Guards Division in a diversionary role met with a tantrum from the Division's commander, Takuma Nishimura. Yamashita wrote in his diary on February 6:

> I handed over my orders at 11 am to all the division commanders for the attack on Singapore. The commanders of the 18th and 5th Divisions said they would do their duty. But the divisional commander of the Imperial Guards looked very annoyed. He obviously has no faith in the plan. This plainly follows the demand he made yesterday that his division should lead the attack so he and his troops would be allowed to show their bravery.

Yamashita's main attack, utilizing the 5th and 18th Divisions, would cross the Johor Strait from the west, landing in the Western Area against the Australians. As in Malaya, Yamashita depended upon the momentum of his blitzkrieg to carry the Japanese troops to a swift victory.

As his X-Day and X-Time, Yamashita picked after nightfall on February 8. In an example of the rare coordination of IJA and IJN assets during the operation, the assault would be preceded a few hours earlier by a late afternoon, long-range bombing attack by an armada of IJNAF G3M and G4M bombers based in Indochina. As the bombers departed, the troops sat patiently in concealed locations in the Johor jungle and waited to move out.

Landing under cover of darkness at about 10:00 pm on February 8, a first wave of 4,000 troops in about 300 boats nearly took the Australians by surprise, but in the darkness the men of the 22nd Brigade could barely see what they were shooting at. Searchlights that had been provided to assist in defending this sector were not turned on.

The Japanese troops stormed ashore in a wooded, swampy area known as Surimbun Beach, and were present in such numbers and traveling with such speed as to throw the defenders into confusion. At the moment when well-entrenched defenders should have had the upper hand against exposed attackers on the water, the system had failed. Once the Japanese were ashore, the genie was out of the bottle and an enemy that should have been kept at bay for months was inside Singapore in force.

"I believe that it was solely due to the weakness of our defenses which resulted from extended fronts." General Percival admits in his postwar book *The War in Malaya*:

> This was aggravated by the fact that again for reasons unknown our artillery defensive fire was slow in coming down. That may have been due to the cutting of the telephone wires by the bombardment or to the fact that it is not easy to see signal lights in that wooded country. On the other hand it seems there was an unfortunate reluctance to use the wireless. It also appears that the beach searchlights were never exposed. Some of them may have been destroyed by the bombardment. The chief reason why the Japanese got ashore was because we were too thin on the ground.

Indeed, the 4,000 attackers faced just 2,500 defenders at the invasion site. Percival, still believing that the main attack would come in the Northern Area, did not send reinforcements to the Western Area until the following morning, when the Japanese were almost atop the RAF field at Tengah.

Shortly after midnight, as Yamashita watched from his palace tower command post, blue signal flares were fired to indicate that the vanguards of both the 5th and 18th Divisions were reporting successful landings. By dawn, the entirety of both divisions had been ferried across to Singapore Island, along with a substantial number of artillery pieces.

In the late afternoon of February 9, the Imperial Guards Division, who had feigned an assault one day earlier, crossed the Johor Strait near the Sembawang Naval Base on the northern side of the island. The defenders had set fire to the huge fuel tanks at the base to keep them out of Japanese hands, and there was some fear that they would have flooded the Johor Strait with burning oil. While the British never purposely resorted to this, the fires ashore were severe, and some Imperial Guards were killed as burning oil did reach the water and the landing area in the adjoining mud flats.

The pouting Nishimura, still angry that his division had not been used as the vanguard, had been in no hurry to send his Imperial Guards across the Johor Strait, and what role this may have played in some of them being burned alive is hard to know.

In his diary, Yamashita wrote:

> I ordered the Imperial Guards who were waiting among the rubber plantations to cross the Strait. I wanted them to go in after the 5th Division's crossing, but then their commander asked for further orders from me. I received a message from him that his troops were hesitating to cross because of oil flames on the surface of the water. It looks to me as if he is still upset about not being able to lead the attack. I ordered him to do his duty.

Meanwhile, the causeway, which had been considered irreparable after it was blown up by the British, was expeditiously rebuilt within 48 hours as a wooden structure by the same practiced engineers who had rebuilt 250 bridges in Malaya. Soon Japanese trucks and tanks were rumbling into beleaguered Singapore across the 251st bridge.

During the first two days, Japanese troops seized the RAF bases at Tengah on the west of the island, and at Sembawang and Selatar on the north. In the west, the defenders pulled back to a defensive line that was anchored on the Kranji River to the north. Called the Jorong Line after the main road which it bisected, this position held only briefly. Percival recalls in his memoirs of the war:

> The result of the various errors of judgement committed on the 9th was that by dawn on the critical 10th February the pivot position at Kranji had been abandoned. The two battalions of 27th Australian Brigade, out of touch with their Brigadier, had taken up positions which gave protection to neither the right flank of the Jurong Line nor the left flank of 3rd Corps.

Bennett had committed his last reserve formation to the static defense of part of the Jurong Line and Percival had no other reserve immediately to hand. Meanwhile, the Western Area command had issued to the commanders of its subordinate formation an order to be acted on in certain circumstances, based on Percival's secret and personal instructions to his senior commanders regarding the taking up of a perimeter position around the city of Singapore.

As Kenneth Attiwill later observes:

> to these weary and distracted officers, sorely in need of reinforcements and encouragement to fight on, despite their difficulties, the receipt of such an order was tantamount to an admission that the higher command regarded the situation as hopeless. The psychological effect of this order undoubtedly had a considerable bearing on their actions during the 10th.

Within the city of Singapore, the mood was eerily surreal. Despite the sounds of artillery and smoke in the distance, life on suburban streets and in large colonial homes carried on. The band was still performing at the Adelphi Hotel, and at the famous Raffles Hotel, military officers in non-combat administrative posts still gathered at the bar. The Singapore daily newspapers continued to publish full editions until February 11.

Flight Lieutenant Arthur Donohue told Attiwill in a postwar interview:

it was cool, quiet and peaceful where we sat on the veranda of the [Seaview Hotel] that morning [February 11], only a few miles from the fighting. The artillery had quieted down with the coming of daylight. Denny and I were enthralled for a while watching an exotic, dark-haired English girl clad in shorts and a light sweater, exercising her two greyhounds among the palm trees out on the lawn. She was swinging a cloth about for them to leap at. Her movements and theirs were so graceful that I thought she must be a dancer, but someone said she was a nurse. It seemed that either she or the approaching enemy and the terrible fighting must be unreal. It just didn't make sense – but neither did a lot of things, in the last days of Singapore.

His memory still vivid, Donohue recalls that

my final memory of Singapore, as it appeared to me looking back for the last time, is of a bright green little country, resting on the edge of the bluest sea I'd ever seen, lovely in the morning sunlight except where the dark tragic mantle of smoke ran across its middle and beyond, covering and darkening the city on the seashore. The city itself, with huge leaping red fires in its north and south parts, appeared to rest on the floor of a vast cavern formed by the sinister curtains of black smoke which rose from beyond and towered over it, prophetically, like a great overhanging cloak of doom.

Until after the war, Donohue had been officially presumed killed in 1942. His "posthumous" Distinguished Flying Cross citation read:

this officer carried out low level reconnaissance sorties and successfully attacked enemy shipping and ground objectives. On one occasion while attacking enemy troops who were attempting a landing in the Singapore area he silenced the enemy fire and enabled the rest of the Squadron to press home attacks with impunity. He has destroyed several enemy planes.

Some expatriates who had remained indifferent until now, or had believed the myth of Singapore's impregnability, suddenly panicked. Bands of them now crowded the port, climbing aboard any boat that they could find and setting sail across the Straits of Malacca, hoping to reach Sumatra. Some made it, but others landed in Japanese-occupied areas, where they were killed or captured. Many were attacked from the air or by Japanese naval patrols.

———————

Though the Japanese had achieved air superiority over the battlefield, General Archibald Wavell, the theater commander, was able to fly into the RAF base at Kallang on the edge of Singapore City on February 10 to meet with Percival. Wavell had earlier thought that the Japanese would attack in the west, as indeed they did, but had deferred to Percival in his erroneous theory that the assault would come in the northeast. On February 10, he chose to overrule his subordinate, insisting that the Jurong Line should be recaptured, with the words:

> It will be disgraceful if we cannot hold our boasted fortress of Singapore to inferior enemy forces. There must be no thought of sparing the troops or civilian population, and no mercy must be shown in any shape or form to any weakness. Commanders and senior officers must lead the troops and, if necessary, die with them. There must be no thought of surrender. Every unit must fight it out to the end and in close contact with the enemy.

Percival writes, "The attempt to launch [a counterattack on the Jurong Line] resulted only in further confusion and in the destruction in detail of the forces involved."

Wavell had also ordered all of the RAF assets in Singapore to relocate to safer bases in the Dutch East Indies and he flew out on one of the last planes himself. It was intended that Hurricanes flying from Sumatra would continue to fly air defense over Singapore, but as

Kenneth Attiwill later recalls, "from that day forward no British aircraft was seen in the sky over Singapore."

On the night of February 10–11, troops from the 5th and 18th Divisions, attacking from opposite sides, captured the fortified heights of 545-foot Bukit Timah, the highest point on Singapore Island, only a few miles from the edges of the city of Singapore. As many historians have observed, and as Percival admits in his memoirs, there was nothing now stopping the Japanese from heading straight into the city.

Masanobu Tsuji writes eloquently in his memoirs, that on February 11, "the morning sun rose peacefully over the island battlefield on Kigensetsu, the anniversary of the coronation of the Emperor Jimmu." This was the date that he had once mentioned as a goal for the Japanese conquest of Singapore. The island had yet to be conquered, but its demise was almost palpable.

However peacefully the sun may have risen, it did not rise over a peaceful battlefield. Fighting still raged from one end of the island to the other. Still, amazing progress could be credited to Yamashita's army. The Tiger of Malaya had invaded an island fortress that was supposed to have held out indefinitely and had captured at least half of it in two days.

With this, he issued his ultimatum to Percival. In multiple copies of a memo that was dropped in small boxes over British lines, Yamashita reminded the British commander that he was isolated from reinforcements, that his brave army was all but defeated, and that "in the spirit of chivalry," he should surrender in order to prevent further loss of life among the million civilians on Singapore Island.

Percival did not respond, and the fighting continued. The Japanese continued to tighten the noose, and British efforts continued to fail despite great gallantry. The 15-inch naval guns, with their armor-piercing rounds, targeted the railroad yards at Johor Bharu, and did considerable damage to trains loaded with Japanese equipment, but this was not known to the British until after the war.

On February 14, the Japanese reached the Alexandra Hospital on the west side of Singapore City. Yamashita wrote in his diary:

The Japanese troops entered the great military hospital at Alexandra, and there a tragedy took place. They claimed that Indian troops had fired from the hospital. Whether they did so or not, I cannot say. As a reprisal they bayoneted some members of the staff and patients including one poor fellow as he lay on the operating table. Next day they murdered 150 of the staff and patients. There were many horrors in the last war but for cold-blooded barbarity this deed will surely rank very high.

Reminiscent of the murder of wounded and medical personnel by Imperial Guards at Parit Sulong two weeks earlier, the Alexandra Hospital Massacre on February 14 ranks as one of the most infamous atrocities committed during the campaign.

On February 15, the day which came to be called "Black Sunday," Australian General Gordon Bennett observed in his diary that "today opened with a hopeless dawn of despair. There is no hope or help on the horizon. The tropical sun is sending its steamy heat on to a dying city which is writing in is agony."

Black Sunday was the 12th birthday of General Arthur Percival's daughter. Margery was celebrating with her mother in England, both of them anxiously hanging on the bad news from across the world that was about to get so much worse.

In Singapore that morning, Percival had received his last message from Wavell, telling him

so long as you are in a position to inflict losses and damage to enemy and your troops are physically capable of doing so, you must fight on. Time gained and damage to enemy are of vital importance at this juncture. When you are fully satisfied that this is no longer possible I give you discretion to cease resistance. Inform me of intentions. Whatever happens I thank you and all your troops for gallant efforts of last few days.

After attending church, Percival convened a meeting of his staff and some of Singapore's civilian leaders, minus Governor Thomas. The general told them of the discretion that Wavell had given him, and put Tomoyuki Yamashita's ultimatum of February 10 on the table. Percival also presented a second memo from Yamashita that had been delivered to him on Friday 13th. It was described as an "Admonition of Peace from the standpoint of the Nippon Samurai Spirit." A rambling manifesto that paid lip service to the Greater East Asia Co-Prosperity Sphere and the notion of Japan as a liberator, the document concluded with a paragraph which read:

> Passionately wishing to avoid the calamities of War. I expect you to consider upon the eternal honor of British Tradition, and you, be persuaded by this Admonition. Upon my word, we won't kill you, but treat you as Officers and Soldiers if you come to us. But if you resist us we will gybe swords.

Whereas the February 10 memo was signed "Tomoyuki Yamashita," this one was signed simply "Singapore Nippon Army." Being an official document, it used the formal "Nippon." Implicit also was that a Nippon army controlled at least a portion of Singapore.

The defenders had retreated into a defensive zone in the southern part of the island, and could have made a last stand, but there were a million civilians to think about, and by this time the fresh water reservoirs and the warehouses stocked with food supplies were in Japanese hands. In his diary, Gordon Bennett wrote, "silently and sadly we decided to surrender."

The British delegation, headed by Colonial Secretary Hugh Fraser and several staff officers, reached the Japanese 5th Division positions at Bukit Timah at 1:00 pm carrying a white flag and a Union Jack as instructed in Yamashita's ultimatum. When Yamashita learned of this, he refused to receive the delegation, insisting that he would deal only with Percival himself.

Percival finally arrived at Yamashita's headquarters and faced the 25th Army commander later that evening, Singapore time. In front of reporters, notably those of Japan's Domei News Agency, Yamashita dictated the terms to the defeated British general and his staff. General Gordon Bennett, commander of the Australian forces, was not present. He had relinquished his command to a subordinate and had escaped from Singapore aboard a purloined sampan.

Getting right to the point, Yamashita told the British general, that "the Japanese Army will consider nothing but unconditional surrender."

"I fear we shall not be able to submit our final reply before midnight," Percival replied.

"Reply to us only whether our terms are acceptable to you or not," Yamashita insisted, raising his voice. "Things have to be done swiftly as we are ready to resume firing in the evening."

"Won't you please wait until you formally file into Singapore?"

"It is impossible," Yamashita replied sternly. "In the first place, why not disarm all the British troops here, leaving only about 1,000 armed gendarmes for maintaining peace? In the second place, under no circumstances can we tolerate further British resistance."

The surrender was signed at 7:50 pm.

The meeting, filmed by newsreel cameras for global dissemination, was widely perceived in the West as a humiliation of Percival, and there is no doubt that it was Yamashita's intention to humiliate the British Empire. In a postwar interview with John Deane Potter, Yamashita explained what was on his mind at the time:

> On this occasion I was supposed to have spoken to Percival rather abruptly. If I did, it was because I now realized that the British army had about 100,000 men against my three divisions of 30,000 men. They also had many more bullets and other munitions than I had. There have been many versions and rumors about my behavior at this meeting, including the story that I said to him, "All or nothing." This is not true. But I knew that if the battle was to be fought in the streets of Singapore, there would be many casualties among the civilian population, and I did not know how long we could carry on, as our munitions were very low. I was preparing an all-out attack on that night and their surrender offer came as a surprise. After making a promise to meet me, the enemy commander was half an hour late.

When the time came to talk, he accepted the unconditional surrender but asked me to postpone the ceasefire until the next day. It looked to me as if the British Army wanted to delay everything but they still estimated the Japanese forces as more than they really were. They seemed to assess our force at about five divisions.

Then Yamashita turned to Potter and admitted that:

I was afraid in my heart that they would discover that our forces were much less than theirs. That was why I decided that I must use all means to make them surrender without terms. My interpreter was very poor. My attack on Singapore was a bluff – a bluff that worked. I had 30,000 men and was outnumbered more than three to one. I knew that if I had to fight long for Singapore, I would be beaten. That is why the surrender had to be at once. I was very frightened all the time that the British would discover our numerical weakness and lack of supplies and force me into disastrous street fighting.

As Japanese rule descended upon Singapore, it was officially renamed as Syonan-to, roughly translated as "the Light of the South." Strict rules of occupation were imposed, and the Kempeitai, the Japanese military police, proceeded to round up and execute many people, mainly ethnic Chinese, who lived in Singapore.

Most of the prisoners of war were shipped out of Singapore, to serve as slave laborers in Japan or on various Japanese engineering projects throughout Southeast Asia, notably the Burma Railway, which was the subject and backdrop of the 1952 novel by Pierre Boulle, *The Bridge on the River Kwai*. An estimated 30,000 of the Indian prisoners later joined the pro-Japanese Indian National Army, which fought against the British in Burma.

Many of those who had escaped in small boats during the final days were also captured or killed. In mentioning the Japanese seizure of people escaping Singapore, reference should be made to the infamous Banka Island Massacre.

The freighter *Vyner Brooke*, named for the "White Rajah" of Sarawak, had escaped Singapore on February 12 filled with wounded troops attended by a contingent of Australian nurses. Shortly after the Japanese capture of Banka Island, the ship was attacked and sunk offshore. A number of survivors, including two dozen of the nurses and some of their patients, managed to reach the island. When they were discovered, the men were shot or bayoneted, while the nurses and a civilian woman were ordered to wade into the surf. When they were waist deep in the water, they were sprayed with machine gun fire. One survivor, Lieutenant Vivian Bullwinkel, was left for dead. She survived and eluded capture for ten days before being found and jailed by the Japanese.

Lieutenant Bullwinkel survived the war and testified at a postwar War Crimes Tribunal. She went on to serve as the director of nursing at a suburban Melbourne hospital and as president of the Australian College of Nursing.

High-ranking military prisoners taken in the Singapore saurrender, as well as British civilian administrators, including General Arthur Percival and Governor Shenton Thomas, were incarcerated at Singapore's Changi Prison. Percival, however, was removed in August 1942, and eventually sent to a POW facility for VIP prisoners in Manchukuo.

Coincidentally, the man who defeated Percival, General Tomoyuki Yamashita, also ended up in Manchukuo. Yamashita, who became a national hero after the defeat of Singapore, was preparing the report which he assumed he would be asked to deliver to Emperor Hirohito personally when he got news of the transfer, effective on the first day of July.

In Tokyo, Yamashita's old rival, Hideki Tojo, had arranged for him to take command of the 1st Area Army of the Kwantung Army, a reserve and garrison force which was officially activated in July, one day after Yamashita's transfer. Tojo had arranged the timing so that there would be no opportunity for Yamashita to stop in Japan on his way his new assignment. It is believed that Tojo, jealous of Yamashita's notoriety, did not want him on Japanese soil, for fear that the emperor might decide that the Tiger of Malaya and the Hero of Singapore might be a good candidate for the post of minister of war, a portfolio retained by Tojo himself when he became prime minister.

The 1st Area Army headquarters were at Mukden, but Yamashita would be quartered in a house at the advance headquarters at Batanko, 60 miles from the Soviet border. Though his wife was later permitted to join him in Manchukuo, Yamashita would not see Japan again for two years, and then for just a week.

If Tojo did not want his rival in Japan, he might have served the cause more usefully by leaving Yamashita in the field in Southeast Asia than sending him into virtual exile on a quiet front. It is easy to imagine a tactician of Yamashita's caliber successfully continuing to lead the remarkable IJA blitzkrieg across Southeast Asia and into India or Australia. Such were the fears of the Allies in the summer of 1942.

The remarkable, lucky, and carefully crafted successes of the Tiger of Malaya had frightened the Allies at the nadir of their morale and contributed to the image of the IJA as an invincible force.

A stunned Winston Churchill, reacting to the almost incomprehensible news from across the globe, called the fall of Singapore "the worst disaster and largest capitulation in British history."

CHAPTER 17

WAR COMES TO BURMA

Burma was a keystone on the strategic map of Southeast Asia. With China to the north, Thailand to the east, and India, the crown jewel of the British Empire, to the west, it was a crossroads of hugely important centers of gravity in the geopolitics of East Asia.

For China, Burma was a lifeline. In 1937, with major Chinese ports under Japanese control, China, in cooperation with Burma, began building the Burma Road, a 700-mile, largely unpaved highway that ran across the rugged mountains of northern Burma, connecting Burma's port of Rangoon with the Chinese city of Kunming, by way of the Burmese city of Lashio. Utilizing the labor of an estimated 200,000 workers, the Burma Road had opened in 1938. Most of China's military supplies came via this precarious thoroughfare.

For Thailand, Burma was a buffer between itself and the British center of gravity in India. For the British, Burma was India's doorstep. For these reasons, Burma was of utmost importance strategically to all three.

Japan's desire to occupy this Southeast Asian keystone was directly associated with Burma's importance to China and the British Empire. There was some petroleum production at Yenangyaung in central Burma, but by comparison to that of the Dutch East Indies, Burma's oil fields were inconsequential. Japan wanted Burma the way a chess player desires to place a particular piece on a particular square. The value of Burma was not inherent, but lay in its position relative to other squares on the board.

Because of their ongoing war with China, the Japanese wished to cut the Burma Road supply route. Britain feared that Burma, if captured by the Japanese, would be a stepping stone for an invasion of India itself. A few weeks earlier, such a prospect had been absurd. However, after Tomoyuki Yamashita's apparently effortless conquest of impregnable Singapore, this could not be ruled out. In Allied circles, there was a great and genuine fear that the Germans would capture the Suez Canal and drive eastward across Iraq and Iran – where Axis sympathies ran high – and link up with the Japanese somewhere in India, where anti-British sympathies simmered.

In the propaganda of the Greater East Asia Co-Prosperity Sphere, when mention was made of "Asia for Asiatics," Indians were included. In the manual given to IJA troops, *Read This Alone: And The War Can Be Won*, mention was made about the liberation of "350 million Indians ruled by 500,000 British," and the independence movement in India was sufficiently robust that the British worried about what would happen if the Japanese crossed into India branding themselves as liberators. Once a backwater to regional affairs, Burma was suddenly a precious regional crux.

Throughout the centuries, Burma had evolved and dissolved, alternating between empires and disparate warring states with blurred borders. It is named for the Bamar people, who are the dominant ethnic group (around seven out of ten) in the country. The name "Myanmar," in use officially since 1989, though not universally recognized, is also derived from the term Bamar. In the late nineteenth century, as the French were assembling their own colonial domain in neighboring Indochina, the British invaded Burma in a series of wars, absorbing it into their empire by 1886.

Originally a governor's province of British India, Burma was detached in 1937 as a distinct entity, administered by a separate colonial government. Rangoon, the Burmese administrative center, had been the fourth largest city in British India – after Bombay, Calcutta, and Delhi – with a prewar population of 400,000.

As a figurehead prime minister for Burma, the British picked Dr Ba Maw, a Burma-born, French-educated attorney and legal scholar. As a strong advocate of Burmese independence, Ba became hard to control and a thorn in the side of the British colonial administrators. He was removed by them in 1939, and was jailed for sedition in 1940 for opposing British participation in World War II.

When 1942 began, Lieutenant General Shojiro Iida's IJA 15th Army, which had taken control of Thailand in one day on December 8, was on that country's border with Burma. It was comprised of the 33rd Division under Lieutenant General Shozo Sakurai, and the 55th Division, commanded by Lieutenant General Hiroshi Takeuchi.

Opposing them was the British Burma Army, commanded by Lieutenant General Thomas Hutton, a former staff officer with Britain's General Headquarters India. Within his command, Hutton had elements of the 7th Armoured Brigade, the "Desert Rats," who had recently relocated from North Africa. They were equipped with American-made M3 Stuart light tanks, which were known to the British unofficially as "Honeys." This gave the defenders of Burma an edge that was unavailable to British forces in Malaya. While equipped with Bren gun carriers, the troops defending Malaya had no tanks with which to face the Japanese armor.

In addition to several British regiments, Hutton also had two divisions under his command, the 1st Burma Division and the 17th Indian Infantry Division, both of which consisted mainly of Indian troops, including regiments of the highly regarded Gurkha Rifles. As with most Indian divisions, the officers were mainly British. The 1st Burma had once included Burmese troops, but most had been mustered out before the war and were concentrated in military police units. Even the division's core regiment, the Burma Rifles, was mostly Indian. The division was later redesignated as the 39th Indian Infantry Division. In the back of Hutton's mind, he expected to rely on the support of Chiang Kai-shek's Chinese Army. Chiang did not want to see his tenuous Burma Road lifeline snipped, and Hutton assumed he would fight to protect it.

All four of the divisions which faced one another across the Thailand–Burma border in January 1942 were understrength. Those under Hutton's command were poorly trained and poorly equipped, while Iida's divisions, though well equipped, suffered from having had units detached to support ongoing operations elsewhere.

Just as Iida's 15th Army was a subsidiary of General Count Hisaichi Terauchi's Southern Expeditionary Army Group, headquartered in Saigon, the Burma Army was a subsidiary of General Archibald Wavell's British India Command, headquartered in New Delhi.

Overhead, the IJAAF possessed considerable strength and the use of bases in Thailand, as well as Indochina. On the opposite side, elements of Britain's RAF had deployed to Rangoon, but these were much smaller than the RAF force in Malaya and Singapore, which had been so badly outclassed by the Japanese. However, the RAF was augmented by the American Volunteer Group (AVG), three squadrons of American fighter pilots who had been surreptitiously recruited on orders from President Franklin Roosevelt in 1941 before the United States entered World War II. Known as the "Flying Tigers," their mission was to fly against the Japanese in support of Nationalist China. They were American military pilots who had resigned their commissions in order to fly as civilians as part of one of World War II's most famous "black ops." Between them, the RAF and the AVG managed to impede the initial IJA air raids against Rangoon.

During its initial offensive phase in December 1941, the IJA had not so much invaded Burma, as probed its frontiers, specifically in the Tenasserim (now Tanintharyi) region, an area of steep coastal hills which parallels the long and very narrow "tail" of Burma that extends along the coast south of Rangoon, sandwiched between the Andaman Sea and western Thailand. Because it could be resupplied only by air and sea, this strip was especially vulnerable to a mechanized overland attack from Thailand.

A month later, the Japanese took Victoria Point (now Kawthaung), at the southern tip of Burma, which was more symbolic than anything.

The British chose not to defend it. On January 18, Hiroshi Takeuchi, commander of the 55th Division, sent his 143rd Infantry Regiment across the Tenasserim hills to capture airfields at Mergui (now Myeik) and Tavoy (now Dawei). Two battalions of the Burma Rifles put up a spirited defense before being pushed aside at Tavoy, but Mergui, like Victoria Point, was left undefended.

The main Japanese invasion of Burma by the main force of Iida's 15th Army came on January 22, with the objective – obvious on both sides – being the capture of Rangoon. Takeuchi's 55th Division was to drive due westward to attack Rangoon from the east, while Sakurai's 33rd Division would circle to the north to flank Rangoon and attack from the west.

The distance from the Thai border was a bit less than 150 miles as the crow flies, with the notable terrain features being a series of rivers flowing southward out of central Burma. In the order that they would be confronted by the Japanese, they were the Thaungyin (now Moei), which demarcated the Thai border; the Salween, a parallel tributary of the Thaungyin; the Bilin; the Sittang (now Sittaung); and the Pegu (now Bago). The Irrawaddy, Burma's greatest river and navigable highway of commerce, parallels the other rivers farther west, passing through Rangoon itself. On paper, the broad Sittang was perceived by the strategic planners on both sides as the key defensive point between Thailand and Rangoon.

Hutton's strategy consisted of opposing Takeuchi at each river crossing with his outnumbered and inexperienced Indian soldiers, while hoping that the Chinese would soon intervene in strength. His first line of defense on the rivers would be the 17th Infantry Division, which was under the command of Brigadier (acting Major General) John George "Jackie" Smyth, who had earned a Victoria Cross for bravery in action in World War I.

The first battle took place at the point where the Salween flows into the Thaungyin, but it was little more than a holding action. The problem of defending river crossings is that the defenders have the river to their backs. In this instance, abandoning irreplaceable supplies, they retreated by boat on January 31, coincidentally at about the same time that the defenders of Malaya were retreating across the Johor Strait. The Japanese, having prepared in advance with small boats for river crossings, were hot on their tails.

After a two-day holding action at the narrow and indefensible Bilin River, Smyth withdrew the defenders from the jaws of encirclement, and they retreated under cover of darkness to the Sittang. At the time, Smyth was accompanied by Brigadier David Tennant "Punch" Cowan, a staff officer from Rangoon, whom he sent back to Hutton's headquarters to request permission to withdraw most of his troops and heavy equipment across the Sittang. He considered this to be the safest way to meet Takeuchi's assault.

Hutton initially refused, though he later relented and allowed for a partial withdrawal to the west bank. In the meantime, Smyth was faced with the impossible task of organizing a defense of both the east bank of the Sittang River, and the metal railway bridge which crossed it – while the 17th Division had its back to the river.

Elements of Takeuchi's 214th and 215th Regiments caught up to Smyth's men by February 19, and in the ensuing battle, the Indians fought bravely, despite being frequently outflanked on the eastern bank of the river, and being under constant air attack. The Japanese troops even managed to penetrate as far as the bridge. One of Smyth's big worries by this time was that the Japanese might use an airborne assault, as they had in the Dutch East Indies, to land paratroopers in his rear on the west bank.

Smyth knew that allowing Takeuchi to capture the bridge intact would hasten the IJA advance on Rangoon considerably, so he found himself with a "rock and a hard place conundrum." The bridge would have to be destroyed. The only question was when.

Jackie Smyth blew the Sittang River Bridge at dawn on February 23. It turned out to be a bad choice, but in all fairness, there were no good choices available. Two brigades from the 17th Division, the 16th and 46th – over half of the division's total strength – were trapped on the east side of the river, but Smyth assumed that the IJA would own the bridge before they could make it across, so down it went. Many of the stranded troops finally made it across the river, but in so doing, they abandoned piles of heavy equipment, supplies, and even their small arms.

On March 1, after he learned of the debacle on the Sittang, General Archibald Wavell, the Allied theater commander who headed both the British India Command and the newly formed ABDA Command, sacked both Smyth and Hutton. Punch Cowan succeeded Smyth, taking command of a 17th Division which was now depleted to a mere 40 percent of its authorized strength. Replacing Hutton was recently knighted General Sir Harold Alexander, late of the Southern Command in England itself, who relocated to Rangoon to command the defense of Burma.

———————————

Less well defended than Singapore, Rangoon, like Manila two months earlier, hung at the mouth of the Irrawaddy River like low-hanging fruit.

PART IV

A CROWN JEWEL, FROM ONE EMPIRE TO ANOTHER

CHAPTER 18

THE HEART OF THE DUTCH EAST INDIES

The IJA first set foot in the heart of the Dutch East Indies on February 14, 1942, one day before the fall of Singapore. They came, not across the beaches as in Malaya, Singapore, and the Philippines, but from the sky.

The aircrews of RAF Lockheed Hudson bombers returning to airfields at Palembang on Sumatra found themselves flying through a formation of Japanese transport aircraft heading directly toward them, coming *from* Palembang, where they had blanketed the ground with paratroopers. A half hour or so before, a group of RAF Blenheim bombers had made their final approaches to their landings at Palembang flying through the masses of Japanese airborne troops as they dangled from their parachutes. This was a dramatic beginning of an end for an empire where the Dutch East India Company had first set up a trading post in 1603.

By the "heart" of the Dutch East Indies, we mean the islands of Sumatra and Java, the "home islands" of the 17,500-island archipelago, which officially became a colony of the Netherlands in 1800 when the Dutch East India Company went out of business. Three quarters of the 60 million people in the Dutch East Indies lived on those two islands, with two thirds of them on Java alone. By comparison, Borneo and Celebes had respective populations of three and five million.

Most of the ethnic European population lived in Java. Their numbers had been growing rapidly through immigration from the Netherlands, rising from 170,000 in 1920 to 242,000 in 1940. Many colonial government retirees stayed on, rather than retiring to a Netherlands they barely knew. Because of the longevity of Dutch rule, there were a sizable number among those ethnic Dutch administrators who had been born in the Indies, and who had lived their entire lives there. Some had never even set foot in the Netherlands, and most who had, had been there for a relatively short time.

The Dutch administrative center for the vast colony, the city of Batavia (now Jakarta) on Java, boasted a population of nearly 450,000, making it the third largest city in Southeast Asia after Bangkok and Singapore.

Although Borneo was, in the vernacular of the petroleum industry, the "oil patch" of the Dutch East Indies, Sumatra and Java were not without importance to that industry. There were important oilfields and refineries at Palembang, Sabang Island, and Pangkalanbrandanon on Sumatra, and to a lesser extent around Tjepoe (now Cepu) and Bojenegoro on Java. Meanwhile, 4,488-square-mile Bangka Island, just offshore and administratively part of Sumatra, had been one of the world's most important sources of tin since the eighteenth century.

While a great deal is written about the need of the Japanese economy for Indies oil, the Dutch colony was also commercially important in terms of Japanese exports of manufactured goods. In the two decades before the war, the proportion of the colony's imports that came from Japan increased from 14 to 31 percent. This was just another element in the complex web of relationships within that family of lands and peoples which was being assembled under the heading of the Greater East Asia Co-Prosperity Sphere.

The Dutch colonial administrators in Batavia understood what was coming. In formally articulating the concept of the Greater East Asia Co-Prosperity Sphere in 1940, Foreign Minister Yosuke Matsuoka had expressed the Japanese belief that the colonies of European powers defeated by Germany should rightfully fall into the sphere of Japanese influence, or beneath the *Hakko ichiu* roof of Japanese manifest destiny to dominate Asia. The Dutch in Batavia had seen what the Japanese had done with French Indochina since France fell under the jackboot of the Third Reich in 1940.

The defense by the Dutch of Borneo had been a scorched earth and a scant effort – except for the submarines of Divisie Onderseeboten III – at fighting back. The defense of Sumatra and Java, because of their place as the centerpiece of the colony, would have to be more substantial. The history of the Dutch defense of the Indies in the twentieth century had been a matter of making do. To the powers with the purse in Amsterdam, things seemed to be going fine out in the Indies, so there was no reason for change. No national government likes to spend money on defense in peacetime, and military appropriations for a distant colony where there had been no major threat in modern times were a hard sell. For the lawmakers and strategic planners in the Netherlands, the Indies were very far away, and they were colored in the image of a quiet colonial backwater, a place from which the petroleum, tin, and bales of spices flowing into the Dutch economy were taken for granted.

As the war began, the Royal Netherlands East Indies Army (Koninklijk Nederlands Indisch Leger, KNIL) was under the command of Lieutenant General Hein ter Poorten, an officer who was typical of most of the officers under him in that he had been born in the Indies of Dutch parents, and had spent his entire life and career there, except for a few years at a military staff college in the Netherlands.

Born in Buitenzorg (now Bogor) in 1887, ter Poorten had been chief of staff to his predecessor, Lieutenant General Gerardus Johannes Berenschot, assuming the top job when Berenschot was killed in a plane crash on October 13, 1941 as he was returning to Batavia after a meeting with British Air Chief Marshal Brooke-Popham, then the British commander in Southeast Asia.

When he became KNIL's commanding officer, ter Poorten inherited a difficult job, scant resources, and little support from his civilian boss,

Governor General Alidius Warmoldus Lambertus Tjarda van Starkenborgh Stachouwer, a Dutch nobleman who had assumed the post in 1936. The governor had respected the deceased commander, but did not feel that ter Poorten was up to the task.

"He doesn't have the specific qualities of Berenschot when it comes to working together with civil organizations and problems other than purely military ones," van Starkenborgh Stachouwer complained. "He has a big mouth and operates with less tact."

Ter Poorten's biggest problem in the spring of 1942 was in fact a military one. On the eve of the war, his command numbered 35,000 officers and men – the majority of which were ethnic Indonesians. These were augmented by 40,000 *Stadswacht Landstorm* (home guard) troops, who were mainly Indies-born ethnic Europeans. Meanwhile, there were several small, nominally independent *Vorstenlanden* (Princely States), which the Dutch had allowed to exist in central Java, of which Surakarta and Jogjakarta (now Yogyakarta) were the largest. The sultans each maintained their own small, ethnic-Indonesian army, but these small palace guard detachments were under the KNIL operational command structure.

The majority of these KNIL forces were concentrated on Java, with only about 2,000, commanded by Lieutenant Colonel L.N.W. Vogelgesang, guarding Palembang on Sumatra.

The overall numbers are misleading, given that the KNIL was trained more as a police force than as a modern field army, and was therefore an uneven match for the Japanese armies which were comprised of many veterans of combat in China. Having pacified the last major domestic uprising against Dutch rule around the turn of the century, the KNIL had neither anticipated nor trained for serious combat operations until after the defeat of the Netherlands in 1940. There was a growing independence movement, but it had yet to evolve into an insurgency that would have required sustained military operations.

The KNIL, which functioned as a cross between a garrison force and a military police detachment, was comprised of three infantry divisions, the 1st Infantry Division under Major General Wilbrandus Schilling, the 2nd Division under Major General Pierre Cox, and the 3rd Division under Major General Gustav Ilgen. Each division was organized into motorized battalions – though many of their vehicles were antiquated – and the 1st and 2nd each had modest numbers of 75mm and 105mm field guns. The 2nd Division did have about 20 light tanks.

The KNIL air force, the ML-KNIL, commanded by Lieutenant General Ludolph van Oyen, possessed more than 350 aircraft, most of which were unsuitable for combat operations. Of those which were considered first-line aircraft, 80 were twin-engine Martin Model 139 and Model 166 bombers (the export equivalent of the US Army's B-10), which had only recently been phased out as obsolete by the USAAF. Eclipsed by newer types being built in the United States, the Martin bombers were also inferior in both speed and range to Japanese twin-engine bombers, such as the Mitsubishi G4M, which was widely used by the IJN in Southeast Asia operations. Parenthetically, the G4M had been the key weapon in the sinking of the *Prince of Wales* and the *Repulse* in December 1941.

When it came to air-to-air combat, the ML-KNIL was equipped with 36 Curtiss Hawks (used by the US Army as the P-36), and 72 Brewster Buffalo fighters (used by the USN as the F2A), which had been such a disappointment to the British in Malaya. Both were thoroughly outclassed in terms of speed and maneuverability by the first-line Japanese fighters, notably the IJA's Nakajima Ki-43 Hayabusa and the IJN's Mitsubishi A6M Zero.

Virtually the entire ML-KNIL was based on Java or at Palembang, although, as seen in earlier chapters, some aircraft were forward-deployed to Borneo, and there had been an effort made at building additional airfields throughout the archipelago. Also as noted earlier in this book, the backbone of the Marine Luchtvaartdienst (Netherlands Naval Aviation) was the Dornier Do 24, a German-built flying boat, of which the service had about two dozen. By the end of 1941, these were augmented by a half dozen recently delivered, American-built Consolidated Catalina flying boats.

After the beginning of hostilities in Malaya in December 1941, the ML-KNIL began cooperating with the British RAF and the RAAF, flying sorties in support of the British operations in Malaya. In January, as things heated up in the skies over the Malay Peninsula, RAF and RAAF aircraft withdrew from Malaya and Singapore to use ML-KNIL airfields in Sumatra, farther from Japanese air bases.

Even before the formal activation of the Joint American–British–Dutch–Australian (ABDA) Command on January 15, 1942, there was a great deal of cooperation between the Allies. Given that the Netherlands were then under German occupation, there was no possibility of Dutch reinforcements arriving in the Indies. However, Wavell, who headed the ABDA Command, anxiously attempted to reinforce the Dutch with British Commonwealth troops.

By mid-February, the RAF and RAAF air units based in Sumatra and Java consisted mainly of remnants and survivors of the Malay campaign, although they were augmented by the 48 Hawker Hurricanes that had recently arrived aboard the aircraft carrier HMS *Indomitable*, and which filled out RAF No. 226 Group. The USAAF also forward-deployed aircraft from the build-up of American air assets in Australia.

The airfields at Palembang, about 450 miles due south of Singapore, had been selected in December 1941 to become a major joint bomber base. The military field needed paving, and the commercial field, with its hard surface runway, needed to be expanded to host a large number of ML-KNIL, RAF, and RAAF aircraft, as well as USAAF bombers. The military field, called Palembang 2, was so primitive that even KNIL pilots had trouble finding it. So too, did Japanese bombers who came to attack Palembang.

In retrospect, this decision to upgrade the Palembang airfields, as well as additional fields on other islands, came at least half a year too late – though at the time, the speed of Tomoyuki Yamashita's 25th Army dash through Malaya was still unthinkable. In fact, the big construction project was overtaken by events, and the multinational ABDA air force used the Palembang fields as is.

The first Japanese air raids against Palembang 1, the commercial field, came on February 6, 1942. The Singapore operation had reached its turning point, and the RAF Blenheim bombers which had been routinely striking the Japanese lines of communications on the Malay Peninsula had relocated from Malaya and Singapore to Sumatra.

In the air battle which ensued during the middle of February, the Allied air forces took a terrible beating from the Japanese. Even the illustrious Hurricanes were not a match for the Zeros and Oscars. Four Hurricanes were lost and two damaged on February 6 alone.

———

Just as the ABDA defensive plan called for a lightly reinforced defensive contingent in Sumatra and a major stand on Java, so the Japanese plan called for a proportional commitment of forces. The core of the Japanese Sumatra invasion force was Colonel Toshishige (aka Toshinari) Shoji's 230th Infantry Regiment, as well as one battalion from the 229th, both drawn from the 38th Division, which had taken part in the conquest of Hong Kong. As noted in Chapter 15, the division's third regiment, the 228th, had been assigned to the invasion of Ambon Island.

Also included in the order of battle for Sumatra was the IJA 1st Parachute Force, four airborne companies under Colonel Seiichi Kume. Taking a page from the playbook of the IJN Special Naval Landing Forces over Celebes on January 11 and 12, the IJA intended to use its own airborne troops to drop in behind the coastal defenses on February 14, two days before the amphibious troops came ashore.

The surface invasion fleet, which departed for Sumatra from Cam Ranh Bay, was escorted by an IJN contingent under Vice Admiral Jisaburo Ozawa, commander of the Japanese Southern Expeditionary Fleet, and of naval operations in the South China Sea. Ozawa's command had also supported the Celebes operations. This fleet carried an advance force of the 229th Infantry Regiment aboard eight transports, followed by a main force of 229th and 230th troops aboard

14 troop carriers. Supporting warships included the heavy cruiser *Chokai*, Ozawa's flagship, and the cruisers *Kumano*, *Mogami*, *Mikuma*, *Suzuya*, and *Yura*, and ten destroyers, as well as minesweepers and other supporting ships. Also part of the fleet was the aircraft carrier *Ryujo* with the IJN 3rd Air Group.

This fleet was observed sailing toward Sumatra by a British reconnaissance aircraft on February 13, even as those same waters north of Palembang were filled with the numerous smaller vessels filled with refugees escaping the doomed Singapore – which were then being strafed by the occasional Japanese fighter.

The following day, the skies over Sumatra were filled with both Japanese and Allied aircraft as the airborne troops headed south and squadrons of RAF Hudsons and Blenheims were sent north to attack the invasion fleet – with special attention to the *Ryujo* and the troop ships. The carrier survived, but at least one transport was sunk.

Just as the Dutch had been surprised by the Japanese airborne attack a month earlier over Celebes, the British at Palembang were not expecting to see the sky filled with parachutes. The nearly three dozen IJA transports were identified by various sources as either Mitsubishi Ki-57 variants of the Ki-21 twin-engine bombers, or Kawasaki Ki-56s, copies of the American Lockheed Model 14 Super Electra. Apparently, Ki-21s were also present to drop supplies for the paratroopers, so this may have played into the misidentification. These aircraft, assigned to the 1st, 2nd, and 3rd Chutai (troop carrier squadrons) had arrived over the drop zones unchallenged, escorted by Ki-43 Hayabusa fighters of the 59th and 64th Sentai (fighter squadrons).

A call went out for the RAF Hurricanes of No. 226 Group, which were out on a mission. They only barely returned in time to see the paratroop planes escaping, out of range of the Hurricanes, running short of fuel as they came back to their bases in Malaya. The Japanese did acknowledge the loss of one Ki-57.

The Hurricanes turned their guns on the Japanese troops, who had landed near the Palembang 1 airfield and the refineries. None had come near Palembang 2, which was still not known to the Japanese, so the Allies were able to use that field even as they fought the invaders from the sky who were now swarming across the landscape.

Approximately 350 airborne troops came down into two drop zones. Those who were tasked with capturing the Palembang 1 airfield were under the command of Colonel Seiichi Kume, and those landing near the refineries were reportedly led by Lieutenant Hirose Nobutaka. The latter contingent managed to capture all or part of the refinery complex, which had not yet been damaged by the Dutch, and the refinery was recaptured by *Stadswacht* antiaircraft troops in a major firefight and at great cost. However, the entire action actually bought time for the Japanese as it delayed any efforts to sabotage the refinery.

On February 15, as Tomoyuki Yamashita was preparing to accept the surrender of the British in Singapore, an additional airborne landing, involving nearly 100 paratroopers under Lieutenant Ryo Morisawa, was made in the vicinity of the Palembang 1 airfield.

The results of the airborne assault were mixed. On one hand, it was a very costly exercise. Just as the Germans had suffered monumental losses to achieve their airborne victory in Crete, the IJA airborne troops had suffered around 80 percent casualties, and had failed to capture and hold their objectives.

On the other hand, the airdrops were certainly disruptive, and they had the psychological effect of enveloping the defenders with parachuting enemy troops. Further, the survivors were never decisively defeated, and they managed to elude capture.

The amphibious landings on February 16 came in two parts, with the advance force of the 229th Infantry Regiment landing on Bangka Island, and the main force of troops from the 229th and 230th coming ashore across the narrow Bangka Strait on the Sumatra coast near Palembang. Artillery support came from the 8-inch guns of Admiral Ozawa's cruisers, as well as naval gunfire from the lesser guns of his destroyers, while the aircraft from the *Ryujo* lent air support.

Allied airmen, meanwhile, found the narrow confines of the Bangka Strait, crowded with a dozen ships and countless landing barges, to be a target-rich environment. A force of 22 Hurricanes, 35 Blenheims, and a few Hudson bombers that were assembled at Palembang 2, struck the invasion fleet hard. A tremendous air battle ensued as Hurricanes attacked Japanese bombers, Zeros from the *Ryujo* attacked RAF bombers, and the Hurricanes and Zeros tangled with one another high over the straits. The transports were damaged, and numerous landing craft were destroyed by the RAF aircraft.

The IJA invaders paid a high price, but their superior numbers and their own momentum propelled them forward. The barges carried the troops upstream on coastal rivers and estuaries, permitting them to disembark deep into the Sumatran coastal plane, well beyond the shoreline. Overwhelmed by the Japanese momentum and an enemy in their rear, and under orders from ABDA commander Wavell, the remaining defenders torched the petroleum facilities and stocks of rubber, and followed other Allied troops who were already withdrawing from Palembang and from Sumatra itself.

For several days, there had been a huge exodus of retreating Allied personnel from the major port of Oosthaven (later Telukbetung, now Bandar Lampung) at the southeastern tip of Sumatra, located about 200 miles from Palembang and about 50 miles across the Sunda Strait from Java.

On February 16, the last of the Allied aircraft on Sumatra were flown out to fields on Java, and on February 17, the last evacuation boat, the Dutch liner *Rosenbaum*, pulled out of Oosthaven with the last refugees. In addition to 4,390 British Army and RAF personnel, 700 KNIL troops, and around 1,000 civilians made their escape, as the Australian corvette HMAS *Burnie* shelled the docks and fuel storage area in the port.

On February 20, when the IJA did not follow up the occupation of Palembang with an immediate drive on Oosthaven, an RAF team under Group Captain G.E. Nicholetts sneaked back into the city aboard an Australian ship to recover an important stock of aircraft parts.

Amid the despair, confusion, and pyres of burning oil at Oosthaven, it was a scene reminiscent of the last days of Singapore as they had played out earlier that week. The only thing missing was the Japanese, who had intercepted many of the Singapore refugees.

CHAPTER 19

TIGHTENING THE NOOSE ACROSS THE INDIES

As Malaya and Borneo were the battlegrounds of Southeast Asia, Sumatra and Java had existed for a time both literally and figuratively as islands in a swirling sea of conflict. The gradual isolation of the "home islands" of the archipelago was in part a function of the expansive vision of the mileposts on the Southern Road as imagined by Hideki Tojo and his generals during their conference in Tokyo in November 1941.

The overnight collapse of all but Java of the main islands of the Dutch East Indies – after more than a century as an immense integrated colony – can be blamed in part on the Dutch vision of their distant empire. Using just a handful of battalions to defend the outer islands, especially Borneo, which made the colony the world's fourth largest oil producer, seems counterintuitive.

Of course, with their mother country in chains, the Dutch in the Indies had to make do with what they had, and Java, as the jewel in their colonial crown, deserved the greatest weight of their available resources. And as we have seen in following the Japanese advance through Borneo,

Celebes, and Sumatra, the resources which the Dutch had available in the Indies were modest at best. The KNIL, functioning as a mere garrison force, was simply not ready to fight an army of the caliber of the IJA. It was poorly equipped when it came to basics such as mechanization or artillery, and had little or no training in modern battlefield warfare against a disciplined and determined foe. The prewar defense scheme for the Indies with such a force rested on the shaky foundation of focusing the preponderance of KNIL resources within the narrow perimeter of Java, and holding on until reinforcements arrived.

In the spring of 1942, the flaw in this non-strategy was apparent. Reinforcements were not coming. The British had lost an army in Singapore, and they were not coming. The Americans still had brave men fighting in Bataan that could not be rescued by either the US Army or the US Navy. The Australians were exhausted by Malaya and had committed their AIF troops to help the British in North Africa. Now, with the Japanese capture of the airfields on Celebes and Ambon, the Australians were worried about their own survival. If the increasing vulnerability of Java was illustrated by the Japanese capture of Borneo, Celebes, and now Sumatra, the vulnerability of Australia was painfully underscored by the massive air raid on Darwin that came on February 19 – which included land-based bombers flying from Celebes and Ambon.

Also on February 19, the Japanese tightened the noose of advanced airfields even further with simultaneous invasions of the island of Timor, halfway between Ambon and Darwin, and the island of Bali, which was closer to eastern Java than Sumatra was to western Java.

The 11,883-square-mile island of Timor had been the colonial possession of two European countries since the mid-nineteenth century, with the Netherlands in the west and Portugal ruling a slightly larger slice of the island in the east. The seat of the Dutch government, Koepang (now Kupang), was and is the largest city. Near Koepang, Penfui (now Poeloeti) was the largest airfield. The 600-man KNIL garrison, commanded by Lieutenant Colonel Nico van Straten, was mainly an infantry contingent, and possessed only four 75mm guns.

In mid-December 1941, a week after the start of the war in the Pacific, Australia had forward-deployed troops to help protect the airfields on Ambon and Timor, the latter being only 500 miles from Darwin. As Gull Force was sent to Ambon, the 1,400-man Sparrow Force, commanded by Lieutenant Colonel Bill (later Sir William) Leggatt, arrived on Timor on December 12. Centered on the AIF 2/40th Battalion of the 23rd Brigade, Sparrow Force also included antitank and artillery batteries, as well as 2/2nd Independent Company under Lieutenant Colonel Alexander Spence, which later had the distinction of being one of the few Allied ground units to survive the action in the Indies to fight again later in the war.

Though the ML-KNIL had no combat aircraft based at Penfui, the RAAF sent a dozen Hudson bombers. The airfield was proving to be an important link in the American air bridge between Australia and the beleaguered Philippines, and ABDA considered it to be a vital part of Allied strategy in Southeast Asia. While Leggatt's 2/40th Battalion set up to defend Koepang and Penfui, Spence's 2/2nd Company and a contingent of Dutch troops prepared to invade Portuguese East Timor in order to secure the entire island against the Japanese.

In Lisbon, the government of Antonio Salazar complained loudly, declaring that Portugal, neutral in the war in Europe, was also neutral in the Pacific, a strategy that would save Macau from the fate of Hong Kong.

While it had been three decades since the Dutch and the Portuguese had formally agreed on a border across Timor in 1912, there was still an institutional memory of the open warfare that had transpired between the two colonial parties back in the nineteenth century. In Europe, diplomats representing all the parties had met to decide what to do, and it was agreed that the Portuguese governor in Timor could formally request aid if he felt threatened by the Japanese.

Embarking on the yacht *Canopus*, Spence traveled to Dili, the Portuguese administrative center, on December 17. Here he met with Governor Manuel de Abreu Ferreira de Carvalho even as the Dutch and Australian troops made an unopposed landing nearby.

Japanese aircraft were overhead, and had already strafed the Allied positions and had destroyed Portuguese property, but Carvalho insisted on the pretense of neutrality, and he refused to ask for Allied intervention in the absence of an actual, boots-on-the-ground Japanese invasion. Furthermore, he announced that he considered himself a prisoner of the Allies. By the end of 1941, an agreement was reached whereby the Dutch would withdraw from Portuguese Timor, leaving the Australian Diggers of Alexander Spence's 2/2nd Company as the official occupation force.

During January and February 1942, minimal reinforcements were sent to Timor, including the British 79th Light Anti-Aircraft Battery, which arrived in at Koepang on February 16. A contingent of Portuguese troops from Angola was also being sent.

All of this was overtaken by events, as Japanese attacks against key locations throughout Timor increased in intensity, and the RAAF pulled out the small contingent of bombers that had been deployed in December. As had happened prior to the Japanese invasion of Ambon, the defenders were left without air cover to defend against Japanese bombers, based in Celebes and Ambon, that were able to attack Timor at will.

In the meantime, the aerial bombardment was augmented by naval gunfire from some of the same ships from Ibo Takahashi's IJN Eastern Force that had helped hammer Ambon into submission. Arriving aboard his flagship, the cruiser *Nachi*, Rear Admiral Takeo Takagi brought a covering detachment that included the cruiser *Haguro* and four destroyers. Escorting the Timor invasion fleet, meanwhile, were other veterans of the Ambon battle. Rear Admiral Raizo Tanaka, aboard his flagship, the cruiser *Jintsu*, was joined by ten destroyers and several minesweepers.

As this fleet headed south, the Allies were scraping together further reinforcements to send to the Timor garrison. It had been decided that Sparrow Force should be doubled to two battalions. Brigadier William Veale had arrived on Timor on February 12 with his headquarters, and was awaiting the arrival of the 2/4th Infantry Battalion, as well as the US Army's 49th Field Artillery Battalion. However, en route from Australia, the transports carrying these troops were intercepted and attacked by Japanese bombers, and compelled to turn about and retreat.

As at Borneo and Ambon, the assault on Timor was planned as a joint IJA–IJN operation. The 228th Infantry Regiment of the 38th Division, which had landed at Ambon a little less than three weeks earlier, had shipped out aboard nine troop transports under the command of Colonel Sadashichi Doi. Meanwhile, the 3rd Yokosuka Special Naval Landing Force, under Lieutenant Commander Koichi Fukumi and staging out of Kendari on Celebes, was tasked with making an airborne landing east of Koepang.

Though it should not have been that way, the Japanese amphibious landings on the night of February 19–20 took the defenders off guard. While most of the Allied defenses around Koepang were on the north side of the southwest tip of Timor, the main force of the IJA 228th Regiment, 4,000 strong, came ashore on the southern side, essentially outflanking the entrenched positions overlooking the harbor. Meanwhile, in Portuguese Timor, when 1,500 troops of the 228th came ashore near Dili, they were initially mistaken for the Portuguese contingent from Angola, who were scheduled to arrive on February 19!

Having failed to stop the Japanese on the beaches south of Koepang, the defenders mounted a determined early morning defense at the Penfui airfield on February 20 that cost Doi's troops around 200 casualties. Leggatt then ordered his men to pull out, detonating previously planted demolition charges as they went.

Their withdrawal eastward toward more defensible positions put them in exactly the right place to intercept Koichi Fukumi's 3rd Yokosuka paratroopers as they descended into fields near Usua, about 15 miles east of Koepang at mid-morning. More than half of the airborne troops in the first drop were killed by gunfire or thrust bayonets as they landed in the midst of this Aussie hornets' nest, or in further actions on the ground as they attempted to capture the village of Babua later in the day.

A second airborne attack came on February 21, and gradually the Japanese ground and airborne troops surrounded the isolated remnants of the 2/40th Battalion. On the morning of February 23, after consulting his subordinate commanders, Bill Leggatt decided to surrender his command to prevent their being annihilated. Though Leggatt survived his ensuing captivity, a sizable number of the Sparrow Force troops who surrendered with him did not. Shortly after he was captured, a Japanese officer admitted to him that only 78 men in the first parachute drop had survived.

Brigadier Veale was among the Australian forces that had managed to successfully escape into the interior of the island, and when they learned of Leggatt's surrender, they sought to link up with Allied forces in Portuguese Timor.

When the invasion came, the Allied contingent in eastern Timor included both Spence's 2/2nd Company and a 150-man Dutch contingent led by van Straten. As the latter attempted to get back to Dutch Timor, Spence's men fought a delaying action, then melted into the mountains and jungles of the interior. Having been trained for small-unit actions and living off the land, they essentially became a guerilla force. By March, both Veale and van Straten had linked up with Spence.

On both Borneo and Celebes, unsuccessful attempts had been made by escaped Allied troops to operate as guerrillas, but in these cases, the stragglers were captured after a relatively short time. In Timor, it was a different situation entirely. Despite Sadashichi Doi's best efforts to catch them, Sparrow Force managed to elude capture while embarrassing the Japanese commander with deadly hit-and-run attacks.

Having cobbled together a radio, the fugitives were able to contact Australia and apprise Allied leaders of the situation, and by May, clandestine supply runs and evacuations of wounded were taking place, first with seaplanes, and later with ships. Veale and van Straten were pulled out in May, leaving Spence in command. During August 1942, the 48th Division under Lieutenant General Yuitsu Tsuchihashi, who had defeated the Americans in northern Luzon in December, undertook a major push to capture Sparrow Force, but they were pulled out for redeployment to New Guinea without having achieved this objective.

In the meantime, Allied ships managed to reach Timor with supplies and fresh troops. The Australian government even sent documentary filmmaker Damien Parer to Timor, where he shot the film *Men of Timor* about the exploits of Sparrow Force. Parer is best remembered as the cinematographer on the 1942 documentary about the New Guinea campaign, *Kokoda Front Line!* This film won a 1943 Academy Award. Parer was killed by a Japanese bullet in 1944 while filming the US Marines on Peleliu.

Spence was evacuated in November, followed by the last of Sparrow Force, who were pulled out by January 1943. They had killed 1,500 Japanese troops, while losing 40 of their own men.

The remarkable, albeit relative, success of Sparrow Force is in contrast to the fate of their fellow "Birds," Gull on Ambon, and Lark on New Britain. While this book focuses on the Southeast Asia Theater, mention of the fate of Lark Force provides an opportunity to discuss the way in which activities in Southeast Asia intersected the operations which were taking place in the Southwest Pacific. On the chessboard of the Southwest Pacific, the strategic planners in Tokyo saw the Bismarck Archipelago, especially the island of New Britain, east of Southeast Asia and the Indies, as the linchpin of their future strategy. It was also a space on the board that would have to be occupied in order to check any Allied moves which might be made from Australia. Indeed, it would be the key to a ground offensive against Australia, should this long-discussed strategic option be given a green light.

Specifically, they had their eyes on the port city of Rabaul, 1,700 miles east of Timor and 3,000 miles east of Batavia. Located at New Britain's eastern tip, it was 800 miles closer to Australia than the huge IJN base on the island of Truk. Rabaul was to become the forward operating base.

The timetable for the Rabaul operation, code-named Operation *R*, was set for a month before the Timor invasion and it paralleled Japanese operations in Dutch Borneo. The invasion fleet had departed from Truk on January 14, midway on the calendar between the Tarakan landings on January 10, and those at Balikpapan two weeks later.

As they were doing across Southeast Asia, the Japanese went after Rabaul with a determined efficiency and a force that substantially outnumbered the Allied defensive assets. The IJA force assigned to the Rabaul mission was the South Seas Detachment, a brigade-sized IJA force commanded by Major General Tomitaro Horii, who had led the invasion of Guam in December. Formed under the command structure of the IJN South Seas Force (based on the 4th Fleet) it was intended for offensive operations in the Pacific islands. For the Rabaul operation, the detachment was centered on the 144th Infantry Regiment, and other units detached from the 55th Division, including a battalion of the 55th Mountain Artillery Regiment, a squadron of the 55th Cavalry Regiment and engineer, antiaircraft, and other support units.

Sailing south from Truk, the IJA troops were escorted by an IJN task force under the command of Vice Admiral Shigeyoshi Inoue which included seven cruisers, 14 destroyers, and the aircraft carriers *Akagi* and *Kaga*, both veterans of the Pearl Harbor attack.

Lark Force, commanded by Lieutenant Colonel John Scanlon, numbered around 1,400 men, was centered on 23rd Brigade's 2/22nd Battalion, and contained two artillery batteries, one antiaircraft and one antitank. It was a minimal contingent with minimal obsolete air support – and one of its companies was detached to defend Kavieng on the island of New Ireland. As Bruce Gamble points out in his histories of the Rabaul campaign, the Australian numbers included local militia units and a battalion band that had been recruited in its entirety from the Salvation Army!

After a series of air attacks, Horii sent as many as 4,000 troops ashore on New Ireland on January 22, while a 5,000-man contingent landed on New Britain just after midnight the following day. Lark Force met the troops of Colonel Masao Kusunose's 144th Infantry Regiment on the beaches near Rabaul, but the overwhelming Japanese superiority in numbers allowed Kusunose to land troops at additional locations that were undefended. By the end of the day, all of Scanlon's defensive positions were overrun. Most of the men of Lark Force were captured, but 300 managed to escape westward to New Guinea.

The Japanese quickly turned Rabaul into their pivotal operational crossroads in the South and Southwest Pacific. It became the principal forward operating base for the IJA and the IJN and the air arms of both services. Around Rabaul, major airbases were built at Lakunai, Rapopo, Tobera, and Vunakanau. Rabaul became for the Japanese in World War II what Singapore had been to the British for the previous century, a formidable and heavily fortified keystone to their overall military strategy – and their empire. By 1943, the Japanese would have more than 100,000 personnel stationed at Rabaul.

In fact, it became what Singapore might have been for Britain's RN – if the British had not lost that great base – and it was certainly more important to the Japanese than Singapore was now. Indeed, after the Japanese victories in Malaya and the Dutch East Indies, Singapore was lying serenely in the middle of a vast Japanese sea.

CHAPTER 20

BEAUTIFUL BALI, STEPPING STONE TO JAVA

February 19, 1942, the day that the Japanese came ashore in Timor and the day that Japanese bombs fell on Darwin, was also the date that the Japanese invaded Bali.

The IJA had no intention of occupying all 17,500 islands of the Dutch East Indies. The five largest, of course, were the highlight of their operations, to which were added places such as Ambon, with its strategic airfield, and New Guinea, the stepping stone to Australia. Bali was not on the original list for IJA operations, but a curious fluke of especially poor weather over Borneo and Celebes, which restricted air operations, and clear weather farther south, made airfields on Bali an important part of the plan for the invasion of Java. It did not hurt that Bali was only a 3-mile ferry ride from Banyuwangi on Java.

Bali has always had a reputation as a unique place among the 17,500 islands. Historically, it was the island where Hinduism held sway after Islam swept the rest of the archipelago that became the Dutch East Indies. Today, it is a globally recognized leading tourism destination for travelers in search of diversions from sandy beaches and nightlife, to spas and yoga retreats. In the decade which preceded World War II, it was a place whose singular culture and arts had uniquely inspired the imagination of the West.

The Bali of the eve of World War II was the Bali that had been discovered, almost as a time capsule, by a succession of artists and anthropologists in the 1930s. They had described it with wide-eyed amazement as a magical Shangri-La. The Bali into which the IJA stepped on February 19, 1942 was not like the other islands of the Indies. It was not a landscape of oil wells, but a delicate panorama of temples and the captivating music of the gamelan.

Among the wide-eyed who discovered it in the 1930s was the anthropologist Margaret Mead, whose prewar field studies of life and sexuality on South Pacific islands, and in particular on Bali, alternately stunned or titillated Western sensibilities at the time, but also helped inspire the sexual revolution of the 1960s. The gamelan of Bali greatly intrigued the modernist composer Colin McPhee when he visited as an amateur ethnomusicologist, and he helped introduce Balinese culture to the *avant garde* salons of prewar New York.

The man who had done the most to recreate Bali as an icon in Western popular culture was the Mexican-born New York artist Miguel Covarrubias, who honeymooned on Bali in 1930 with his wife, the choreographer Rosa Rolando (originally Rosemonde Cowan). His paintings of Balinese life, especially of sensual, bare-breasted young women were a sensation when they were exhibited in New York in 1932.

Bankrolled by a Guggenheim Fellowship, the two returned in 1933, gathering material and snapping pictures for the book *Island of Bali*. Dr Anna Indych-López, an associate professor of art history at the City College of New York, writes that "Covarrubias idealized Bali as a pristine and enchanted land that embodied a vision of social harmony and beauty," adding that he "was drawn to the exoticism of the South Sea Island paradise."

When the book was published by Knopf in 1937, it created a groundswell of interest in Balinese culture, and this preoccupation found its way into textile design and decorative arts. As Dr Indych-López points out:

> *Life* magazine and *Vanity Fair* reported on Covarrubias's work on Bali, which inspired a "Balinese vogue" among fashionable New Yorkers as epitomized by the window displays at the Fifth Avenue department store, Franklin Simon, which included fabric designs with Bali prints by the artist. Even before *Island of* Bali's appearance in mid-November 1937, Knopf ordered a second printing to satisfy demand.

Theodore Friend, in his book *Indonesian Destinies*, writes that mesmerized westerners described Bali as "an enchanted land of aesthetes at peace with themselves and nature."

Among the western artists most charmed by Bali was the German painter Walter Spies, who lived in Bali off and on from 1927, and who was well liked by the Balinese themselves. As a German national, Spies was interned in 1940 after the German occupation of the Netherlands. On January 19, 1942, exactly one month before the Japanese arrival in Bali, Spies was aboard a ship carrying internees being relocated when it was attacked and sunk by an IJN patrol boat. The exotic home in the mountains at Iseh that he built in 1937 survived the war to eventually become a high-end tourist retreat catering to the rich and famous.

While so many of the Indies were "lightly defended" when the Japanese arrived, Bali was essentially entirely undefended. There were no KNIL troops on the island, only Lieutenant Colonel W.P. Roodenberg and his Korps Prajoda, a native auxiliary corps of about 600, to guard the 2,232-square-mile island.

The invading force consisted of the "Kanemura Detachment," which centered on the 3rd Infantry Battalion, commanded by Major Matabei Kanemura. The battalion and supporting troops had been detached from the 48th Division, then earmarked for operations in neighboring western

Java. They traveled to Bali in two transport ships, escorted by four destroyers, and a covering force under Rear Admiral Kyuji Kubo, whose flagship, the cruiser *Nagara*, was accompanied by another three destroyers.

For Kubo, the Bali experience was just the opposite of that at Ambon Island three weeks earlier. The requirement for naval bombardment at Ambon was in contrast to the sleeping shores of Bali which had no coastal artillery with which to duel. However, offshore, Ambon had been undefended by an Allied naval presence, whereas at Bali the Japanese ran into one of the biggest naval battles in the Dutch East Indies to date, an action described in detail in the following chapters.

Matabei Kanemura's objective was the airfield at Denpasar on Bali's southern coast, which would eventually evolve into today's Ngurah Rai International Airport, one of Indonesia's busiest. In 1942, though, the place was almost a ghost town, as the ML-KNIL had based no aircraft there, and non-military flights were a rarity by this time. When Roodenberg ordered his troops to detonate the demolition charges without delay, they misread the message to understand that he was ordering a delay. Kanemura's men captured the airport intact by 10:30 pm and the land battle of Bali was essentially over.

The following morning, the Mitsubishi Zeros of the IJN Tainin Kaigun Kokutai (Tainin Air Group) arrived on Denpasar's runway in preparation for the Dutch East Indies endgame on Java. This group had the distinction of being the home of some of the IJN's most famous and most successful fighter pilots. The cream of the crop, these aerial samurai included Hiroyoshi Nishizawa, who is credited with 87 aerial victories and is considered to be Japan's leading ace, as well as Saburo Sakai, who scored 62 victories, and Takeo Omura, who had 50.

War had come to the "enchanted land of aesthetes at peace with themselves and nature," and the last island stepping stone to Java was under new management.

CHAPTER 21

TIGHTENING THE NOOSE IN THE JAVA SEA

With the fall of Borneo, Sumatra, and all the islands culminating with beautiful Bali, the attention of both sides focused on the crown jewel of the Dutch East Indies. Java now found itself in the crosshairs at the center of a rapidly narrowing circle of carnage, surrounded by a raging tempest. Within those turbulent seas, the last half of February 1942, the two weeks following Singapore's demise, were filled with a cascading series of naval actions.

As the perimeter contracted, so too did General Archibald Wavell's ABDA Command. After the battle of Balikpapan, when four USN destroyers had laid waste to the Japanese invasion fleet off lightly defended Borneo, the mission of the ABDA combined fleet fell into line with that compressed strategic outlook. Recognizing ABDA's limitations, Wavell now focused his attention on protecting Java.

On February 2, after Allied reconnaissance aircraft had observed an invasion fleet being assembled at the island of Jolo, Dutch Vice Admiral Conrad Emil Lambert Helfrich, the Dutch naval commander in the Indies, suggested to the USN's Admiral Thomas Hart, the overall commander of all ABDA naval assets, that a combined strike force should be created for the express purpose of stopping the Japanese invasion of Java.

The ABDA Combined Strike Force was placed under the command of Dutch Rear Admiral Karel Doorman, and headquartered at the big Dutch naval base at the port of Surabaya (in Dutch, Soerebaja), the second largest city on Java.

The Allied naval strength in the seas between Malaya and the Philippines and through the waters surrounding the Dutch East Indies was clearly inferior to that of the IJN. With the loss of the heart of the USN's Pacific Fleet at Pearl Harbor, the USN presence consisted of the former Asiatic Fleet, which had escaped from the Philippines. Doorman's strike force had no battleships or aircraft carriers, and just two heavy cruisers, the USS *Houston* and the HMS *Exeter*, the latter famous for having helped to defeat the German pocket battleship *Graf Spee* in 1939. His light cruisers included the Dutch warships HNMLS *Tromp*, HNMLS *Java*, and HNMLS *De Ruyter*, his flagship, as well as the USS *Marblehead* and HMAS *Perth*.

The great battleships of the USN and the RN had been knocked out of action in the first three days of the war in the Pacific, and the Dutch had none to begin with. It might not have been that way, had far-sightedness in Amsterdam been rewarded, not ignored. Even before World War I, noting the increased Japanese expansionism in northeast Asia, and the lopsided Japanese victory in the Russo-Japanese War, a Dutch Royal Commission had proposed in 1913 that the Koninklijke Marine should build nine large battleships. The idea was to use four to ensure Dutch neutrality in Europe, and five to augment the modest naval forces in the Indies.

Parliamentary debate about funding ensued, the idea came and went during the interwar years before emerging on the eve of World War II with a proposal to buy three battle cruisers. Nothing had been done about this by the time that the Netherlands surrendered to Germany. The biggest Dutch ships in the Indies at the time were light cruisers. Indeed, corners had been cut and armament was limited to less-than-6-inch guns on these, including Admiral Doorman's flagship in the Indies, the *De Ruyter*, which had been launched in 1936 during the depths of the Great Depression.

By contrast, the IJN, the beneficiary of a prewar naval building boom, was able to concentrate multiple task forces on the scale of the total ABDA Command at various locations throughout the South China Sea and the Dutch East Indies. Furthermore, with the myriad airfields that the IJA had captured from Malaya to Borneo, and which the IJN had captured in Celebes, Japanese airpower from both services dominated the skies throughout the region as the shrinking Allied perimeter withdrew into Java.

For the final assault on Java, the two IJN surface fleets, which had been operating independently since December, would converge. The Western Force under Vice Admiral Jisaburo Ozawa, commander of the Southern Expeditionary Fleet, fresh from the operations off Sumatra, would support landings in western Java, while the Eastern Force under Vice Admiral Ibo Takahashi would support the invasion of eastern Java.

The ABDA Combined Strike Force barely had the opportunity to form up in the waters north of Java when it was put through the same wringer from Japanese airpower that had sunk the *Prince of Wales* and *Repulse* two months earlier. The specific place was off the Kangean Islands in the Flores Sea about 300 miles east of Surabaya, south of the Makassar Strait between Borneo and Celebes, and north of the Lombok Strait near Bali. The battle is known variously as the "Battle of" one or the other of these areas of ocean.

On February 3, as the ABDA Strike Force was heading north into the mouth of the Makassar Strait, it was observed but not attacked by Japanese aircraft. Shortly before 10:00 am the following morning, though, Japanese land-based bombers came overhead in force, and the bombs began to fall. The Japanese bombardiers naturally targeted the cruisers, the largest ships in the fleet below. The Japanese pilots returned to their bases, proudly bragging of having sunk three Allied cruisers, but in fact, only two had been damaged, albeit seriously.

The *Marblehead* was effectively put out of action, although she limped west to Ceylon, and was eventually repaired in South Africa.

The Japanese believed they had sunk the *Houston*, but she was soon able to rejoin combat operations after repairs in Surabaya. She had, however, lost the use of her aft turret.

One of the Houston's next assignments was to join the task force that departed Darwin, Australia on February 15, escorting reinforcements bound for the garrison at Timor. The convoy came under heavy air attack the following day and turned back to Australia upon learning that a substantial IJN surface fleet was offshore to support the invasion of Timor, and that it was supported by aircraft carriers. By now, the crew of the *Houston*, aware that the Japanese had reported her sunk at least once, had given her the nickname "Galloping Ghost of the Java Coast."

The next major surface action in the Dutch East Indies came in the late evening of February 19, the same day as the widely separated Japanese invasions of Timor and Bali, and the infamous Japanese air attack on Darwin. The place was the Badung Strait, east of Bali, and the antagonists were the Bali invasion fleet versus an ABDA fleet headed by the Dutch cruisers HNMLS *Java* and HNMLS *De Ruyter*, the Dutch destroyer HNMLS *Piet Hein*, and two USN veterans of the battle of Balikpapan, USS *John D. Ford* and USS *Pope*.

The two troop ships had just landed the Kanemura Detachment for its unopposed landing on Bali's south coast, and were pulling away, escorted by the destroyers *Arashio*, *Asashio*, *Michishio*, and *Oshio*. All five Allied ships opened fire at 10:25 pm, with little effect, and the destroyers proceeded to fire torpedoes. The Japanese destroyers replied with their own torpedoes, with the *Asashio* scoring a fatal hit on the *Piet Hein*. Rear Admiral Kyuji Kubo, aboard cruiser *Nagara* and accompanied by another three destroyers, steamed toward the battle, but remained out of range.

The two sides disengaged, but at around 1:30 am on February 20, the Japanese invasion fleet was intercepted by a second ABDA force, the cruiser HNMLS *Tromp* and the destroyers USS *John D. Edwards*, USS *Parrott*, USS *Pilsbury*, and USS *Stewart*. When the *Tromp* engaged the *Asashio* and the *Oshio*, all three suffered damage. *Michishio* was badly damaged by gunfire from the *Tromp* and two of the American destroyers. As the two sides disengaged, she was left dead in the water, but she did not sink and came under tow. Once again, as in the earlier engagement, Kubo and his contingent were out of range.

―――――――

In the space of three weeks, the last of Celebes, followed by Ambon, Timor, Bali, and most of Sumatra had each slipped under the big roof of the Greater East Asia Co-Prosperity Sphere, destined for bleak years of no prosperity. During those weeks, the great invasion fleet tasked with the final subjugation of the Dutch East Indies embarked from Cam Ranh Bay in Vietnam, bound for the beaches and jungles of Java.

The instrument of this subjugation, the IJA 16th Army, commanded by Lieutenant General Hitoshi Imamura, was comprised of two components. That which was tasked with invading western Java and capturing Batavia assembled at Cam Ranh Bay, and was comprised of Imamura's 16th Army headquarters, as well as the 2nd Division and the 230th Infantry Regiment from the 38th Division, which had taken part in the conquest of Hong Kong. The second detachment, assigned to land in eastern Java, assembled at Jolo Island in the Philippines, and consisted of the 56th Infantry Group, which had served in the Borneo operations, and the 48th Division, which had spearheaded the initial 14th Army victories in the Philippines.

The IJN support for Imamura's assault included perhaps the largest concentration of Japanese warships in Southeast Asia thus far. Divided into two detachments, they were under the overall command of Vice Admiral Ibo Takahashi, whose flagship, the cruiser *Ashigara*, was flanked by the cruiser *Myoko* and the destroyers *Ikazuchi* and *Akebono*.

Imamura and the force targeting western Java embarked on February 18 aboard a huge convoy of 56 transports escorted by the cruisers *Yura* and *Natori*, as well as 14 destroyers and other ships under the command of Rear Admiral Kenzaburo Hara. They were joined by another force under Vice Admiral Takeo Kurita, whose cruisers *Mogami* and *Mikuma* had participated in the battle for Sumatra.

Imamura's second detachment, bound for eastern Java, was to be supported by the IJN Eastern Force. They departed from Jolo Island on

February 19, a day after Imamura, aboard 41 troop ships. Their escort, commanded by Rear Admiral Shoji Nishimura, included the light cruisers *Naka* and *Jintsu*, supported by 14 destroyers. Covering the convoy and these escorts, and commanded by Rear Admiral Takeo Takagi, were the heavy cruisers *Nachi* and *Haguro*, as well as the destroyers *Ushio* and *Sazanami*. When the Eastern Force met the ABDA Combined Strike Force, the warships would operate under Takagi's command.

————————

On the ground inside Java, General Archibald Wavell, the commander of the ABDA Command, pondered his situation. The plan to pull the majority of Allied assets into Java after having committed relatively few to the defense of the other islands had looked good on paper, but now that it was done, his hand did not look so strong after all. The combined ABDA fleet had been essentially obliterated. ABDA airpower was scarcely more intact than the ABDA fleet, consisting mainly of battered remnants. The ABDA ground troops, which had been preserved for a last stand in Java, were comprised of brave men, but they were exhausted men who knew they were a match for the Japanese only in the remotest corners of the imagination. ABDA was no longer a cohesive Joint American–British–Dutch–Australian force, but the KNIL, with small contingents from the other armies attached. Wavell decided that the short-lived command should be deactivated, and that command of the Allied defense of Java should go to a Dutch general. He proposed this to Winston Churchill on February 21. Only two weeks had passed since the fall of Singapore.

"I am afraid that the defence of ABDA area has broken down, and that defence of Java cannot now last long," a despondent Wavell wired Churchill.

> It always hinged on the air battle … Anything put into Java now can do little to prolong the struggle; it is more [a] question of what you will choose to save … I see little further usefulness for this HQ. Last about

myself. I am, as ever, entirely willing to do my best where you think best to send me. I have failed you and President [Roosevelt] here, where a better man might perhaps have succeeded. If you fancy I can best serve by returning to India I will of course do so … I hate the idea of leaving these stout-hearted Dutchmen, and will remain here and fight it out with them as long as possible if you consider this would help at all. Good wishes. I am afraid you are having [a] very difficult period, but I know your courage will shine through it.

The following day, the prime minister wrote back, telling Wavell, "When you cease to command the ABDA area you should proceed yourself to India, where we require you to resume your position as Commander-in-Chief to carry on the war against Japan from this main base." In *The Hinge of Fate*, the fourth volume of his wartime memoirs, Churchill observed that "I admired the composure and firmness of mind with which Wavell had faced the cataract of disaster which had been assigned to him with so much formality and precision."

ABDA officially went out of business at 9:00 am on February 25, and Wavell departed two days later, winging his way to New Delhi to resume his post as commander-in-chief of the British India Command. In 1943, by then promoted to field marshal, Wavell became the penultimate viceroy of British India.

On the ground in Java, ter Poorten accepted his new role as Allied commander, firmly stating in a broadcast that he thought it better to "die standing rather than to live on our knees."

———————

On February 27, even as Wavell was in the air, having left Java for the final time, things were reaching a climactic moment in the seas north of the crown jewel island. Admiral Doorman and what had been earlier been known as the ABDA Combined Strike Force had departed from Surabaya the day before to intercept the IJN Eastern Force and the invasion fleet bound for eastern Java.

Doorman had two heavy cruisers to match the Japanese two, the *Nachi* and *Haguro*. These were the HMS *Exeter* and the USS *Houston*, which had just returned to Surabaya after the failed mission escorting reinforcements to Timor. The Japanese heavies, however, outgunned the Allied ships, especially the *Houston*, which had just four 8-inch guns after having lost her aft turret. This compared to ten guns of the same caliber aboard the Japanese heavy cruisers.

Doorman's strike force also included three light cruisers, the HMAS *Perth*, the HNLMS *Java*, and his flagship, the HNLMS *De Ruyter*, as well as nine destroyers, the USS *Alden*, HMS *Electra*, HMS *Encounter*, HMS *Jupiter*, USS *John D. Edwards*, USS *John D. Ford*, HNLMS *Kortenaer*, USS *Paul Jones*, and HNLMS *Witte de With*.

Meanwhile the IJN fleet, commanded by Rear Admiral Takeo Takagi, consisted of two heavy cruisers, *Nachi* and *Haguro*, and two light cruisers, *Naka* and *Jintsu*, as well as 14 destroyers, the *Amatsukaze*, *Asagumo*, *Harusame*, *Hatsukaze*, *Kawakaze*, *Minegumo*, *Murasame*, *Samidare*, *Sazanami*, *Tokitsukaze*, *Ushio*, *Yamakaze*, *Yudachi*, and *Yukikaze*.

At about 4:15 pm on February 26, Doorman was alerted by Admiral Helfrich to the presence of the Japanese invasion fleet. They were reported to be 200 miles, north by northwest, from the Allied fleet. Doorman was ordered to intercept and attack the Japanese that night under cover of darkness. He sailed north at about 6:30 pm conducting a sweep of the Java coast north of Madura Island, near Surabaya, where the Japanese seemed to be headed. The Allies saw no sign of the Japanese during the night, but at about 9:00 am several Japanese aircraft attacked. They did little damage, but they were able to report the location of the Allied fleet.

Around 2:30 pm on February 27, Doorman was returning once again to Surabaya when he received word that Allied reconnaissance aircraft had observed not one, but two, Japanese convoys within a short distance of Java. From the air, or indeed from the surface, the convoy, strung out across the Java Sea for 20 miles, was hard to miss. In his postwar memoirs, Commander Tameichi Hara, the captain of the IJN destroyer *Amatsukaze*, observed that the convoy "was quite a spectacle.

An obvious laxity prevailed in the transports with their ill-trained crews. Many transports emitted huge clouds of black smoke from their funnels … Most disturbing, however, was the dreadfully slow pace of the trailing heavy cruisers."

Turning his strike force about, Doorman led his five cruisers and nine destroyers to engage the enemy. The British destroyers formed a screening force, while the USN ships brought up the rear. Japanese aircraft had also spotted the Allied ships, and attacked. As with the Japanese aircraft observed that morning, there was no effort at a serious air strike, and the Allied force steamed ahead.

Clouds of black smoke aside, the two battle fleets first had eyes on one another shortly after 4:00 pm and the first salvo erupted from the Japanese cruisers at 4:16 pm at a range of about 16 miles. The guns of the *Houston* replied a few minutes later, though the majority of the smaller-gunned Allied cruisers remained out of range, and the battle of the Java Sea was joined.

Takagi aimed for the classic "Crossing the T" maneuver, in which his fleet would pass perpendicular to the line of the Allied ships, each one able to fire broadside with all main turrets at the Allied ships, who would be in line, and therefore unable to use all their turrets. In the meantime, the Japanese ships began laying down a smokescreen. They fired two salvos of torpedoes in the battle's first 45 minutes, sinking the *Kortenaer* and severely damaging the *Exeter.*

Doorman reformed his fleet for an attack, which was led by the destroyers *Electra, Encounter*, and *Jupiter* shortly after 6:00 pm. The *Electra* managed to hit the Asagumo's engine room, but, in response, a withering barrage of Japanese fire blanketed the *Electra*, which was sunk at 6:16 pm.

As the sun went down, Doorman broke off the attack, and was leading his cruisers in an effort to get around the Japanese warships and attack the troop ships. The problem was that he had not seen them, and his only notion of where they might be relative to the warships was based on hours-old intelligence from aerial reconnaissance flights which had to be relayed to him from ashore.

Having failed at this effort, Doorman then led his warships back toward the north coast of Java by the light of a full moon to wait for the Japanese fleet. The *Jupiter* exploded at 9:16 pm, having struck a Dutch mine laid earlier in the day, and sank. With this, Doorman moved his ships farther offshore to search for the Japanese.

Shortly after 11:00 pm, the Allied ships spotted and engaged Takagi's two heavy cruisers, *Nachi* and *Haguro*, at a distance of about seven miles. Both Japanese vessels responded with gunfire and torpedoes, which found their mark shortly after 11:30 pm. The *Java* and the *De Ruyter*, Doorman's flagship, were each hit by single torpedoes moments apart. The order to abandon ship was given, but the ships sank quickly. Doorman's last order was to the surviving cruisers *Houston* and *Perth*, instructing them to break off the attack and withdraw to Batavia. Doorman was witnessed on the bridge of the *De Ruyter*, going down with his ship.

The other Allied ships also broke off the attack and retired toward Surabaya, while the Japanese fleet regrouped. The Allies had lost two cruisers and three destroyers sunk, and the *Exeter* seriously damaged. She would be repaired, but she was lost in her next battle.

The Japanese had suffered only the *Asagumo*, left dead in the water, but later repaired to fight again and again in later battles. The Eastern Force troop ships were never touched by Allied guns. Eastern Java had not been spared the invasion that was supposed to have taken place overnight on February 27–28, but this "inevitable" had been delayed by one day.

As the *Houston* and *Perth* headed west, the Allied destroyers that survived the battle of the Java Sea followed the *Exeter*, escorted by the *Witte de With*, south to Surabaya. Because the big Dutch naval base was vulnerable to air attack, and the Allies were thin on fighters capable of flying top cover, the decision was made to get the ships back out to safe ports as soon as they could be patched up and refueled. By the end of the day, four of the American destroyers, *Alden*, *John D. Edwards*, *John D. Ford*, and *Paul Jones* departed for Australia by way of the Bali Strait east of Java.

The badly damaged, but seaworthy *Exeter* was ordered to sail from Surabaya to Ceylon for repairs. The ideal route would have been to follow the other ships, and to steer west toward Ceylon after they were safely south of Java. However, the Bali Strait was too shallow for the *Exeter*, so she departed westward through the Java Sea, escorted by the HMS *Encounter* and the USS *Pope*, intending to turn south through the Sunda Strait at the western end of Java.

By the end of the day on February 28, the only major warship left in Surabaya was the *Witte de With*, which had developed mechanical issues.

At the same time that the disbursal of vessels was taking place at Surabaya, the HMAS *Perth* and USS *Houston*, the "Galloping Ghost of the Java Coast," were galloping westward across the Java coast by themselves, reaching Tanjung Priok, the port of Batavia, at 1:30 pm on February 28.

The two cruisers arrived amid the chaos of both Tanjung Priok and Batavia being under continuous Japanese air raids, and found a safe harbor. Indeed, they sailed in just as there was a great flurry of urgency for ships to evacuate the port. A couple of hours later, as soon as they were refueled, the *Perth* and *Houston* departed. They did not even have time to wait for the Dutch destroyer HNLMS *Evertsen*, which had been ordered to accompany them.

They sailed west, planning to transit the Sunda Strait between Java and Sumatra, and to gallop the south coast of Java toward Tjilatjap (now Cilacap), and rest the crews, who had slept little if at all for several days, before resuming the fight.

At around 11:30 pm, as they passed Bantam Bay (now Banten Bay), on the northwest tip of Java, near the mouth of the Sunda Strait, the *Perth* spotted another ship, five miles ahead in the darkness. Thinking it to be an Australian corvette that they expected to meet, signal lights were flashed. When the reply came back unintelligible, the *Perth* realized what was going on. Much to their surprise, the two Allied cruisers had run into the midst of an enormous amphibious landing operation.

The Allies knew that this landing was coming, but if aerial reconnaissance had ascertained the when and where, nobody had told Captain Hector Waller of the *Perth*, or Captain Albert Rooks of the *Houston*. The Japanese, in contrast, were aware of the two cruisers, and the destroyer *Fukubi* had been shadowing them at a discreet distance, unseen by them in the inky darkness.

The night before, they had chased about on the Java Sea, searching in vain for the troop ships of the Japanese *eastern* landing force. Now, 24 hours later, as they approached the Sunda Strait, they found themselves in the midst of the Japanese *western* landing force disgorging its troops at Bantam Bay.

There were 56 troop ships carrying the bulk of Lieutenant General Hitoshi Imamura's 16th Army, including Imamura himself, traveling aboard the *Ryujo Maru*, coincidentally the same transport that had delivered General Tomoyuki Yamashita to the Malay Peninsula in the early morning hours of December 8, 1941.

Surrounding these ships and sailing about screening them, was Rear Admiral Kenzaburo Hara's battle fleet, including the light cruiser *Natori* and the destroyers *Asakaze, Fubuki, Harukaze, Hatakaze, Hatsuyuki, Murakumo, Shirakumo*, and *Shirayuki*. Farther away from the transports, and out of range for the ensuing battle, was the force commanded by Vice Admiral Takeo Kurita that included the cruisers *Mogami* and *Mikuma*, recent veterans of the Sumatra operations, as well as cruisers *Kumano* and *Suzuya*, and the aircraft carrier *Ryujo*, another veteran of the Sumatra campaign.

The first salvo, a brace of torpedoes, in the battle of the Sunda Strait was fired by the ship that the *Perth* had mistakenly signaled, possibly the *Harukaze*. Both Allied cruisers returned fire.

In the ensuing naval battle, which lasted until after midnight, the *Harukaze, Mikuma,* and *Shirayki* all suffered serious damage, but remained seaworthy. A minesweeper and four of the troop transports were sunk – two by friendly fire – with these including the *Ryujo Maru*, with Hitoshi Imamura still aboard.

Both of the Allied cruisers were sunk, with the *Perth* losing 55 percent of her crewmen, and the *Houston* losing 65 percent. The fate of these ships was unknown to the Allies until late in 1942, and details of the battle were not known until the captured survivors were released from Japanese custody after the war. Both Rook and Waller, like Doorman the night before, went down with their ships.

Imamura also went down with his ship, but he was rescued from the water and taken ashore soaking wet. It was not the way he had hoped to first set foot on Java.

The HNLMS *Evertsen* arrived on the scene as the battle was ongoing, and steered away. She was, however, ambushed by the destroyers *Murakumo* and *Shirakumo*, and damaged so severely that she was deliberately run aground.

At 4:00 am on March 1, as the swirling muck on the bottom of the Sunda Strait was still settling over the *Perth* and the *Houston*, and as the grounded *Evertsen* still burned, the HMS *Exeter* and her escorts, the HMS *Encounter* and the USS *Pope*, turned into the Sunda Strait. Observing Hara's fleet, and being in no shape to engage it, the three Allied ships turned about and attempted to escape to the northwest, back into the Java Sea.

Had they been able to escape south of Java, they might have had clear sailing all the way to Ceylon. To the north, however, they sailed into the massing of Japanese naval power that was forming the noose around Java.

At 9:35 am, by the light of day, the three Allied ships sighted the heavy cruisers *Haguro* and *Nachi* and other ships from Takagi's fleet, which had mauled the Allies so badly less than two days earlier. Again, they turned to escape, but when they were about 100 miles south of Borneo, they found themselves on a collision course with Vice Admiral Ibo Takahashi's flagship, the cruiser *Ashigara*, which was accompanied by the cruiser *Myoko* and other ships.

The Japanese gunners opened fire at 11:20 am. The *Exeter* returned fire, but was blanketed with a relentless barrage. She wound up dead in the water, and the *coup de grace* was delivered in the form of a torpedo from the destroyer *Inazuma* at around 11:45 am.

The Allied destroyers, laying a smoke screen, attempted to escape into a rainstorm. The *Pope* did manage to elude the enemy, but the *Encounter* was sunk by gunfire from the cruisers. Shortly before 2:00 pm, though, aircraft from the carrier *Ryujo* found the *Pope*, and sent her to the bottom as well.

At about the same time, back at the harbor at Surabaya, other Japanese aircraft destroyed the crippled destroyer *Witte de With*, the last Allied surface warship left in the Dutch East Indies.

Just as the IJA had developed a well-justified reputation for invincibility, the IJN had wiped the Dutch East Indies clean of an Allied naval presence, and they had done so in less than 48 hours without the loss of a single warship.

CHAPTER 22

THE AXE FALLS ON JAVA

As he watched the sun rise over the jungled hills of western Java on the first day of March 1942, Lieutenant General Hitoshi Imamura had much on his mind. He thought about the ignoble dunking that he had experienced in the waters of the Sunda Strait just after midnight the night before. He tried *not* to think about his horror in these dark waters, and the fear that he would drown like a kitten in the surf before he had a chance to prove himself with his conquest of the crown jewel of the Dutch East Indies. An inheritor of the samurai spirit, he had no fear of death in battle, only the fear of dying clumsily without having had the chance actually to do battle.

A career IJA officer, Imamura had graduated from the IJA Academy in 1907, two years behind Hideki Tojo and Tomoyuki Yamashita. As Yamashita and Tojo had served as military attachés in Switzerland and Austria in the wake of World War I, young Captain Imamura had gone to the United Kingdom in that capacity in 1918. In 1927, he was posted as military attaché in British India. After a series of staff jobs at IJA headquarters, he was promoted to major general and sent to Manchukuo in 1936 as deputy chief of staff of the Kwantung Army. From 1938 to 1940, now a lieutenant general, Imamura commanded the 5th Division, then involved in the war in China, after which he served a stint as deputy to General Otozo Yamada, the inspector general of military training, and one of the most powerful men in the IJA.

In June 1941, Imamura was given command of the 23rd Army, a garrison force that had been formed in China, and which would later be tasked with the invasion of Hong Kong. He was in this job when he was summoned to Tojo's office in Tokyo in November 1941 to take command of the 16th Army for the Dutch East Indies operation.

As the sun ascended into the sky and he put on a dry uniform, Imamura, like his counterparts offshore and in the air, was feeling quite invincible. The superiority of the IJA had been proven in Malaya, Singapore, and the other Dutch East Indies. The superiority of the IJN was manifest in the fact that it had sent the Allied fleet to the bottom of the Java Sea.

With the IJN having tightened the noose, the axe of Imamura's 16th Army fell upon Java with blows at opposite ends of the island, two in the west, and one in the east.

The landings in the west were intended to bracket Batavia in preparation for a pincer attack. One force landed at Bantam Bay, and the adjacent town of Merak, which had been the Java terminal for ferries arriving from Sumatra. This placed them roughly 60 miles west of Batavia. The other prong of the pincer went ashore at Eretanwetan, near present-day Pamanukan, about 80 miles east of Batavia.

The eastern Java force came ashore in the vicinity of Kragan, about 100 miles west of Surabaya. Here, operations were conducted by the 56th Infantry Group, commanded by Major General Shizuo Sakaguchi, which had captured Tarakan and Balikpapan on Borneo in January, and the 48th Division commanded by Lieutenant General Yuitsu Tsuchihashi, which had played an important role in the 14th Army's early successes in the Philippines in December 1941.

In the west, where Imamura himself came ashore at Bantam Bay, the principal unit was the 2nd Division under Major General Masao Maruyama. As its designation suggests, the 2nd Division was one of the oldest units in the IJA, tracing its origins to the Sendai garrison force in the 1870s. It had seen action in all of Japan's twentieth-century wars, beginning with the

Russo-Japanese War, and including its being in the spearhead of the IJA invasion of Manchuria in 1931, as well as its involvement in the China Incident, especially the battle of Suchow (now Xuzhou) in 1938. The following year, the 2nd Division was assigned to the 6th Army as a strategic reserve unit during the Nomonhan Incident, and was preparing to go into action against the Soviets when the ceasefire was signed on the eve of World War II.

The 2nd Division's new commander, Masao Maruyama, had led a career that roughly shadowed that of his 16th Army boss, Hitoshi Imamura. A 1911 graduate of the IJA Academy, he graduated from the Army War College in 1919, four years after Imamura, and followed him into his posts as military attaché to both the United Kingdom and British India.

Maruyama's assignment to the IJA General Staff in 1930 found him running the Anglo-American military intelligence apparatus, and four years later he was back at the Japanese embassy in London. In 1937, Maruyama commanded the 4th Regiment of the Imperial Guards Division during the China Incident, and in 1938, promoted to major general, he took command of the 6th Infantry Brigade. These added combat experience to a long series of staff jobs.

For operations in Java, Maruyama had divided his 2nd Division into three combat components, or detachments, named for their commanders in typical IJA form. The Nasu Detachment, commanded by Major General Yumio Nasu, was centered on the 2nd Infantry Group, and included two battalions of the 16th Infantry Regiment, as well as a pair of motor transport companies.

The Fukushima Detachment was led by Colonel Kyusaku Fukushima, commander of the 4th Infantry Regiment, and included two battalions of that regiment, as well as the 5th Antitank Battalion. The Sato Detachment was commanded by Colonel Hanshichi Sato, commander of the 29th Infantry Regiment, and included that regiment along with the division's 2nd Tank Regiment. Engineer units, as well as elements of the 2nd Division's 2nd Field Artillery Regiment, were assigned to each of the three detachments.

The fourth prong of the Western Force was Colonel Toshishige Shoji's veteran 230th Infantry Regiment, which Toshishige had led into Hong Kong in December and into Sumatra two weeks before coming to Java. The 230th was augmented by a mountain artillery battalion, an antiaircraft battery, an antitank battalion, and a light tank company. Toshishige was also accompanied by engineers and – reminiscent of the Malaya campaign – a bridge-building company.

Unlike the situations on other islands of the Dutch East Indies, where roads were confined only to the handful of coastal enclaves, Java had a modern paved highway system like that which the British had constructed on the Malay Peninsula, and which the Americans had built on Luzon. The gem of the Java highway system was the North Coast Road, which dated back to its role as part of the nineteenth-century Great Post Road. It is now Indonesia's National Route 1, and partly contiguous with the AH2 freeway. The North Coast Road ran for nearly 900 miles from the Sumatra ferry port at Merak to the Bali ferry port at Banyuwangi, traveling fairly close to the northern coastline of Java the entire way. Both Batavia and Surabaya were on the North Coast Road, and it was so near the Japanese invasion beaches that the invaders could include the road in their beachhead perimeter within an hour or so of landing.

As with Tomoyuki Yamashita and his 25th Army in Malaya, Imamura planned to exploit this and other roads that the Dutch had built on their favorite of the Indies. The 16th Army landed with trucks and bridge-builders. Like Yamashita, they also brought plenty of bicycles.

Opposing the Japanese forces, the backbone of the Allied ground force was the KNIL, commanded by Lieutenant General Hein ter Poorten, who became the Allied commander when ABDA was formally dissolved and General Archibald Wavell made preparations to retire to India. Consisting of three infantry divisions, the KNIL had begun the war with a manpower strength of 35,000 officers and men, but had suffered losses of around 10,000 men killed or captured on the outer islands. The number of *Stadswacht Landstorm* (home guard) troops had been reckoned at around 40,000 but these were not considered potentially effective against an army such as the IJA.

After the staggering losses at Singapore, Wavell had made an effort to obtain British and Australian reinforcements for Java. By February 27, 12 days after the Singapore surrender, as Wavell departed, the British force in Java numbered around 5,500. Commanded by Major General Hervey Sitwell, these troops consisted mainly of artillery and antiaircraft artillery units.

Sitwell's command also included B Squadron of the 3rd King's Own Hussars, a light tank regiment which had been part of the 7th British Armoured Brigade, fighting the Germans in North Africa. They had been dispatched as reinforcements for Singapore, but had arrived in the area after the British defeat and most were redirected to Burma. The 3rd, with a total of 21 tanks, was first sent to Sumatra on February 17, but was quickly pulled out and dispatched to Java, where it arrived on February 26.

Operationally, Sitwell concentrated his forces at the western and eastern ends of Java, correctly anticipating that the major Japanese objectives would be to capture Batavia in the west, and the naval base at Surabaya in the east, as well as the Java oil patch, which was centered on Tjepoe (now Cepu) and Bojenegoro, 50 miles west of Surabaya.

A further location which was important to the Dutch was the city of Bandoeng (now Bandung), 60 miles southeast of Batavia. Located in the mountains at an elevation of 2,500 feet, it had the sort of climate that was favored by European expatriates, and as such it had grown into a popular resort city for weekend getaways from Batavia. Indeed, it had become so fashionable among the wealthy set as to have earned the nickname "the Paris of Java." The long-term plan for the Dutch East Indies had involved moving the administrative functions from Batavia to Bandoeng. Some government buildings and military barracks had already been constructed by 1941, but the plan had not been implemented. Nevertheless, the city was selected as the fall-back bastion from which the KNIL would manage its defense of Java.

Also of importance was the port city of Tjilatjap (later known as Cilacap or Chilachap) on the south coast. It was correctly surmised that the Japanese assault on Java would come on the north side of the island, impacting all the major ports from Batavia to Surabaya, leaving Tjilatjap as a key point of access for resupply. There was nothing between this port and Australia but open water. With this in mind, the British assigned two batteries of the 77th Heavy Anti-Aircraft Artillery Regiment under Lieutenant Colonel H.R. Humphries, and one from Major P.P. Andrews's 21st Light Antiaircraft Artillery Regiment to protect Tjilatjap. They had brought in all their guns by March 3.

The Australian ground contingent in Java was commanded by Brigadier Arthur Blackburn and known as "Blackforce." It was comprised of about 3,000 men. Their heaviest armament consisted of machine guns, mortars, and a few antitank guns. The Australian 6th and 7th Infantry Divisions, which had been pulled out of the North Africa campaign, had been committed to the Java campaign, but they were not expected to arrive until the end of February at the earliest.

Also coming in from Australia were a battalion of the US Army 131st Field Artillery Regiment and the 26th Field Artillery Brigade Headquarters, a total of 750 men.

During the second and third week of February, an additional 12,000 troops were added to the Allied totals. These were men who had escaped from either Singapore or Sumatra. Most were stragglers that constituted no intact units, virtually none had any equipment, and large numbers were support troops untrained for combat. There were many aviation ground crews, who were unneeded because Wavell's air assets had dwindled so considerably. The RAF and RAAF were down to around 25 operational Hurricanes, and a like number of bombers and reconnaissance aircraft, but the Dutch ML-KNIL and the USAAF could add two dozen fighters and two dozen bombers to these totals.

Throughout March 1, the RAF and the Dutch ML-KNIL managed a series of air strikes against the Japanese beachheads, but these met a determined antiaircraft response and did little damage. The Dutch still had a handful of Martin bombers, but the RAF contribution involved mainly the Hurricanes, which could do little against the enemy troops other than to strafe those ashore and the barges carrying men and materiel from the troop transports. By the end of the first day of the Java battle, though, most of the Allied aircraft had been downed or damaged.

Given that they were the closest units to Batavia, the overall mission of the Japanese 2nd Division was to surround and capture the Dutch administrative capital. The idea was to overwhelm any and all Allied armed resistance, then to move quickly, using trucks and bicycles, and to seize bridgeheads across the two major north–south rivers in western Java. These were the Tjoedjoeng (now Ciujung) and the Tjidoerian (now Cidurian), which were 40 and 10 miles west of Batavia, respectively, as well as upstream tributaries such as the Tjianten (now Cianten).

Rather than make a direct eastbound approach to Batavia along the North Coast Road, the majority of 2nd Division troops turned inland, generally toward the city of Buitenzorg, located about 30 miles due south of Batavia, which was coincidentally the hometown of KNIL commander Hein ter Poorten. From here, Batavia could be approached though its back door.

All four of the 16th Army detachments in western Java had come ashore intact, and with minimal resistance except for air strikes and the failed attack by the *Houston* and *Perth*. All four moved out toward their objectives within a few hours of coming ashore on March 1.

The Nasu Detachment faced only sporadic resistance from KNIL units, which were mainly consumed with blowing up the bridges along the Tjoedjoeng River. Early in the afternoon, the Dutch dramatically destroyed the big bridge that crossed to Rangkasbitoeng (now Rangkasbitung), just as Nasu's advance reconnaissance unit reached it. Undaunted, the Japanese found and seized another bridge at Serang, and eradicated its defenders. With this bridge under control, they moved across and ahead, reaching Rangkasbitoeng, on the east bank, by 9:00 pm.

During March 1, the Fukushima and Sato Detachments found the going slower than Nasu had, given that the Allies had destroyed so many bridges on smaller rivers. By the end of the day, they had only just barely reached the Tjoedjoeng.

By 11:00 am, however, the advance units of the 230th had overcome initial opposition from a KNIL cavalry unit and had secured the main road between Batavia and Bandoeng, cutting off direct communications between the two.

East of Batavia, Shoji's 230th Regiment had come ashore harassed, but not impeded, by aircraft from the airfield that was to be their initial objective. They were to capture the Allied air base at Kalidjati about 20 miles inland from their beachhead at Eretanwetan, on the shores of Ciasem Bay. Still an airport today, Kalidjati was one of the best aviation facilities on Java at the time. As such, it was seen as an ideal operational field for Japanese tactical aircraft supporting the 16th Army ground operations on the island.

At Kalidjati, the defense was in the hands of the British and under the command of Group Captain George Frederick Whitsondale of the RAF. His defenses were tailored to air attacks, not a ground attack, and his biggest guns were in two antiaircraft batteries. Aside from this, the defenders on the ground consisted of around 350 British troops and RAF ground crewmen, and about 150 KNIL infantrymen, all armed only with rifles and machine guns. The official word from Allied headquarters was that Kalidjati was in no danger of a Japanese ground attack, and that the RAF men should stand by what was left of their battered fleet of aircraft and await orders.

Shoji, apparently unaware that Kalidjati was "not endangered" by his advance, arrived shortly before noon. At the sound of an RAF Hudson bomber taking off, the Shoji Detachment attacked. Supported by artillery and tanks, they made quick work of the defenders, and by 12:30 pm the battle of Kalidjati was over. About a third of the

The public market in San Pablo, Laguna, southeast of Manila after a Japanese air attack on Christmas Day in 1941. (NARA)

Imperial Japanese Army troops assault an American position near Subic Bay in the Philippines after an artillery bombardment. (NARA)

The Type 95 Ha-Go light tank was widely used by the IJA throughout its campaigns across Southeast Asia. This particular action was in Bataan in early 1942. (NARA)

A 14th Army infantry unit on the attack near Mount Samat on the Bataan Peninsula in April 1942. (NARA)

IJA troops employ a flamethrower in an assault on an American or Filipino position during the fighting on Bataan in 1942. (NARA)

Imperial Japanese Army infantry troops hitch a ride aboard a Type 95 Ha-Go light tank as it crashes through the Bataan jungle during the offensive in early 1942. (US Air Force)

The Japanese battle flag flies over the Philippine island of Mindanao after the Japanese victory in 1942. (NARA)

On the border of Thailand, IJA troops prepare for their invasion of Burma in January 1942. (Author's collection)

Troops of the 15th Army celebrate the fall of British colonial rule at Government House in Rangoon, March 1942. (NARA)

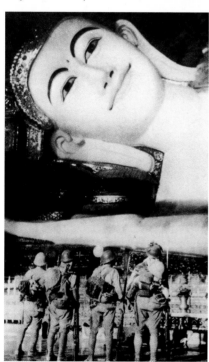

IJA troops visit the famous, 177-foot Shwethalyaung Reclining Buddha at Bago, about 50 miles northeast of Rangoon, during their conquest of Burma in 1942. (Author's collection)

The Imperial Japanese Army adopts a local means of transportation during operations in Burma. (Author's collection)

The massive air attacks on Darwin, Australia in February 1942 were compared to the similar attacks on Pearl Harbor two months earlier. All four of the Japanese aircraft carriers that launched aircraft against Darwin had done so against Pearl Harbor. (Author's collection)

Hideki Tojo inspects Imperial Japanese Army garrison troops in Manila during a visit to the Philippines. (NARA)

The dollar currency that was issued by the Japanese government during the occupation of Malaya, Brunei, Sarawak, and North Borneo was known locally as "Banana Money" because of the illustration of a banana tree. Japanese guilders were issued in the Dutch East Indies. (Author's collection)

Japanese government currency denominated in Australian shillings. The Australian currency was issued in areas such as New Guinea and the Solomon Islands where Australian currency was used before the war. The rumor still persists that the Japanese printed substantial quantities in anticipation of their occupation of Australia proper. (Courtesy of Don Johnson)

A wartime painting by Japanese war artist Kei Sato, entitled "Deadly Jungle Fighting: New Guinea Front." (NARA)

defenders died or were captured, including Captain Whitsondale, who was killed in action.

———————

More than 400 miles to the east, daybreak on March 1 found Lieutenant General Yuitsu Tsuchihashi's 48th Division and General Shizuo Sakaguchi's 56th Infantry Group ashore on a northeast-facing beach at a place near Rembang called Kragan, which is so small that it still does not show up on most maps of Java. Having crossed this once pristine tropical beach, Tsuchihashi's men immediately raced a few miles west to capture the modest port facilities at Rembang so that their heavy equipment could more easily be unloaded.

As with the other units in the west, the invasion fleet had been subjected to more or less continuous Allied air attacks. They suffered some serious losses of men and materiel in strafing attacks, as well as a high-altitude strike by USAAF B-17s flying from Australia. Conversely, the Japanese ships and Japanese troops ashore had put up a fire storm of antiaircraft fire that cost the Allies dearly.

As with the Western Force aiming toward Batavia, Tsuchihashi's main attack on Surabaya would not be a frontal attack along the main North Coast Road. Rather, the principal elements of the Eastern Force tasked with capturing Surabaya would drive south and encircle the city, an effort which would also serve to cut off a potential Allied retreat into the interior mountains of Java. In addition to taking Surabaya, Tsuchihashi was also tasked with capturing the oil facilities around Tjepoe and Bojenegoro, which were conveniently located less than 35 miles due south of his beachhead.

Tsuchihashi subdivided his 48th Division into four task forces, each essentially a reinforced regiment. Two of them, comprising the majority of the division's resources, were sent inland to outflank Surabaya and attack it with a pincer movement from the south. These were the 47th Infantry Regiment, with the 48th Infantry Group headquarters attached, under the command of Major General Koichi Abe, which constituted the left, or western part of the pincer. Simultaneously, the 1st Formosan Infantry Regiment under Colonel Hifumi Imai would be the pincer's right wing.

Meanwhile, Colonel Tohru Tanaka, commander of the 2nd Formosan Infantry Regiment, would lead a command centering on his regiment to capture Tjepoe, while Lieutenant Colonel Kuro Kitamura and his 48th Reconnaissance Regiment were tasked with the capture of Bojonegoro. All the detachments but Kitamura's would each have a mountain artillery battalion and an engineer company attached.

As Tsuchihashi's men turned eastward toward Surabaya, Shizuo Sakaguchi's 56th Infantry Group departed from the beachhead in the opposite direction, following the North Coast Road toward Semarang, which would initially be bypassed in order to turn inland and cut Java in half at its midsection.

Leading the 124th Infantry Regiment under Sakaguchi was Colonel Kyohei Yamamoto, who had served heroically under him in Borneo three weeks earlier. Yamamoto was the officer who had earned high marks from his commander for having led the 3rd Battalion of the 146th Infantry Regiment through mountains and malaria to launch a successful land assault on Bandjarmasin at the climax of the Borneo campaign.

All day on March 1, the advances made by the Japanese in eastern Java were subject to Allied air attacks of an intensity that had not been experienced elsewhere in the Dutch East Indies. The troops on the ground, meanwhile, encountered many roadblocks and were subjected to numerous ambushes involving both small arms and artillery.

However, in no place on Java, either east or west, were the Allied forces able to stave off the Japanese landings. At no place were they able to confine the 16th Army to its beachheads. In most cases, the defenders had made advances difficult and costly, but it was clear that the momentum in Java, as it had been throughout the Dutch East Indies, was with the invader.

CHAPTER 23

FOUR DAYS ON JAVA

As he stood in his command post, watching the sun rise over the jungled hills of western Java on the second day of March 1942, Lieutenant General Hitoshi Imamura of the Japanese 16th Army reflected on the immense battles that had transpired the previous day. Beginning at midnight, he had witnessed the battle of the Sunda Strait first hand – and had almost been a casualty himself. Nevertheless, all the beachheads on which Japanese boots had touched the fine straw-colored sand were now secured, and the sounds of armed combat had moved inland.

Throughout the day, Imamura's men had endured attacks from the air and had done battle with first-line defenders on the ground across Java. They had pushed them back, in some cases more easily than others, and the men of the 16th Army had taken losses.

By daybreak on March 2, elements of the 2nd Division in the west had reached and secured crossing points over the Tjoedjoeng and Tjidoerian Rivers, the major natural barriers to an eastward advance, although it would be the end of the day before all of the division's offensive detachments were on the eastern bank.

The Nasu Detachment, the primary 2nd Division contingent, commanded by Major General Yumio Nasu, had crossed the rivers and had overcome all the initial Allied roadblocks. Nasu had captured the city of Serang, and was chasing a retreating enemy toward Buitenzorg, a major city south of Batavia.

This was part of Imamura's plan to circle south of Batavia and attack from the rear, rather than making a frontal attack along the North Coast Road. Inside the city, the Allied commander, Lieutenant General Hein ter Poorten, had marshaled the forces of the KNIL 1st Infantry Division, under Major General Wilbrandus Schilling, to defend their city.

At the same time that the first defenders of western Java were withdrawing toward Buitenzorg, the Australians were preparing to block the Japanese pursuit at the Tjianten River, 15 miles west of that city. Blackforce, the 3,000-man Australian contingent under Brigadier Arthur Blackburn, was heading for the east bank of the Tjianten south of Leuwiliang, to take up positions abandoned by KNIL troops that had been pulled out to meet the attack east of Batavia by the Japanese 230th Infantry Regiment. Blackburn protested an order to move part of Blackforce to meet the 230th, arguing that dividing his command would put it in a weaker position at both locations, and the order was rescinded.

KNIL engineers had blown up the bridge on the Tjianten at Blackburn's position, so after noon on March 2, the Aussies dug into concealed positions from which they could watch the advance guard of Nasu's 16th Infantry Regiment as they arrived on the west bank to ponder their next step in getting across the yellow, muddy river. Through the day, more and more Japanese troops had arrived and were milling around in increasing numbers, waiting for the order to start across.

Finally, in the late afternoon of March 2, the men of the Blackforce 2/2nd Pioneer Battalion decided that a critical mass of Japanese troops was in the kill zone of their guns. They opened fire from their concealed positions, killing a large number of 16th Infantry Regiment troops. For that day, Allied lines west of Buitenzorg had held.

March 3 saw the battle for a Tjianten River crossing at Leuwiliang, west of Buitenzorg, begin early. Under cover of darkness, the men of Yumio

Nasu's 16th Infantry Regiment made a nearly impossible effort to get across the rain-swollen river to outflank Arthur Blackburn's Blackforce troops. By 4:00 am they had succeeded in establishing a bridgehead on the east bank, but they came under fire from the Australian gunners. In turn, Blackforce launched an all-day, and ultimately successful, counterattack against the small Japanese enclave, supported by tanks from the British 3rd King's Own Hussars, the light tank regiment which had recently arrived from North Africa.

Meanwhile, tanks from Nasu's detachment were coming under fire from four guns of the US Army 131st Field Artillery Battalion, which had been attached to Blackforce. It was a textbook case of artillery work. Using trained forward observers, the gunners destroyed Japanese tanks and vehicles as far from the river as possible, creating a roadblock, which prevented those closer to the river from escaping. The gunners then "walked" their subsequent fire toward the river, accurately striking all the vehicles in the path of their barrage. It was a rare Allied success story in the western Java campaign when the Tjianten River line held for a second day, while Blackforce was inflicting heavy losses on the Nasu Detachment.

On March 4, though, the tide turned on the road to Buitenzorg. Troops from the Nasu Detachment made a second effort to get across the Tjianten River in the early morning darkness, and this time they came in sufficient numbers to hold their bridgehead. The 2/2nd Pioneer Battalion remained to engage them and to cover the withdrawal of the remainder of Blackforce.

By now, it was clear that the turning point in the campaign had passed. What had begun as an effort to protect Buitenzorg in order to prevent a Japanese assault on Batavia from the south, had turned into an effort to protect Buitenzorg so that refugees fleeing Batavia could pass through Buitenzorg to escape to the mountain haven of Bandoeng.

Just as Douglas MacArthur had abandoned Manila and designated it an open city, Hein ter Poorten decided that Batavia could not be defended. He and Wilbrandus Schilling had made the decision to withdraw, and they asked Arthur Blackburn to hold the Japanese 2nd Division for 24 more hours while Schilling's Dutch 1st Division joined the river of civilian evacuees withdrawing through Buitenzorg to Bandoeng. As storm clouds, both literal and figurative, gathered on the horizons, it was time to say goodbye to the old colonial city with its broad avenues and colonnaded neo-classical government buildings. Few who had walked these streets in March 1941 could have imagined that this day would come just 12 months later.

The holding actions by Blackforce were complicated by their being in retreat and by the heavy rain which had moved into western Java. The pursuing actions by the Nasu Detachment were also made difficult by the weather, but were further complicated by the numerous roadblocks and fallen bridges that Blackforce had left in their path. The Australian units became separated, and found themselves in bitter small-unit actions. Late in the afternoon of March 4, one surrounded Blackforce contingent counterattacked with a bayonet charge to extricate themselves.

With the appearance of a collapsing Allied front, the IJA 2nd Division commander, Major General Masao Maruyama, prepared for a final swing of the axe. Ahead lay the contested Buitenzorg. To his left was the jewel of the Indies, Batavia, devoid of defenses and awaiting him. Toward the latter, he sent Colonel Hanshichi Sato and his detachment, which included the 29th Infantry Regiment as well as the 2nd Tank Regiment. The undefended city surrendered at 9:30 pm on March 5. Governor General Tjarda van Starkenborgh Stachouwer, meanwhile, fled with the generals to Bandoeng.

Two years earlier, it had taken the German Army four days to capture Amsterdam. Now, it had taken the IJA four days to capture Batavia.

Back on the battle line to the south, Masao Maruyama had assumed that the pivotal position at Buitenzorg was as well defended as its approaches had been. Therefore, he augmented Yumio Nasu's detachment with a battalion each from the Fukushima and Sato Detachments. Maruyama ordered this attack to go in after nightfall on March 5.

Given that Maruyama attacked blindly, having conducted no reconnaissance of this strategic city, the attack might have been a disaster. Recalling that Blackforce had stopped the Nasu Detachment in its tracks for two days, anything might have happened inside Buitenzorg. However, luck was with the attacker that night. The KNIL had left only two infantry companies, some artillery, and a battalion of *Stadswacht* guards nicknamed "Buitenzorg" who were essentially fighting for their home turf.

During the four days that it had taken Maruyama to take Batavia and Buitenzorg, the force that landed at Eretanwetan, 80 miles east of Batavia, was also making progress. The 230th Regiment under Toshishige Shoji had captured the Kalidjati air base from the British on March 1, and at about 5:00 am the next morning, an advance unit of the 230th, led by Shoji personally, had taken the nearby town of Soebang (now Subang).

However, much to Shoji's surprise, the KNIL 5th Infantry Battalion under Major Carel Gerrit Jan Teerink launched a vigorous counterattack about three hours later. Supported by tanks, the Dutch were able to overwhelm the small number of Japanese in Soebang, although they never detected Shoji himself, who had taken cover. Some of the tanks even penetrated as far as the Kalidjati air base, but they had outrun the infantry, and without infantry support, they were compelled to pull back to Soebang.

Teerink was a notable individual, one of those swash-buckling, Indiana-Jones-style adventurers who populated the colonial jungles of the world in the years before World War II. Born in Amersfoort in the Netherlands 44 years earlier, he had gone abroad to seek excitement, joining the KNIL as a second lieutenant in 1919. He stayed on in the Indies, and as a KNIL captain, he accompanied the great zoologist Richard Archbold of the American Museum of Natural History on his historic 1938–39 exploration of New Guinea. Various scientific databases, including those of Harvard University, list Teerink as a botanist with important contributions to the Archbold Expedition.

By noon on March 2, as more Japanese troops arrived on the scene, Teerink's audacious little force pulled back under fire, having lost most of its tanks and several other vehicles. The KNIL troops that had been pulled away from Blackforce west of Buitenzorg were supposed to have taken part in a follow-up attack on Soebang, but they did not arrive in time. The battle was over, and despite their dauntless few hours in the city, the Dutch were now in retreat.

As the KNIL withdrew toward Bandoeng, pursued by the Shoji Detachment, the IJAAF began arriving at Kalidjati. While burnt-out hulks of Hurricanes still smoldered on the tarmac, aircraft from three air units were flown in on the afternoon of March 2. These included reconnaissance aircraft of the 16th Sentai, Ki-51 attack bombers of the 27th Sentai, and Ki-43 fighters of the 59th Sentai, which had been operational in the Sumatra campaign. Larger Ki-48 medium bombers of the 75th Sentai began to fly in the following day.

Meanwhile, the Japanese troops were moving toward the Allied airfield at Andir. This base was being subjected to a sustained Japanese aerial bombardment on March 2, even as the badly mauled Allied air force attempted to use it to consolidate their remaining strength. Thanks to the air bases that had been secured on the islands close to Java, the Japanese were able to bring considerable resources to bear in this attack, and the Allies did not have a chance.

As their air forces had ceased to be an effective fighting force, the Allies were beginning to consolidate their ground forces in and around Bandoeng, about 25 miles from Soebang. March 3 found Shoji's 230th Infantry Regiment locked in see-sawing battle south of the air base at Kalidjati which his men had captured two days before. The loss of this airfield, which had come so quickly on the first day of the invasion, was deeply troubling to the Allies, and a great deal of effort was being expended to take it back. General ter Poorten committed elements of the KNIL 10th, 14th, and 15th Infantry Battalions, supported by KNIL field artillery to the project.

This force, known as Groep Toorop after its commander, Colonel C.G. Toorop, succeeded in reaching the perimeter of the Kalidjati base by around 2:00 pm on March 3, and attacked without waiting for a contingent of ten light tanks and 60 trucks full of troops which were making their way north from Bandoeng.

For the second day in a row, Dutch troops had reached Kalidjati, and for a second day they were thrown back. Shoji had one advantage of which Toorop could only dream. He had total air superiority. Japanese aircraft taking off from the same airfield that was under attack set their sights on the attackers. Meanwhile, Japanese tactical airpower had also spotted the tanks and trucks of the relief column, and had attacked them as well.

Planning ahead, Shoji was also expanding his initial beachhead, sending his troops east and west along Java's North Coast Road. To the east, his men defeated the tanks and troops of the KNIL 2nd Cavalry to capture Kandanghaoer (now Kandanghaur) on March 3.

To the west, Shoji's objective was to reach the intersection between the North Coast Road and the highway south to Bandoeng that is now Indonesia's National Route 4. Controlling this intersection, near Tjikampek (now Cikampek), which was about 40 miles west of the beachhead and 40 miles north of Bandoeng, would effectively sever one of the last highway links between Batavia and Bandoeng. Both of these were still under Allied control at the moment, but General ter Poorten was taking his steps to abandon Batavia and declare it an open city when Shoji's men reached this crossroads.

On March 4, Shoji's 230th Infantry Regiment plan could be summarized as a two-pronged drive on Bandoeng, with the two prongs being the 1st Battalion under Major Masaru Egashira, and the 2nd Battalion under Major Mitsunori Wakamatsu. Coming west from Soebang, Wakamatsu captured Poerwakarta (now Purwakarta) at around 7:00 am while Egashira reached Tjikampek early in the afternoon, finding it abandoned.

Moving quickly, using motor vehicles and their ubiquitous bicycles, the two battalions raced to catch the withdrawing Allied stragglers before they could be integrated into the defensive positions around Bandoeng.

The next major battle took place late on the afternoon of March 5 at a pass south of Tjikampek as the Wakamatsu ran into the entrenched positions of the 1st KNIL Infantry Battalion, backed by the 5th Infantry Battalion under Carel Teerink, whose powerful, tank-backed counterattack at Soebang three days earlier had very nearly cost Colonel Toshishige Shoji his life. This time, the battle would cost Teerink his.

To the west, sundown on March 5 found the IJA 2nd Division under Major General Masao Maruyama also closing in on Bandoeng from the west, as Shoji's 230th was closing the circle on the "Paris of Java" from the north.

To the east, March 4 found the 124th Infantry Regiment under Colonel Kyohei Yamamoto, part of the advance guard of General Shizuo Sakaguchi's 56th Infantry in the *Vorstenlanden*, the quasi-autonomous Princely States that the Dutch had allowed to exist in central Java. They found that KNIL troops had been dynamiting bridges, and that the soldiers of the sultanates of Surakarta and Jogjakarta were willing to put up a token resistance. By the evening of March 5, though, the advance guard of the troops who had served heroically under Yamamoto in Borneo three weeks earlier had bicycled into the city of Jogjakarta and were disarming the troops of Sultan Hamengkubuwono IX. Having ascended to the throne two years earlier in March 1940, the sultan got his job back after the Japanese occupation and ruled until 1988.

In eastern Java, Lieutenant General Yuitsu Tsuchihashi's 48th Division had continued its two-pronged advance on Surabaya, with Major General Koichi Abe's 47th Infantry Regiment on the left, and the detachment built around Colonel Hifumi Imai's 1st Formosan Infantry Regiment on the right.

By the end of the day on March 5, they were southwest of the city and overcoming modest KNIL resistance. Imai's unit was approaching Modjokerto (now Mojokerto) about 25 miles southwest of Surabaya, and Abe was approaching Porong on the southern fringes of the city. Colonel Tohru Tanaka, whose 2nd Formosan Infantry Regiment had captured the oil fields of Tjepoe on March 2, was now at Djombang (now Jombang) about 40 miles southwest of Surabaya.

As he looked at a map of Java five nights after the invasion, Lieutenant General Hitoshi Imamura could see that his 16th Army controlled less than a quarter of the land area of the crown jewel island of the Dutch East Indies. However, he was in possession of Batavia, and a continuous stretch of the North Coast Road from his original beachhead at Bantam Bay to the gates of Surabaya. At the same time, he had almost the entire Allied army backed into corners at Bandoeng and Surabaya. Overhead, Japanese aircraft ruled the skies, and attacked Allied ground troops who could respond with little more than ineffective small arms fire. The noose that a week ago had been a loosely looping lariat in the Java Sea, was now a pair of hangman's knots.

CHAPTER 24

THE CONQUEST OF THE DUTCH EAST INDIES

Lieutenant General Hein ter Poorten greeted the sunrise over Java on the morning of March 6 knowing that his days as an officer in command of an army, and as a free man in the land of his birth, were numbered. A week before, the notion of Japanese boots on Java was a real probability, but still an abstract notion that had yet to materialize. Now, the Japanese were the civil authority in Batavia, a city that had been a monument to Dutch culture and political power for 300 years.

For more or less a dozen generations, the Dutch, expatriates and Indies-born, had sat in Batavia, ruling a subject people across an archipelago of 17,500 islands. Today, the sun rose upon nearly a quarter of a million Dutch people, who, after 300 years, were 48 hours into their new status as the subjects of Emperor Hirohito.

For the moment, Hein ter Poorten was in a state of suspended reality. He sat in Bandoeng, the Paris of Java, with its crisp modern art deco buildings, a city that might have been in Europe, were it not for the muggy heat. Bandoeng was as Dutch on March 6 as it had been a week ago, as Dutch as it had been a year ago. Tomorrow? That was another story.

There was an urgency in the air, but it was not the urgency that had prevailed in Batavia a few days ago. Then, it had been an urgency to escape.

Today, there was nowhere to go.

Across the mountains to the south, a bedraggled relative few were making for Tjilatjap and other points along the southern coast, but that too, was a dead end. Where could anyone go? Australia was the goal, but it was as far away as the dark side of the moon for refugees in small boats when the Japanese controlled the seas.

There was relatively little fighting in western Java on March 6. There were some skirmishes in and around places such as Tjibadak, a few miles to the north of Bandoeng, but, for the most part, the Allied troops who could make it had already arrived in Bandoeng and were digging in for a final stand.

Hein ter Poorten was corralled here with his boss and nemesis, Governor General Tjarda van Starkenborgh Stachouwer. They stood at odds, the Netherlands-born nobleman and the soldier who had been born just across the horizon in Buitenzorg, a city that had breathed its last as a Dutch colonial city in the predawn darkness of this very day. But they stood together, emblems of a dying epoch.

The soldier knew that the nobleman disliked him and derided him as a tactless man with "a big mouth," but they could agree on the obvious. They were doomed to a common fate. There was nowhere to turn, and out there, in the verdant green landscape, the enemy was tightening the hangman's knot.

They knew that Hitoshi Imamura was using the excellent highways built for Dutch colonialism to bring in the artillery, the tanks, and the troops for the final assault. It was especially galling to know that the Japanese soldiers were also traveling by train on the railroads that had been designed and built to bring Dutch tourists from Batavia on holiday excursions to Bandoeng.

———————————

Having disarmed the palace guard in the Sultanate of Jogjakarta the night before, Kyohei Yamamoto's 124th Infantry Regiment continued to press southward toward the coast on March 6. Opposition was fierce when it cropped up, but incidents were sporadic and short-lived. At Keboemen, they met, but overwhelmed a contingent of about 100 *Stadswacht* troops. The highway bridges across the Serajoe River had been destroyed, but the Japanese troops had encountered such obstacles before, and a pontoon bridge was put in place. By around 8:00 pm on March 7, they were moving across.

Just past noon on the following day, Yamamoto's bicycle blitzkrieg reached the south coast of Java, and entered the port city of Tjilatjap. The scene was one of chaos. Beneath skies in which three batteries of British antiaircraft artillery pecked away at Japanese bombers, Dutch civilians, and not a few Dutch troops were scrambling aboard small boats.

Earlier, when Lieutenant Colonel H.R. Humphries, the senior British artillery officer, reached the KNIL command center in Tjilatjap, he was told that Lieutenant Colonel C.H. Statius Muller, the commander of the KNIL garrison, had abandoned the city and had escaped to Wangon, the headquarters of the KNIL Central Army District. The British were invited to do the same. This they did, although to move more quickly they disabled and abandoned their guns.

When Humphries and his men caught up with Muller later on March 7, he found the KNIL officer demoralized. Humphries offered the services of his troops, who were armed with rifles and submachine guns, but the KNIL officer declined. As Humphries wrote in his postwar after-action report,

> fruitless efforts were made to prevail upon him to accept the offer pointing out the advantages of his having approximately 1,000 well armed and extremely mobile ground troops at his disposal. The determination and morale of all ranks was of the highest order, the Dutch Commander could not however be persuaded.

"I have no orders, you must go on to Tasikmalaya," Muller said, absurdly deferring to the absence of proper paperwork at a critical moment.

"I took this to be a definite indication of the Dutch lack of intention to fight at this juncture," Humphries recalled. "[I] was in no way surprised when subsequent events took the form they did."

———————

March 7 was a crucial day across Java. By reaching Tjilatjap, the Japanese had effectively cut the island in half, although that had little significance, given that the defenders were surrounded in pockets, notably their great citadels at Bandoeng and Surabaya. In these places, the nooses had been tightened to the point of asphyxiation. In the east, the Japanese troops were already motoring and bicycling through Surabaya's suburbs. In the west, they were in Lembang, only 7 miles from Bandoeng.

General ter Poorten met with Major General Hervey Sitwell, who commanded the British forces in Java, to discuss options. Sitwell told the KNIL commander that, if the Dutch were going to head for the hills as a guerilla force, his men would fight at their side. Ter Poorten said that they would not do that. For such an undertaking to be viable, they would have to live off the land with the assistance and support of Java's indigenous people. This same population had long been yearning for independence from the Netherlands. As ter Poorten explained, the erstwhile Dutch subjects could not be counted upon to provide aid and comfort to colonial troops in the defense of a colonial regime that most wanted to see ended.

There was ample evidence that the pro-independence organizations within the Dutch East Indies had seized upon the "Asia for Asiatics" aspect of the Greater East Asia Co-Prosperity Sphere propaganda, and many people were embracing the Japanese as the agents of an end to Dutch rule. The Indonesian people were already looking beyond the prewar status quo.

Brigadier Arthur Blackburn's Blackforce troops still numbered 8,000. Despite the fact that their positions were essentially untenable, they were still, as late as the morning of March 8, ready and willing to fight on.

In Bandoeng, however, the inevitable came calling that morning, and its message was clear. At 9:00 am, ter Poorten went on the radio to broadcast his order of the day to all the KNIL troops still resisting the Japanese. It was over, he told them, and they should lay down their arms. Sitwell phoned him an hour later to say that the British were following suit. He had no choice. A British surrender was implicit in the Dutch surrender. To fight on under these circumstances would risk reprisals against British POWs.

With this, ter Poorten and the governor general, accompanied by Major General J.J. Pesman, commander of the Bandoeng garrison, headed north to the former Dutch air base at Kalidjati on the south side of Batavia. Here, on the afternoon of March 8, they met the enemy, not in combat, but in subjugation.

Lieutenant General Hitoshi Imamura greeted them across the table on the afternoon of March 8 to dictate terms. Among other things, Imamura insisted that the KNIL commander make a second broadcast the next day, explicitly ordering all troops, including the British, Australians, and Americans to surrender. When all of the Japanese demands had been dictated and accepted, ter Poorten surrendered an army. Tjarda van Starkenborgh Stachouwer surrendered three centuries of Dutch history.

That night, Bert Garthoff, the announcer for Nederlands-Indische Radio, signed off from the studio in Bandoeng, saying, "*Wij sluiten nu. Vaarwel tot betere tijden. Leve de Koningin!*" ("We close now. Farewell until better times. Long live the Queen!") The station then played the Netherlands national anthem. When he heard this, Imamura told the military police, the Kempeitai, to find out who at the station had played the "provocative" anthem and execute him. This was done.

On the southern coast, when Colonel Kyohei Yamamoto's fast-moving troops caught up with C.H. Statius Muller, late of the Tjilatjap garrison, at around noon on March 9 in Wangon, they were met with a white flag.

Major General Pierre Cox, commanding the random fragments of what had been the KNIL Central Army District, was ready to surrender. He was taken to General Shizuo Sakaguchi's 56th Infantry Group headquarters, where he formally surrendered central Java to the Japanese on March 10.

At around 2:00 pm on March 10, Imamura, his staff, and their substantial entourage drove into Bandoeng. The victorious general looked around at the art deco buildings of the Paris of Java and relished the next step on his career ladder. He then strode into the erstwhile Dutch headquarters and took on the trappings of the next governor of the formerly Dutch East Indies.

One of Imamura's first administrative objectives in his new post was to begin erasing the Dutch influence and presence in the archipelago. Dutch civil servants at every level, who had expected to stay on in the job under the new masters, were sent to concentration camps and replaced by Japanese administrators. From government documents to signage, the Dutch language was replaced with Japanese. The Indonesian people, who had initially welcomed the removal of the colonial government, adjusted to life under new masters. The official narrative of the Greater East Asia Co-Prosperity Sphere propaganda spoke of the "national independence and happiness" of Japan's new subject population. In reality, the Japanese took no steps toward creation of an independent Indonesia. Instead of considering the happiness of the people, Japan looked at the Indies, with the largest population in Southeast Asia, as a vast labor pool, which Japan needed to build infrastructure across Southeast Asia to support its war effort. According to documents in the Library of Congress, at least four, and perhaps ten million Indonesians were conscripted as *roumsha*, or slave laborers, and sex slaves. Most of the quarter million who were sent elsewhere in the region, especially those who would help build the infamous Burma Railway, never returned.

Imamura remained in his new post until November 11, 1942, when he was assigned to command the 8th Area Army in the Solomon Islands campaign against the Americans.

With the announcement of the Allied surrender in Java, the Sumatra campaign entered its final act. On March 8, the Imperial Guards Division, which had been part of General Tomoyuki Yamashita's 25th Army during the Malaya and Singapore campaign, embarked from Singapore. Though the war in the Dutch East Indies was technically over, and the Allied fleet was at the bottom of the Java Sea, the Japanese took no chances. The Imperial Guards were escorted by elements of the same IJN task force which had supported the Palembang/Banka Island invasion. Led by Admiral Ozawa's flagship, the *Chokai*, this force included the cruisers *Kumano*, *Mogami*, *Mikuma*, and *Suzuya*, as well as a bevy of destroyers and other supporting vessels.

With the Allies having largely abandoned Sumatra, the landings faced no more serious obstacle than high surf. The objectives were generally clustered in two areas. The first centered on the port of Medan – now Sumatra's largest city and then second to Palembang – which is located on the Malacca Strait, due west of Kuala Lumpur, Malaya. The objectives in this area included Medan itself, as well as the oil fields and refineries around Pangkalanbrandan, where Royal Dutch Petroleum, the predecessor to Royal Dutch Shell, had been active since the 1890s.

The second objective was on the northern tip of Sumatra in the province of Aceh – still, after many centuries, a haven of pirates, and an area made famous as the epicenter of the disastrous earthquake and tsunami of December 2004. In Aceh, the city of Koetaradja (later Kutaraja, now Banda Aceh) was a major petroleum center, as was Sabang Island offshore. By occupying these, the Imperial Japanese war machine, once desperately short of petroleum, now possessed in their entirety the immense resources and infrastructure of the fourth largest producer in the world.

As the Japanese troops who had subdued Singapore, and now Sumatra, looked west across the vast Indian Ocean from Sabang, the oil port in the Dutch East Indies that was closest to Europe, they did so with the confidence of knowing that the great oil petroleum resources of Southeast Asia had been swept into the Greater East Asia Co-Prosperity Sphere in the space of two months. If there was a feeling of invincibility in the warm salt air that day in March 1942, it was not without justification.

PART V

THE UNSTOPPABLE
FIRE OF THE
RISING SUN

CHAPTER 25

THE BATTLE OF AUSTRALIA

"Why, there were hardly enough Australians to have organized an effective resistance to the Japanese Army," General Tomoyuki Yamashita told John Deane Potter after the war, explaining his view of a possible Japanese invasion of that country. "All they could ever hope to do was make a guerrilla resistance in the bush. With even Sydney and Brisbane in my hands, it would have been comparatively simple to subdue Australia."

Indeed, this sort of strategy had worked in China. Japan had taken control of the Chinese east coast, the analog of Sydney and Brisbane in China – though Japan had not and probably never would have conquered all of China, the Chinese had not, could not, and never did, regain Japanese-occupied eastern China by force of arms.

Could Australia have been invaded and occupied, even in part? On February 19, 1942, it seemed frighteningly possible. When Japanese bombers came over Darwin that day, many Australians felt that this was the opening act of what Australian Prime Minister John Curtin had dubbed "the Battle of Australia." Was Australia, no farther from the Dutch East Indies than Timor was from Java, the next step for the invincible IJA?

After February 19, it was virtually impossible to find anyone in the land down under – from the military leadership in Canberra to the sheep herders in the outback – who could answer definitively in the negative.

Initially detected by coastwatchers at 9:35 am, the first wave of Japanese bombers began dropping their bombs on the ships in Darwin's harbor at 9:58. The strike force consisted of 188 aircraft, including 81 B5N torpedo bombers and 71 D3A dive bombers, escorted by 36 A6M Zero fighters, whose pilots came in low for strafing runs. For at least 40 minutes, they attacked Darwin's civilian airport, the RAAF field, the army base, and oil storage facilities, but saved most of their wrath for the ships anchored below. The transport ships SS *Mauna Loa*, USAT *Meigs*, MV *Neptuna*, and MV *Zealandia*, were sunk, as was a coal barge and the tanker MV *British Motorist*. So too was the patrol boat HMAS *Mavie*. Ironically, this sailship had been Japanese-owned before December 1941. Perhaps the biggest prize was the USN destroyer USS *Peary*.

There were comparisons to Pearl Harbor, two months earlier, and on the Japanese side, it was much the same cast of characters. The strike force was under the command of Commander Mitsuo Fuchida, who had also led the first wave against Pearl Harbor. The aircraft were launched by the aircraft carriers *Akagi*, *Hiryu*, *Kaga*, and *Soryu*, all of which had taken part in the Pearl Harbor raid. These facts were unknown to anyone on the ground at the time, but the similarities to that attack, fresh in the memories of all, was lost on no one.

Just before noon, the air raid sirens heralded the arrival of the second wave. If the first attack was long on Pearl Harbor symbolism for the attackers, the second was long on underscoring the new reality of Japanese air bases in the Dutch East Indies. This time, the bombers overhead were not single-engine, carrier-based aircraft, but 54 larger twin-engine medium bombers. Again, it was an IJN operation, with equal numbers of G3M and G4M aircraft based in Celebes and Ambon.

If the morning attack was reminiscent of December 7, the attacks by the larger, more heavily loaded medium bombers in the noon strike suggested the Heinkel He-111s that had struck London during the Blitz of 1940. The second wave focused on the RAAF base, but a small third attack by a few dive bombers later in the day sank two transport ships. In all, eight vessels were sunk and another 28 were damaged or grounded. There were 30 Allied aircraft destroyed, mainly on the ground. An investigation at the time estimated that 243 people were killed, although a detailed investigation lowered the total to 235. A plaque on display in Darwin uses the figure 292. In any case, the damage and the death toll were less than at Pearl Harbor.

However, it did not feel that way in Australia at the time. In the Australian psyche, Darwin was a stunning turn of events that even to this day looms large in the institutional memory of World War II, and it is still widely referred to as "Australia's Pearl Harbor." The fact that only four Japanese aircraft were shot down only exaggerated the feelings of vulnerability.

Though the psychological value from the Japanese perspective was both calculated and considerable, there was also a tactical benefit to these dramatic strikes. At Pearl Harbor, the largest capital ships of the USN's Pacific Fleet – less the soon-to-be-vital aircraft carriers – were taken out of the order of battle. At Darwin, the shipping that was destroyed was all part of the resupply efforts for the troops defending the Dutch East Indies. Beyond simply destroying the ships, the attack damaged the port facilities and clogged the harbor with sunk or damaged hulks. This had a domino effect on continued support of the garrisons on Timor and Java, as well as the ability of the Allies to support their fleet in the coming naval actions in the Java Sea.

Was Darwin the opening act of the Battle of Australia? The evidence was there, or so it seemed after the event. This was dramatically underscored just two weeks later as IJN aircraft attacked Broome, Carnot, and Wyndham in Western Australia killing nearly 100 people and destroying two dozen Allied aircraft on the ground. Unlike Pearl Harbor, Darwin was not an isolated tragedy, but the first of nearly 100 attacks, some of them on a very large scale, including four dozen against Darwin, through the end of 1943.

There was also considerable Japanese submarine activity against merchant shipping off Australia's east coast. Between May 31 and June 8,

1942, Japanese midget submarines penetrated Sydney's harbor and succeeded in sinking HMAS *Kuttabul*, a converted ferry. On the last night of this series of attacks, submarines surfaced to bombard Sydney and Newcastle. It was hard not to believe that Australia was under attack when the thud of Japanese canons could be heard in the center of Australia's largest city.

Looking at the global situation – with the British and the Americans still on the defensive and preoccupied with Germany – it was not hard for the Australians to feel defenseless. If the Americans could not save their own people in the Philippines, what could they do for Australia? If the British could not save Singapore, what could they do for Australia?

It was not so much the capture of Singapore, but the apparent dexterity with which it was accomplished, that so shocked the Allies and inspired the Japanese. It was not so much the capture of every main island in the Dutch East Indies, but the apparent ease with which this was accomplished, that so frightened the Allies and emboldened the Japanese. It was not so much the defeat of the Americans in the Philippines and the British Empire forces – from Malaya to Java – that so terrified the Australians, but the fact that the defeated armies in those places were so much larger than the forces available for the defense of Australia.

In September 1939, when Germany invaded Poland, Britain declared war on Germany. Australia, as a part of the British Empire, also declared war, although the country was lamentably ill-prepared. Its navy had just six cruisers and five destroyers, its air force had few modern aircraft, and its army was comprised of just 3,000 troops, most of them administrators. There was a militia, but it consisted mainly of men who had signed up for part-time training exercises.

In World War I, again as a part of its British Empire obligations, Australia had not only followed Britain's lead in declaring war, but also activated the 1st Australian Imperial Force (AIF) to fight with Britain in Europe. In 1939, Prime Minister Robert Menzies announced that Australia would do it again. The formation of the 2nd Australian Imperial Force began in 1939 with the 6th Infantry Division, and within a year the 7th through 9th Divisions, each 20,000-strong, had been formed.

By the end of 1940, Australian ground troops and RAAF units were deploying to North Africa and the Middle East to fight at the side of the British. Australian airmen had also aided in the defense of the United Kingdom during the Battle of Britain.

By the time that the great IJA offensive began on December 8, 1941, three of Australia's four divisions were committed to the Mediterranean Theater, and the 8th Division was in Malaya under British command.

By the time that the first bombs fell on Darwin, the 8th Division had been erased in Malaya and Singapore, with a small part having been sliced off as Bird Forces – only to be themselves erased on the islands to the north. Prime Minister John Curtin, who had succeeded Menzies in October 1941, had requested that the three divisions in the Mediterranean be returned to Australia, but Winston Churchill was reluctant to release them. As it was, they were returned piecemeal, with elements of the 7th Division being sent to Java, where they were lost. Even after allowing the Australian divisions to depart the Mediterranean, Churchill had endeavored to divert them to Burma instead of Australia. Although Curtin won this dispute, the 9th Division was not finally released until October 1942.

It seemed at the time that Darwin was the opening act of an impending Battle of Australia, and only in hindsight do we know that it was not. Most Australians feared that it was. Japanese planners had considered the option, but had rejected it. Indeed Peter Stanley, the principal historian at the Australian War Memorial, believes that, while Japan was interested in Australia and its sphere of influence, the IJA and IJN planners never developed detailed plans for the Australian invasion. Stanley writes:

> Since the sixteenth century Japanese merchants and writers had been intrigued by the "South Seas" or Nan'yo. Business interests developed early in the twentieth century and a rich scholarly literature grew reflecting Japanese interests in the South Seas, including Australia. However, there was no Japanese plan before 1942 to advance beyond the perimeter to be won in the initial conquest.

Citing Nobutaka Ike in *Japan's Decision for War: Records of the 1941 Policy Conferences*, Stanley adds:

> Australia barely rated a mention in the 1941 conferences which planned Japan's strategy. In the euphoria of victory early in 1942 some visionary middle-ranking naval staff officers in Tokyo proposed that Japan should go further. In February and March they proposed that Australia should be invaded, in order to forestall it being used as a base for an Allied counter-offensive (which of course it became). The plans got no further than some acrimonious discussions. The Army dismissed the idea as "gibberish," knowing that troops sent further south would weaken Japan in China and in Manchuria against a Soviet threat. Not only did the Japanese army condemn the plan, but the Navy General Staff also deprecated it, unable to spare the million tons of shipping the invasion would have consumed.

One of the "visionary middle-ranking naval staff officers" was Commander Sadatoshi Tomioka, an Operations section chief on the IJN General Staff. He was the son of Admiral Sadatoshi Tomioka, who was made a baron for his heroism in the Russo-Japanese War. The younger Tomioka saw a Japanese-occupied Australia as a barrier against American interference with the southern perimeter of the Greater East Asia Co-Prosperity Sphere.

While it is true that Hideki Tojo considered the Australia option to be gibberish – and because of his position, it was his opinion that mattered – this characterization was not universal in the IJA. Tojo's old friend and professional rival, Tomoyuki Yamashita, saw the option as not only viable, but desirable. Having just brilliantly succeeded in defeating the British Empire in Malaya and Singapore, Yamashita spoke with infinitely more authority than a middle-ranking staff officer.

"Singapore, the great British bastion in the Far East, has fallen into our hands. The Allies are effectively sealed off," Yamashita wrote to Tojo shortly after the capture of Singapore, beginning his lengthy communiqué outlining his plans for the virtually defenseless land down under. As John Deane Potter explains, instead of an advance farther west into Burma and perhaps India, his plan was to leave a strong garrison in Malaya and Burma and strike down the Pacific to the coast of Australia. Yamashita's plan to conquer Australia was practically identical with his successful campaign in Malaya. He intended to land on each side of the major Australian cities and cut them off, first making a series of dummy landings to draw off the pitifully few Australian troops.

Tojo's reply at the time is not known, but after the war, he told Allied interrogators:

> We never had enough troops to [invade Australia]. We had already far out-stretched our lines of communication. We did not have the armed strength or the supply facilities to mount such a terrific extension of our already over-strained and too thinly spread forces. We expected to occupy all New Guinea, to maintain Rabaul as a holding base, and to raid Northern Australia by air. But actual physical invasion, no, at no time.

There are still many who believed then, and believe now that the Japanese invasion was imminent. A poll carried out by the *Daily Telegraph* in February 1942 reported that 54 percent of those responding believed that Australia would be invaded. In 2002, while two thirds of those responding to a survey conducted by Peter Stanley believed that a Japanese invasion plan had been in the works.

The evidence is sketchy and inconclusive, but it exists. In October 1942, a document reached John Curtin's desk by way of the Australian legation in Chungking, where it had been dropped off by Admiral H.C. Yang, the Director of Military Intelligence for Nationalist China. It was a detailed overview of an operational plan for an invasion of Western Australia accompanied by a diversionary attack on Darwin, all of which was displayed on an accompanying map. Yang had dismissed the map as a fake, and the Australian Chiefs of Staff agreed.

In any case, the plan indicated that the invasion would be executed in May 1942, and the map came to light five months later, and the invasion had obviously not taken place. Nevertheless, Curtin seems to have kept an open mind, accepting the possibility that it might have been a real plan for a cancelled operation.

The conventional wisdom today is that it was a hoax, but there was never any confirmation either way. As Peter Stanley notes, the actual map is still on display in the Research Centre of the Australian War Memorial, so anyone may draw his or her own conclusion.

From the opposite perspective, John Deane Potter writes:

the government machinery for ruling Australia was also prepared. Several Japanese diplomats who had represented their government in Canberra were briefed to follow the Japanese armies into Australia and rule the country for the Emperor. One of them, whom I met later in Osaka, had been nominated as governor general.

Later in World War II, caches of currency, issued by the Japanese government but denominated in Australia shillings, were discovered by Allied troops. A great deal of this currency exists in private hands as war souvenirs, and it is still traded between collectors.

Discussing "what ifs" and hypothetical "might have beens" is always an interesting, though inconclusive, exercise. The Japanese invasion of Australia did not happen, and the postwar conventional wisdom has always held to Tojo's opinion that it would not have. As he had said, such an operation was impossible because Australia was so large, and it was beyond the limit of Japanese supply lines.

Tomoyuki Yamashita told Potter in 1945:

I would never visualize occupying it entirely. It was too large. With its coastline, anyone can always land there exactly as he wants. But it is a long way from anywhere and I could have poured in enough troops to resist effectively any Anglo-American invasions. Although the Japanese General Staff felt my supply lines would have been too long, so would the American or British lines. They might never have been able to reach the place at all. We could have been safe there forever.

CHAPTER 26

THE BATTLE OF AMERICA

For the better part of two centuries, strategists had said with calm assurance that the United States was protected from the military might of any overseas enemy by two vast oceans. Indeed, for all the years between 1814, when the British burned Washington, DC, and September 11, 2001, this assertion was generally true. However, like Australia, the United States came to fear a Japanese invasion in the dark days of 1941 and 1942. In retrospect, this was much less probable than a Japanese invasion of Australia – but the attack on Pearl Harbor, and the subsequent successes of the IJA across the Far East made the Americans feel that anything was possible.

Today, it is largely forgotten that in 1942, American soil was repeatedly attacked by a foreign enemy. Indeed, the IJA did invade and hold territory in Alaska that is today part of the United States – the Aleutian Islands of Attu and Kiska – and the IJN did attack the West Coast of the United States from the sea and from the air.

While the Aleutians and the West Coast are beyond the geographic scope defined for this book, the attacks on the United States are worth mentioning for they serve to underscore the perception of the invincibility in 1942 not only of the IJA, but of the IJN as well.

On the night of February 24–25, 1942, less than a week after the great air attack on Darwin, Australia, searchlights stabbed the sky, antiaircraft shells flew and air raid sirens screamed all night throughout Los Angeles County, California. The government said it was just a weather balloon, but many people cried "cover-up." The "Battle of Los Angeles" is still an element of popular culture, and to this day, there are conspiracy theorists who still claim that there was more to it than "war jitters."

Only one day earlier, the Japanese submarine I-17 really did surface long enough to lob two dozen shells at an oil field in Santa Barbara County, California. Indeed, Japanese submarines were operating up and down the coastline, watching American harbor lights with impunity, just as German U-Boats were doing the same along the Eastern Seaboard.

Meanwhile, the Japanese were building submarines capable of carrying observation aircraft while submerged. A total of 20 of these were completed, a dozen of them before the end of 1941. The aircraft of choice was the Yokosuka E14Y two-place floatplane, which was designed for rapid reassembly on a narrow deck while at sea. Nicknamed "Geta" after the Japanese sandal with the dual pontoon-like structures on the sole, the E14Y was later code-named "Glen" by the Allies.

One such submarine that played an important, albeit largely ignored, role in the history of the war in the Western Hemisphere was the I-25, which was commissioned in October 1941. It would cross the breadth of the Pacific Ocean three times over the ensuing 11 months, captained by Commander Meiji Tagami. During December 1941, the I-25 began attacking coastal shipping along the West Coast. On the night of June 21, 1942, during its second American cruise, the I-25 surfaced off Astoria, Oregon long enough to lob several shells from its deck gun at Fort Stevens. This was a prequel to what was to come in September.

Nobuo Fujita, the pilot of the I-25's Geta, was a plucky and innovative combat pilot who had bombed Shanghai in 1937 while flying off the flagship of the Third Combined Fleet. In 1942, since being assigned to the I-25, he had made daring overflights of the major port cities of Sydney and Melbourne in Australia, and Auckland and Wellington in New Zealand. Fujita later claimed to have had the idea of using the submarine's E14Y as a bomber. Inspired by the success at Pearl Harbor, he imagined attacks by submarine-launched bombers against major targets, such as the big aircraft plants that were just a few minutes flying time from the coastline in Southern California. As the story goes, he submitted a written proposal to I-25 Executive Officer Lieutenant Tasuo Tsukudo, who passed it up through the channels.

In late July 1942, orders made their way back down through those channels. Fujita was assigned the mission of which he had dreamed – although it would not be against as exciting a target as he might have craved. The IJN had got creative, but they were still being cautious. They had decided that the best use of the delicate and vulnerable Geta would be not against a heavily defended, high-value target such as the Douglas Aircraft factories in Santa Monica, or the Lockheed factories in Burbank, but against the vast forests of the Pacific Northwest. In 1936, a major forest fire had devastated the town of Bandon and a large swath of the southern Oregon coastal range, and this inspired Japanese planners to imagine that an incendiary attack could do major psychological and practical damage.

The I-25 began its third cruise to the United States on August 15 and was off the Oregon Coast two weeks later. Having waited a week for rough waves to subside, the crew awoke on September 9 to seas sufficiently calm to launch the floatplane. When the vessel surfaced, the Geta was assembled for flight, and it was armed with two incendiary bombs. With his navigator-bombardier, Petty Officer Shoji Okuda, in the rear seat, Fujita took off from a point about 20 miles offshore. The E14Y crossed the foggy Oregon coastline near Brookings, about 5 miles north of the California border. Fujita turned northeast toward Mount Emily, about 5 miles inland, circling the mountain in a clockwise direction.

Several observers on the ground heard the Geta, and at 6:42 am local time, Howard Gardner, a US Forest Service observer, on duty at the Mount Emily fire lookout, visually spotted a westbound unidentified aircraft. He saw it dropping its incendiaries, which burst into flame amid the cedars. Gardner reported the aircraft to the Air Warning Service filter center in Roseburg, but no immediate action was taken. It seemed so improbable that a lone aircraft over the remote Klamath Mountain Range could constitute an attack by Imperial Japan against the United States. It was not until late afternoon, when Gardner and three others went to investigate and contain the fires, that they found a crater and bomb fragments – and made the connection.

Fujita had guided the aircraft back to the submarine without incident, but as the I-25 was submerging, a USAAF bomber on a routine patrol out of McChord Field near Tacoma, Washington spotted it and attacked. The submarine received only minor damage, and Commander Tagami decided to remain in American waters for a follow-up air attack.

Nearly three weeks later, Fujita made his second aerial attack against Curry County, Oregon. On the morning of September 29, he took off from a point about 50 miles from shore, and made landfall about 50 air miles north of Brookings near Cape Blanco. A number of people ashore reported hearing the aircraft, and two Aircraft Warning Service observers reported seeing smoke, but this had dissipated by the time that US Forest Service personnel undertook a search. Evidently, the incendiaries had started a small fire which burned out in the damp forest. Unlike the aftermath of the September 9 attack, no traces of bomb fragments were ever found.

Each year, to this day, forest fires consume great swaths of the American West. However, the planners who picked the targets for Fujita's Geta had failed to take into account the misty dampness of the Oregon Coast after an especially wet summer. The only air attacks against the United States during World War II had failed. Nevertheless, the I-25 remained in American waters, and did sink two tankers off the Oregon Coast with torpedoes before returning to Japan.

There were no further air strikes, but later in 1942, perhaps inspired by Fujita's unprecedented flights, the IJN made the conceptual transition from building submarines that happened to carry airplanes to developing submersible aircraft carriers for offensive operations. Three of a planned 18 *Sen Toku* "special" boats of the I-400 class were commissioned in 1944. They were the largest submarines to be built until the development of ballistic missile subs a quarter century later. The high priority targets imagined for the I-400s included the Panama Canal, as well as major cities such as New York and Washington, DC.

On July 23, 1945, two I-400s departed from Japan, bound for the Panama Canal – but this mission ended on August 15 when Emperor Hirohito broadcast his order for all Japanese forces to lay down their arms. The I-25, meanwhile, had been sunk on September 3, 1943 in the New Hebrides by the USS *Patterson*.

Infinitely more serious than submersible aircraft carriers was the invasion of Attu and Kiska. The Aleutian operations were a simultaneous part of the same great June 1942 strategic projection as the planned capture of Midway Island, all of which was masterminded and spearheaded by Admiral Isoroku Yamamoto, the architect of the Pearl Harbor attack. The idea was to expand the Japanese perimeter in the Pacific eastward and closer to the mainland United States.

The Midway operation, which was thwarted in the great turning point naval battle of the same name, would have given the Japanese an airbase 1,300 miles from Pearl Harbor and changed the dynamics of operations throughout the Pacific. The capture of Attu and Kiska would place impediments in the way of an American effort to use the island chain as stepping stones for an attack against Japan itself. According to Lieutenant General Kiichiro Higuchi, who commanded the IJA Northern District Army (aka Northern Army), and the overall IJA commander for the campaign, the Aleutians were also considered as potential air bases to support future operations.

The first Japanese action against Alaska was the June 3 air attack launched against the naval base at Dutch Harbor, nearly 800 miles west of Anchorage, by aircraft from the carriers *Junyo* and *Ryuijo*. This was followed on June 6 by the IJN Number 3 Special Naval Landing Force coming ashore on Kiska, 1,500 miles west of Anchorage. The following day, the 301st Independent Infantry Battalion of the IJA Japanese

Northern District Army landed on Attu, which is located 1,800 miles west of Anchorage and about 2,200 miles northeast of Tokyo.

At Kiska, the invaders were met by a ten-man USN weather detachment. On Attu, they discovered Charles and Etta Jones, along with 45 Aleut people living in a small town at Chichagof. They were relocated to Hokkaido, where a third of them died in Japanese custody.

Attu was abandoned briefly in September, but at the end of October Lieutenant Colonel Hiroshi Yanekawa arrived with a contingent of 500 to establish a permanent fortified base at Holtz Bay. Under the command of Colonel Yasuyo Yamasaki, the garrison grew to a force of around 2,300 within five months.

Meanwhile, the USAAF conducted periodic bombing raids against Attu and Kiska, and the USN eventually was able to cut them off and isolate them from resupply. When the United States launched an effort to recapture Attu on May 11, 1943, Yamasaki's men resisted fiercely. Severe cold and frostbite, which had plagued the Japanese all winter, now seriously impacted the Americans. In the final battle, on May 29, the Japanese launched an infantry charge that penetrated the American rear area. When it was over, 580 Americans and 2,351 Japanese were killed in action, while 28 Japanese troops surrendered.

For the August 15, 1943 invasion of Kiska, the Allies assembled a 34,000-man joint US–Canadian force, supported by 95 ships including three battleships. However, the Japanese managed to withdraw their Kiska garrison to Little Kiska Island before the armada arrived. The IJN force that was sent to rescue them mistakenly bombarded the smaller island.

The Aleutian adventure ended poorly for the Japanese, having accomplished little aside from demonstrating that the IJA had, or at least had once had, the ability to project itself to all corners of the Pacific, and to hold American territory for extended periods of time.

CHAPTER 27

CLIMAX IN BURMA

As March 1942 began, and as the last act of the battle for the Dutch East Indies was being played out, the situation in Burma mirrored that on Java. The IJA was proving itself invincible, and the Allies were running low on resources. Lieutenant General Shojiro Iida's 15th Army had crossed the border in strength on January 22, and a month later they reached the Sittang River, considered by the Allies to be the best defensive line between Thailand and Rangoon.

Iida's offensive consisted of the 55th Division under Lieutenant General Hiroshi Takeuchi driving due west toward Rangoon, with Lieutenant General Shozo Sakurai's 33rd Division circling north to outflank the city and attack it from the west.

The British defense of the Sittang River had been a debacle, having essentially opened the road to Rangoon for the Japanese. The defeat had cost Brigadier Jackie Smyth the command of the 17th Indian Infantry Division, and left his successor, Brigadier David Tennant "Punch" Cowan, a unit that was 60 percent depleted and dangerously short of weapons and other equipment.

The defeat also led General Archibald Wavell of India Command to the decision to order the Burma Army, under General Harold Alexander, to pull out of Rangoon. Neither Wavell nor Alexander wanted another

Singapore on his hands – especially when it looked as though Java's doom was sealed. On March 6, Alexander ordered a tactical withdrawal to Prome, about 200 miles north of Rangoon on the Irrawaddy River. Prome lay on Burma's main trunk road which ran via Prome to Mandalay, Burma's second largest city, 400 miles to the north.

Meanwhile, Sakurai's 33rd Division had crossed the Salween and the Sittang farther north and was closing in on the city of Pegu, upstream from Takeuchi and 40 miles northeast of Rangoon. It was at Pegu that Wavell had ordered a counterattack on March 3, which was supported by the 7th Queen's Own Hussars, an armored cavalry regiment from the 7th Armoured Brigade. This set the stage for the first tank battle between British and Japanese troops. Both the M3 Honey and the Japanese Type 95 Ha-Go were light tanks armed with 37mm guns, and were therefore evenly matched technically. They were both designed to support infantry advances, and the Type 95 had excelled in this role in Malaya. At Pegu, the tables were turned, with the Hussars successfully destroying at least four Japanese tanks before withdrawing.

Sakurai continued his advance, circling north of Rangoon. On March 7, even as the evacuation was getting underway, the Japanese reached Taukkyan, on the Irrawaddy north of Rangoon. Here, the Pegu road crosses the main trunk road leading upriver to Prome and farther north to Mandalay.

Had Sakurai turned south at this moment, he would have intercepted – and probably smashed – Alexander's escape from Rangoon, but he was operating under the assumption that the British would not attempt a breakout, and that the best option for assaulting the city was from the west. Therefore, he continued his westward march, leaving only the 214th Infantry Regiment, commanded by Colonel Takanobu Sakuma. They were left behind, not to intercept a tactical withdrawal, but merely to guard the rear of the main body of the 33rd Division. Once the latter had reached its predetermined position west of Rangoon, the 214th was to pull out of the crossroads and join them.

Later in the day, as Alexander's northbound column reached the crossroads, it ran into Sakuma's regiment. A firefight ensued in which the British were forced back. Assuming that he had halted an attempt to outflank the 33rd, Sakuma remained in place only until the latter were safely at their destination. He then pulled up stakes and followed.

When the British regrouped and attacked the Japanese positions, they found them abandoned. Thus it was that the Japanese unwittingly lost the battle of the Taukkyan Roadblock, and the battered Burma Army escaped to fight another day.

———————

With the undefended Rangoon now in Japanese hands and the Burma Army still operational, both sides reinforced to prepare for the next phase of the Burma Campaign. The Allies regrouped and reorganized. The Burma Army, with its roots as a prewar garrison force, was now augmented by the newly created Burma Corps. This served as the umbrella organization for the 1st Burma Division under the command of Major General Bruce Scott, Punch Cowan's 17th Indian Infantry Division, and 7th Armoured Brigade, commanded by Brigadier John Henry Anstice. Burma Corps was commanded by Major General William J. "Bill" Slim. Harold Alexander, his immediate superior, came to defer the actual hands-on work to Slim.

Meanwhile, the Nationalist Chinese had now arrived in the form of the 1st Route Expeditionary Forces (aka the Chinese Expeditionary Force) under Lieutenant General Lo Cho-ying (now spelled Luo Zhuoying). Lo commanded a sizable force, consisting of the 5th, 6th, and 66th Armies, each with three divisions assigned.

The Japanese had also been getting reinforcements. With IJA operations in the Malaya–Singapore Campaign and the Dutch East Indies Campaign successfully concluded, a division from each of the field armies on each of those fronts was detached and relocated to the Burma front. From Singapore – or Syonan-to as the Japanese had renamed it – the 25th Army's 18th Division, under Lieutenant General Renya Mutaguchi, was sent to Rangoon. Likewise was the 56th Division, under Lieutenant General Masao Watanabe, who had contributed troops to the operations on Java. This put four Japanese divisions on the ground in Burma. By this measure, it was the largest concentration of operational IJA ground forces in Southeast Asia to date.

The first major clash between the Japanese and Lo Cho-ying's Nationalist Chinese forces in Burma came on March 8, the same day that Rangoon fell, when one of the Chinese 5th Army units, the 200th Division under Major General Dai Anlan, arrived in the city of Toungoo (also spelled Taungoo). This position was astride the Sittang River, about 150 miles north of the Sittang River crossing that Hiroshi Takeuchi's 55th Division had captured from the 17th Indian Infantry Division two weeks earlier.

As Dai's troops dug in to defend the Sittang crossing at Toungoo, Takeuchi's troops turned north to dig them out. The first shots in their exchange were fired on March 18, but the main attack came on March 24. Takeuchi launched a frontal assault on the city with his 112th Regiment, while sending his 143rd Regiment to encircle the Chinese positions, cut off access to the north and attack Dai's position from behind. When the service troops in his rear were overrun, Dai overreacted, withdrawing his entire command into the defensive perimeter in the center of Toungoo.

Early on the morning of March 25, Takeuchi's two regiments began attacking from the south, west, and north. The eastern side was the Sittang River, so Dai Anlan found himself in the same situation as Jackie Smyth a month earlier, that is, with his back against the Sittang. The situation differed in that Smyth's Indian troops had been in rural terrain, whereas Dai was in the confused terrain of an urban environment. This made it relatively easy for the Japanese to employ a favorite IJA tactic of infiltrating enemy positions. Meanwhile, it became difficult for either side to use artillery, so the battle became, in many cases, close-quarter, hand-to-hand fighting.

The battle continued into March 26, with heavy losses traded as the Japanese captured the west side of the town. A lull on the following day found both sides pulling back to lick their wounds, a disengagement which only meant that the Japanese could use their artillery and employ their air superiority in conducting air strikes.

Toungoo was turning into the biggest battle in Burma thus far, and both sides were sending reinforcements. From the north, Lo Cho-ying dispatched the Chinese 22nd Division to relieve the beleaguered 200th, while the IJA 56th Division, recently redeployed to Burma, was being sent straight into the battle.

The threat from the 22nd Division required Takeuchi to send a detachment of his 143rd Regiment to impede their progress, while also demanding that he redouble his efforts to finish off the 200th quickly. Alas, the Chinese failed to cooperate, stubbornly resisting Takeuchi's repeated assaults on March 28 and 29.

Beginning late on March 29, and continuing into the following day, Dai Anlan began to withdraw his forces across the Sittang River, even as Watanabe's IJA 56th Division began arriving from the east. By the end of the day, Takeuchi's 55th had occupied most of Toungoo, now largely abandoned by the Chinese, and had linked up with Watanabe's 56th, who had secured the bridge across the Sittang. Meanwhile, the two Chinese divisions linked up at Yedashe, about 50 miles to the north, to block any further Japanese movements up the Sittang River Valley.

At the beginning of April, the Allied objective was now to organize the defense of central Burma and to obstruct the Japanese advance south of Mandalay. It now seemed that with the support of the Nationalist Chinese, the Allies might have the critical mass to finally thwart the unstoppable momentum of the IJA.

With four divisions now assigned to his 15th Army, General Shojiro Iida's objective was naturally to continue his forward, northward momentum, which was manifest in three parallel movements. In the center, Takeuchi's 55th Division, supported by Mutaguchi's 18th, were to continue the drive through the Sittang River Valley, dislodging the Chinese 22nd and 200th at Yedashe, and to push on toward Mandalay.

To the east, Watanabe's 56th Division was to push north by northeast with the objective of capturing Lashio, the southern terminus of the

Burma Road, thus severing the only access for further Chinese reinforcements that might be sent to Burma.

In the west, Sakurai's 33rd Division continued its pursuit of the retreating British Burma Corps. Sakurai's immediate objective on this trajectory was to capture the Yenangyaung oil fields and other key locations through the Irrawaddy River Valley, up to and beyond Mandalay. Tactically, the Japanese were overrunning the British wherever they paused in their withdrawal. As Slim attempted to organize counterattacks, he would find himself being encircled by the enemy and forced back to the defensive, and then back to withdrawal.

The story of the defense of the petroleum facilities at Yenangyaung by the 1st Burma Division against Shozo Sakurai's 33rd Division, which began on April 11, was like that of the defense of Palembang on Sumatra two months earlier. In both cases – unlike at Balikpapan in January – the Allies had a reasonable, though ultimately insufficient, force. It is axiomatic that defenders have a force-multiplying advantage, but the defense of petroleum facilities is a special circumstance. Oil fields and refineries are delicate and therefore difficult to protect. Ultimately, the only defense is to deny them to the enemy, as the Dutch did to the Japanese at Balikpapan and Palembang.

On April 15, Slim reluctantly gave that order, but by this time Bruce Scott's 1st Burma Division was essentially surrounded, trapped, baking in the 100-degree equatorial temperatures, and choking on the smoke from burning crude oil. In the sky, the Japanese were maintaining air superiority and raking the encircled Allied troops. Beyond the Allied perimeter, Sakurai's troops were preparing to deal a death blow.

What happened next only served to illustrate the dysfunction of the Allies in the face of the well-oiled IJA war machine.

The Nationalist Chinese 38th Division, part of the force upon which the British depended to tip the balance in their favor in Burma, was in the area and might have intervened – as the Chinese 22nd Division had been doing at Toungoo three weeks earlier. Harold Alexander sent a request to the Chinese by way of US Army Lieutenant General Joseph "Vinegar Joe" Stilwell, who served as chief of staff to

Chiang Kai-shek, as well as being the commander of the newly formed China Burma India (CBI) Theater. The request went back down the chain of command to General Lo Cho-ying of the 1st Route Expeditionary Forces, who flatly refused.

Hearing this, the 1st Burma Division's Bruce Scott personally contacted General Sun Li Jen of the 38th Division, explaining the situation and asking for help. Sun agreed, but was overruled by Lo. Finally, Sun contravened Lo's orders and took his undermanned 113th Regiment and headed south, accompanied by Brigadier John Henry Anstice's 7th Armoured Brigade. Against all odds, this undermanned rescue mission, as well as Scott's attempts to break out of the encirclement succeeded, but just barely. Scott finally linked up with the relief column on April 19. All of the units involved, especially the 1st Burma Division, suffered considerable losses in men and materiel.

Meanwhile, the biggest Japanese successes during the third week of April were being achieved by the 56th Division, the easternmost of Iida's three-pronged 15th Army northward offensive. The spirited stand by the 200th Division at Toungoo had been the high-water mark for the Chinese in Burma. Unable to muster their superior numbers decisively, the Chinese divisions collapsed under the weight of Watanabe's IJA forces. It was like 1937 in northern China all over again as the IJA cut through and scattered Lo Cho-ying's ineffective attempts to stop them.

As had been the case in Malaya in January, the good paved roads built by the British before the war aided the Japanese blitzkrieg. Watanabe was able to race northward faster than the British and Indians could erect defensive positions.

When a collapse begins, it is extremely hard to stop it, and the Chinese units were collapsing into a headlong retreat toward the Chinese border. By April 20, as Sakurai's 33rd Division was resuming his pursuit of the 1st Burma Division north from Yenangyaung, Watanabe was already in Lashio, having succeeded in cutting off the Burma Road. By the first day of May, just as the monsoons began, Takeuchi's 55th Division and Mutaguchi's 18th were in Mandalay, Burma's second largest city.

A footnote to the story of the war in Burma during May 1942 is that of the intervention by Thailand's Phayap (Northwest) Army under Lieutenant General Charun Ratanakun. A sizable force consisting of four divisions, Ratanakun's command, entered Burma on May 10, after the British had withdrawn, and participated mainly in actions against retreating and disorganized Chinese units. Their ultimate objective, however, was the occupation of the Burmese states of Kayah and Shan – roughly the eastern half of central Burma – which the Japanese had promised to Thailand as a territorial adjustment. For the Japanese, this positioned the Phayap Army as a garrison force in a 70,000-square-mile buffer between China and the strategic areas of western Burma.

Also in play during the British retreat from Rangoon to Mandalay, and from there westward into India, was the Burma Independence Army. Not to be confused with the British-organized and Anglo-Indian manned Burma Army, the Burma Independence Army was a fighting force which had been surreptitiously organized by the Japanese before the war to fight the British. Japan had been covertly active throughout Southeast Asia, but only in Burma did this extend to activating a clandestine, indigenous army. The man behind the project was Colonel Keiji Suzuki of the IJA, who visited Burma in 1940, making contact with political opposition leaders and sounding them out on his idea for an army to fight the British.

Meanwhile, Suzuki had also met a popular communist-leaning nationalist and revolutionary named Aung San, who had organized student uprisings in the 1930s. He was associated with Dr Ba Maw, the figurehead of British rule, who had been jailed by them in 1940 for sedition. Also wanted by British authorities, Aung San was the subject of a British arrest warrant. He escaped to China, where he was captured by the IJA while on the run. If his name sounds familiar to modern readers, it is because he is the father of Aung An Suu Kyi, the contemporary Burmese political leader and 1991 Nobel Peace Prize laureate. She was born in 1945, shortly before the end of World War II.

Because of his prominence in anti-British Burmese circles, Aung San was one of several such activists who were brought to Tokyo. Here, he received military training and became part of the Minami Kikan, a secret Japanese intelligence operation inside Burma, as well as of Suzuki's scheme for the Burma Independence Army, of which he became an important leader.

The Burma Independence Army assisted the Japanese invasion in a support and intelligence-gathering role, and by the time that Rangoon fell, they had attracted large numbers of recruits and numbered more than 10,000, roughly the size of an infantry division. Thereafter, they participated in combat operations against British and Indian units.

The importance of the Burma Independence Army was not so much in its fighting skills, as in the fact that it existed as a tangible symbol of proactive rank and file Burmese opposition to British rule. As in the Dutch East Indies, where the Dutch could not depend upon the loyalty of an indigenous population they had ruled for centuries, the British were in a position of having to look over their shoulders as they fought to hang on to a colony.

———

The situation in Burma in May was like that in Malaya at the end of January or that on Java six weeks later. Allied resistance had completely collapsed. The IJA was the very definition of the term "invincible." By the time that the last Allied escapee reached India or China, the Allied casualty toll stood at around 30,000. The Japanese had suffered fewer than a quarter of that number.

A big difference was that in Malaya and Java, the vanquished Allied troops had nowhere to turn, but, with hands raised, to the victors. From Burma, there was the possibility of escape, though the overland escape routes were over steep mountains, through treacherous terrain and beneath monsoon skies. Roads were few and poor, and were clogged with civilian refugees. An escape by airplane was made amid the twin hazards of weather and Japanese air superiority.

The story of the Allied retreat from Burma has been told in great detail elsewhere, but suffice to say that those who made it to China or

India did so on foot and with great difficulty, and a great many did not make it.

The Japanese pursued the Chinese into Yunnan province, but withdrew. Iida might have used the momentum of his four divisions to press on into India – which was greatly feared by the Allies – but he did not. The same monsoons, uncrossable rivers, and horrible footpath roads that bedeviled the British and Indian retreat slowed the Japanese troops to a crawl.

Meanwhile, the Japanese released Ba Maw from the British jail where he had languished since 1940, and began grooming him to reprise the role he had played for the British in 1937–39, that of the Burmese head of state. Officially declared in 1943, the State of Burma dutifully signed a treaty of alliance with Japan, based on the one signed earlier by Thailand, and declared war on the United States and the United Kingdom. Under the title Naingandaw Adipadi, Ba ruled for less than two years, but wielded considerable local power, answering only to the IJA occupation forces. Aung San served as his minister of war.

After the war, both men were able to resume their careers as nationalist politicians and to play a role in Burma's quest for eventual independence, although Aung San was assassinated in 1947, a year before this was achieved, and Ba Maw found himself back in prison, jailed by rival Burmese politician Ne Win, during the 1960s.

CHAPTER 28

BATAAN AND CORREGIDOR, THE FINAL DAYS

"The President of the United States ordered me to break through the Japanese lines and proceed from Corregidor to Australia for the purpose, as I understand it, of organizing the American offensive against Japan, a primary objective of which is the relief of the Philippines," General Douglas MacArthur told reporters at Batchelor Field in Australia on March 17, 1942. "I came through and I shall return."

Late on the dark – dark in so many ways – evening of March 11, MacArthur had stepped off the dock at the fortress island of Corregidor and aboard the patrol boat PT-41, captained by Lieutenant John Bulkeley. He had been ordered, as he said, by Franklin Roosevelt, to escape to Australia to plan the demise of the Chrysanthemum Empire. A flotilla of four PT boats took him to the island of Mindanao, from which a B-17 flew the general, his staff, and his family, to Australia.

The rest, as they say, is history. It is the history of the integral part played by MacArthur in the ultimate Allied victory in the Pacific.

Indeed, Roosevelt ordered him out of the Philippines because he understood that MacArthur *would* play such a role if given the opportunity. However, the history of this success was at the time, and would always be, tempered by nagging criticism that MacArthur abandoned Corregidor and Bataan at a critical juncture.

MacArthur's departure did not help morale among the ragtag defenders of Bataan, nor did the news that they were hearing from the United States via short wave broadcasts. They listened to Roosevelt's fireside chats, which put Bataan in the context of a global war and America's global responsibilities. The subtext was that the defenders of Bataan were on their own. No help was on the way. With the Pacific Fleet at the bottom of Pearl Harbor and the ABDA Fleet at the bottom of the Java Sea, there would be no rescue ships running the blockade. The troops also listened to radio station KZRH in Manila, now Japanese-controlled. It broadcast a special English language program for the Bataan defenders every night. The theme song was "Ships That Never Come In."

General Masaharu Homma had problems of his own. He had been sitting in Manila, staring into the distance at the smudges of black smoke hanging over Bataan for more than two months. Tomoyuki Yamashita had captured Malaya in seven weeks and mighty Singapore in one.

When Hitoshi Imamura had gone ashore in Java, Homma's troops were skirmishing with the American and Filipino troops on their Bataan reserve line between Bagac and Orion. When Hitoshi Imamura sat in Bandoeng and dictated terms for the surrender of the entire Dutch East Indies, ruled by the Netherlands for centuries and now Japanese-controlled, Homma's troops were *still* skirmishing with the American and Filipino troops on their Bataan reserve line between Bagac and Orion. The only thing of consequence that had happened since January was that Homma had let MacArthur get away. Louis Morton writes in his history of the campaign:

Elsewhere Japanese armies had met with spectacular success and General Headquarters felt that it could now spare the forces necessary to complete the conquest of the Philippines. This decision was in no sense an indication that the Army high command was satisfied with the performance of 14th Army. It was not, and soon made its displeasure evident by shifts in Homma's staff. Inspecting officers from Tokyo visiting Manila had found many 14th Army officers comfortably settled in the capital while the battle for Bataan was at its height.

Imperial General Headquarters had sacked General Masami Maeda, Homma's chief of staff, on February 23.

Meanwhile, from late February through all of March, Imperial General Headquarters was loading the 14th Army with resources. Replacements for losses suffered by the 16th Division and the 65th Brigade were sent. The Nagano Detachment, a 4,000-man contingent from the 21st Division under the command of Major General Kameichiro Nagano was diverted from Indochina to the 14th Army.

Lieutenant General Kenzo Kitano's 4th Division shipped out of Shanghai, arriving in strength by March 15. Homma complained that it was the "worst equipped" division in the IJA. To do otherwise would have been to lose face.

The 1st Artillery Headquarters from Hong Kong, under Lieutenant General Kishio Kitajima, also arrived in March. With him, he brought more 150mm howitzers, as well as immense 240mm field howitzers that had not been used in other campaigns. The IJAAF 22nd Air Brigade under Major General Kizo Mikami landed at Clark Field.

Masaharu Homma scheduled his final offensive to begin on April 3, symbolically the anniversary of the death, by some calculations, of the Emperor Jimmu, Japan's first emperor. For the Christian American and Filipino soldiers on Bataan, April 3 was notable in 1942 for being Good Friday.

Homma delivered a withering six-hour artillery barrage against the II Corps positions that began at 9:00 am, accompanied by a massive air assault. Some US Army officers who had been on the Western Front in

1918 compared it to the great barrages of the Great War. The ground attack, spearheaded by the 65th Brigade and 4th Division, backed by tanks, broke through the II Corps left flank, and swung toward Manila Bay. Stunned by the ferocity of the assault, the American and Filipino defenders fell back. The line collapsed *so* quickly – after holding since January – that even Homma himself was surprised.

During Easter Sunday sunrise services, before the day's barrage began, Protestant Chaplain J.K. Borneman called for "deliverance from the power of the enemy." On April 6, the Monday after Easter, the defenders attempted a counterattack which ran straight into a massed attack by the 65th Brigade and 4th Division. The following day, the whole II Corps front began to disintegrate, and on April 8, the defense of Bataan by II Corps collapsed. Meanwhile, I Corps was still intact, but withdrawing in order to maintain the cohesion of the line as II Corps crumbled. By now, the long-held Bagac–Orion line had ceased to exist. In the face of sudden victory after months of stalemate, Homma's troops were ecstatic, and this euphoria gave them momentum.

Japanese morale was as high as the American and Filipino morale was low. The latter were tired and hungry from weeks on half rations, or less, and were dispirited by their inability to stem the Japanese tide. Watching the death and destruction being wrought by Homma's zealous legions, the senior officer on Bataan, Major General Edward King, now considered something that been unthinkable a week earlier – surrender.

King commanded the two corps on Bataan, with General Wainwright having withdrawn to Corregidor when MacArthur departed to take command of the US Army Forces in the Far East (USAFFE). The latter was renamed as United States Forces in the Philippines (USFIP) on March 22.

In considering surrender, King was on the verge of disobeying orders. MacArthur had ordered Wainwright not to surrender, and Wainwright had ordered King not to surrender – although Wainwright was painfully aware of King's situation.

At dawn on April 9, without informing Wainwright, King sent an emissary through the lines under a white flag. He was taken to Kameichiro

Nagano, who agreed to meet with King at 9:00 am. First-hand accounts on file with the Combat History Division of the US Army report that King later recalled that he was thinking of the words of Robert E. Lee, who, 77 years earlier to the day on April 9, 1865, had surrendered to Ulysses S. Grant at Appomattox Court House.

"There is nothing left to do but to go and see General Grant," King said, quoting Lee, "and I would rather die a thousand deaths."

The first meeting, to which King was late, due to road conditions and a strafing attack, was a comedy of errors of jurisdictional protocol. Nagano, though a general, could not represent the 14th Army, but when the representative from the 14th Army arrived, it was Colonel Motoo Nakayama, an operations officer, who was angry that King was not Wainwright. In fact, at this point, if protocol was strictly observed, only Masaharu Homma himself had the equivalent rank to have spoken on the subject of surrender with either King or Wainwright.

Ultimately, General King surrendered to the colonel. Nakayama, knowing that he had the upper hand, demanded the surrender of all American and Filipino forces in the Philippines, but all King could offer was those on Bataan, and Nakayama finally agreed. He had no choice. King asked that his men be allowed to surrender by unit and to use their own motor transportation to prison camps. Nakayama demanded unconditional surrender, and after some bickering, King agreed. He had no choice.

King's surrender of more than 70,000 troops, about a quarter of them American, was probably the largest surrender of US Army troops in US history, and certainly since Dixon Miles surrendered to Stonewall Jackson at Harper's Ferry in 1862. In a message to MacArthur, Wainwright disavowed any role in the surrender.

Thereafter began the infamous Bataan Death March, in which the surrendered American and Filipino troops walked the 80 miles from lower Bataan to the former US Army post at Camp O'Donnell. The mistreatment of the prisoners on this march is one of the most dishonorable and well-documented incidents in the history of the IJA since the notorious Rape of Nanking. Both American and Filipino troops were subjected to repeated beatings, and some were bayoneted or shot and left to die. Denied food or water for three days, the prisoners were finally allowed to fill their canteens, but only from contaminated pools and paddies. Disease became rampant. Estimates of deaths are anecdotal as no records were kept, but they may have been as high as 10,000 Filipinos and several hundred Americans. The "Asia for Asiatics" doctrine, upon which the IJA troops had been briefed, was ignored by the officers and men of the 14th Army when it came to Filipinos.

"I want my troops to behave with dignity, but most of them do not seem to have the ability to do so," Tomoyuki Yamashita had once observed. "This is very important now that Japan is taking her place in the world. These men must be educated up to their new role in foreign countries." Apparently Masaharu Homma was not on the same page. After the war, Homma, the commander of the troops who had conquered Bataan, who had inspected Bataan while the Death March was ongoing, denied any knowledge of it.

With Bataan captured, the only enemy outpost left to Homma's army was Corregidor. It was built for defense, with miles of underground tunnels cut into solid rock, and numerous coastal artillery batteries, including two 12-inch guns. Here, first MacArthur and now Wainwright planned a last stand. Despite his defensive armament, Wainwright was desperately short of food and water for the nearly 15,000 military and civilian personnel on the island.

In the weeks following April 9, Homma, who was still smarting from the criticism for taking more than three months to capture Bataan, now incurred the wrath of Imperial General Headquarters for not having captured Corregidor yet.

It was not that Homma had ignored the island. He had had it under more or less continuous air attack since December, and these attacks intensified in April, especially with the bombers of Kizo Mikami's 22nd Air Brigade now available, and no further distraction for their services on Bataan. The capture of Bataan also brought Corregidor within range of Kishio Kitajima's arsenal of more than 100 field guns and howitzers, most of them larger than 150mm, ten of which were the 240mm monsters.

The surface assault against the well-armed stone and concrete defenses on Corregidor presented many challenges for landing craft. Homma also had a manpower problem. According to the postwar debriefing of his medical officer, Colonel Shusuke Horiguchi, the 14th Army had 28,000 men hospitalized for malaria after the Bataan campaign.

Other than Homma's bragging that he would take Corregidor in a week, the first serious date for an assault was April 25, but this was pushed back several times to May 5, in part to allow time to train troops for amphibious operations with the 1st Sea Operation Unit, which had seen service with Yamashita's 25th Army in Malaya and Singapore.

After a heavy and lengthy artillery barrage lasting several days, the first landing was conducted by the 4th Division's 61st Infantry Regiment under Colonel Gempachi Sato, supported by armor from the 7th Tank Regiment. A second and larger attack involved Major General Kureo Taniguchi's 37th Infantry Regiment, plus more 7th Tank Regiment armor and a battalion from the 8th Infantry Regiment.

Because of miscalculations of the tide, and general confusion, Soto's force landed late, coming in at around 11:30 pm after moonrise, which exposed them to enemy guns. They also landed at random places along the beach, and were faced with having to organize themselves in the dark and under fire. Taking heavy casualties, they came close to being pushed into the sea in a counterattack, and the reports reaching Bataan caused Homma to believe that they had indeed failed.

However, this worst fear did not materialize and the beachhead held. By sunrise on May 6, the Japanese had captured about half the island and were gradually pushing back the defenders. At 10:00 am, Wainwright made the decision to ask for a ceasefire to stave off further bloodshed. A message to Wainwright from Roosevelt gave him freedom of action to act in the best interests of his troops, and said that the president had "complete confidence" in any decision he made.

The surrender of Corregidor was no less complicated than the surrender of Bataan. Homma sent the ill-tempered Colonel Motoo Nakayama, the man to whom King had surrendered. As he had with King, he ordered Wainwright to surrender all American forces in the Philippines, and Wainwright insisted on speaking only with Homma. Under Japanese escort, Wainwright arrived back on Bataan at 4:00 pm and Homma arrived at their rendezvous point an hour later.

Wainwright offered to surrender Corregidor, but Homma reiterated the demand that he surrender all American and Filipino forces in the Philippines, including those under the command of Brigadier General William Sharp on the southern island of Mindanao. Wainwright told him that Sharp had been released from Wainwright's command and was under MacArthur's command, but Homma refused to accept this explanation.

The following day, fearing that the Japanese would massacre everyone on Corregidor, Wainwright agreed to Homma's terms. General Sharp, who had yet to be defeated, and whose forces were potentially able to hold out indefinitely as guerrillas, faced an even more difficult decision. In the meantime, MacArthur had ordered Sharp to ignore Wainwright, but after members of Wainwright's staff came to see him, he was convinced that his failure to comply with Wainwright's orders might cost POW lives. To MacArthur, Wainwright wrote that he had "withdrawn my order releasing commanders on other islands and directed complete surrender. Dire necessity alone has prompted this action."

Louis Morton writes that by June 9,

all forces in the Philippines, with the exception of certain small detachments in isolated areas, had surrendered ... With the conquest of the Philippines, the Japanese gained the best harbor in the Orient, excellent bases from which to stage and supply their garrisons to the south and east, as well as a large population to contribute to the Greater East Asia Co-Prosperity Sphere.

On that same day, Masaharu Homma proudly told Jonathan Wainwright that "your high command ceases and you are now a prisoner of war."

Homma's tenure in the Philippines was not a smooth one, as a current of *gekokujo* began running strong within his staff. Major General Yoshihide Hayashi, his vice chief of staff, was outspoken in favoring a hard line against the Filipinos, and was responsible for the May 1942 execution of Philippine Chief Justice Jose Abad Santos against Homma's wishes, which caused Homma a great deal of embarrassment. Before the war, Hayashi had been part of the Taiwan Army Research Department, the "Doro Nawa Unit," which planned the war in Southeast Asia. Another member of that unit was Colonel Masanobu Tsuji. The master of *gekokujo* who had been on Tomoyuki Yamashita's staff in Malaya was now on the 14th Army staff.

Tsuji and Hayashi were both involved in the Santos execution, as well as in the attempted killing of Manuel Roxas, the former speaker of the Philippines House of Representatives. In the latter case, Homma intervened to rescind the execution order that had been authorized in his name by his two staffers in a blatant and defiant act of *gekokujo*. Roxas survived, and in 1945, he became the first postwar president of the Philippine Commonwealth.

On August 1, less than two months after consigning Wainwright to a POW camp in Manchukuo, Masaharu Homma was relieved of his command of the 14th Army and as military governor of the Philippines and consigned to a desk in Tokyo, where he spent the rest of his career. He was replaced by Lieutenant General Shigenori Kuroda, a man with a reputation for mediocrity whose only important combat post had been as commander of the 26th Division during early 1940 at the time it lost to the Chinese in the battle of Wuyuan. In the Philippines, Kuroda developed a reputation as a playboy and party animal who remained secure in this post only by his friendship with Hideki Tojo.

PART VI

THE SETTING
OF THE SUN

CHAPTER 29

THE END OF THE BEGINNING

By the time that the IJA had sewn up its occupation of Sumatra and Java in the second week of March 1942, they had possession of those islands among the 17,500 of the Dutch East Indies that mattered. The growing empire of Emperor Hirohito now included the oil fields, and a Japanese governor seated in the jewel of the former Dutch colonial crown. The momentum of the invincible IJA invited – indeed it demanded – a next step.

Looking eastward from the Dutch East Indies lay New Guinea, the second largest of the world's islands. Bracketed by Japanese-occupied Ambon and Timor to the west and Japanese-occupied New Britain to the east, it spanned 20 degrees of the earth's longitude. On the chessboard of the intersection between Southeast Asia and the Southwest Pacific, ownership of New Guinea appeared essential to the Japanese strategy of containing Australia and any offensive that the Allies might launch from Australia.

Aside from its place on the map, and an enormous place it is, New Guinea is probably the most improbable slice of real estate to be fought over by the great world powers of the mid-twentieth century. A land of mystery with an unexplored interior, New Guinea is more than twice the size of Japan, but it had fewer census-counted inhabitants than the city of Kobe. It is still a land of impossible terrain where even in the twenty-first century it has yet to be bisected by a highway. It is a place of such remoteness that even many decades after World War II, it was inhabited by multitudes of species not yet catalogued by biologists, and home to numerous groups of stone-age people whose languages had never been heard by anthropologists.

New Guinea had been largely ignored by Europeans until the middle of the nineteenth century, and thereafter they had shown little interest beyond planting their flags. The Dutch had administered the part – or more properly, outposts along the coastline of that part – west of the 141st meridian as Nederlands Nieuw Guinea. The British and the Germans had each claimed a slice of the eastern part until 1919, when this half had been bestowed upon Australia by the League of Nations as the New Guinea Trust Territory. Today, the former Dutch half is part of Indonesia, while the eastern half is the independent state of Papua New Guinea (or Papua Niugini). It is indicative of New Guinea's "forgotten" status in the affairs of the middle twentieth century that its largest city, Port Moresby on the Australian side, was home to barely 2,000 people in 1941.

It was to this, the eastern half of New Guinea, that the Japanese turned much of their attention after the fall of Java. Specifically, they focused on the 400-mile-long Papuan, or "Bird's Tail," Peninsula at the southeast tip of the island. Strategically, this was the part closest to their mushrooming base complex at Rabaul, and on the south side of the Bird's Tail, Port Moresby was only 300 miles from the Cape York Peninsula in the Australian state of Queensland.

As Port Moresby was the largest city, largest port, and home to a growing concentration of Australian and American forces, it was the ultimate objective of the Japanese New Guinea strategy. In Allied hands, it could threaten Rabaul. In Japanese hands, it could protect Rabaul and be used to threaten Australia.

If most of New Guinea was strategically irrelevant to the Japanese master plan, Port Moresby had been a square on the Southwest Pacific chessboard upon which Japanese planners had been fixating for years. As early as 1938, the IJN had begun drafting plans for its capture as part of anchoring the sea lanes at the southern edge of the Greater East Asia Co-Prosperity Sphere. With the approval of Admiral Isoroku Yamamoto – commander of the Combined Fleet and architect of the Pearl Harbor attack – the plan for the capture of Port Moresby and its use in the chess game against Australia had been designed and filed away for later use. By March 1942, with all of the other pieces in place on the board, it was time to dust off the plans for Operation *Mo* (or *Mo Sakusen*, named for the first two Roman letters in "Moresby").

The opening gambit in Operation *Mo* and the New Guinea campaign came on March 8, even as surrender terms were being dictated on Java. The initial targets were the twin villages of Lae and Salamaua on the north side of the Bird's Tail, 200 miles due north of Port Moresby across the Owen Stanley Mountains, from which air support operations could be launched.

Major General Tomitaro Horii, who had led the operations against Guam and Rabaul, had set sail aboard four troop transports from the latter base three days earlier with the IJA's South Seas Detachment. As described in Chapter 19, this organization was under the command structure of the IJN South Seas Force (based on the 4th Fleet), and was based on the 144th Regiment of the 55th Division. Horii's order of battle for the Lae and Salamaua operation was essentially the same that he had successfully used to capture Rabaul in January. Horii's troops were escorted by a substantial IJN fleet, including destroyers, patrol boats, and ships from two cruiser divisions. From Rear Admiral Aritomo Goto's Cruiser Division 6, there were the heavy cruisers *Aoba*, *Furutaka*, *Kako*, and *Kinugasa*. Contributed by Rear Admiral Marumo Kuninori's Division 18 were the light cruisers *Tatsuta* and *Tenryu*.

The landings on March 8 went like clockwork, just as the IJA had come to expect from their experiences at dozens of beachheads across Southeast Asia since December 8. At Lae, the Japanese troops landed without opposition. At Salamaua, there was sporadic gunfire.

Attempts by a handful of Allied aircraft to attack the invaders were swatted away as more of a nuisance than a threat.

Two days later, the situation was surprisingly different, as American aircraft launched a concentrated attack against the ships anchored off the invasion beaches. USN bombers from the carriers USS *Lexington* and USS *Yorktown*, as well as eight USAAF B-17 Flying Fortresses operating from Townsville, Australia, did considerable damage. Three of the transports were sunk, and one damaged. Also damaged were a cruiser, two destroyers, and several support vessels. It was not a major defeat, but it was a serious blow to the complacency with which the Japanese had been operating. It was also the harbinger of an ebbing of Japanese air superiority.

As the Japanese began the enormous task of reinforcing Lae and Salamaua in advance of their assault on Port Moresby, parallel operations were getting underway more than a thousand miles to the west. The great battles which unfolded in eastern New Guinea later in 1942 have been discussed in great detail elsewhere, but the Japanese operations in western New Guinea, which flowed from the momentum of the Dutch East Indies Campaign, have been virtually ignored.

The battle plan for the western New Guinea operations was a naval plan. The objectives were the isolated Dutch coastal enclaves across the north side of the island, as well as around the 21,469-square-mile Vogelkop (now Kepela Burung) or "Bird's Head" Peninsula, which is like an appendage to the northwest corner of New Guinea just as the Papuan Peninsula, the "Bird's Tail," is the signature geographic feature on the southeast corner of New Guinea. The plan was simply to use a naval force to pluck the isolated coastal communities one by one.

The spearhead for operations in western New Guinea was the IJN Special Naval Landing Forces. Specifically, they were troops under the command of the 24th Special Base Force, which was part of the IJN 2nd Southern Expeditionary Fleet; this was essentially the IJN 3rd Fleet, renamed on March 10 and given the responsibility for activities within the largely pacified Indies. The invasion force, known as Expeditionary Force N and under the overall command of Rear Admiral Ruitaro Fujita, was organized on Ambon immediately after the conquest of Java, and shipped out on the night of March 29.

Outnumbering the transports, the escort included the light cruiser *Kinu*, two destroyers, assorted patrol boats, and submarine chasers. Air support was supplied by the seaplane tender *Chitose*, which had been active in supporting a number of previous landings in the Dutch East Indies. The landing force itself, under IJN Captain S. Shibuya, included a small detachment from the 24th, plus the battalion-sized contingent of infantry from the 4th Guards. It was small relative to those assigned to previous operations because it was correctly assumed that resistance from handfuls of KNIL stragglers would be minimal.

The first objective for Expeditionary Force N was Bula on the eastern tip of the island of Ceram, where there was a small oil production facility. Reaching this on March 31, and finding that it had been abandoned, the Japanese ships steamed westward, making landfall at Fakfak on the western tip of New Guinea proper on April 1. From here, Expeditionary Force N proceeded clockwise around the Vogelkop Peninsula, reaching Sorong on April 4, and Manokwari on April 12. A week later, they reached Hollandia (now Jayapura), near the border with Australian-administered eastern New Guinea, which had been one of the few important Dutch administrative centers on the island.

At each point on this expedition, the Special Naval Landing Forces found their objectives either lightly defended or completely deserted of KNIL troops. Most of the Dutch had long since embarked on a long and difficult escape to Australia, or had escaped into the jungle to conduct guerilla actions against the Japanese. Indeed, in most cases, the defense of western New Guinea had been so insignificant that lightly armed sailors from the warships served as garrison troops. Garrison detachments of IJA forces were not sent to relieve them on a permanent basis for several months. Neither side bothered with the south and southwest coast of western New Guinea, which was inhospitably swampy, and home to few settlements.

Eastern New Guinea, however, was another matter. With the Japanese reinforcing their position at Lae and Salamaua, and the Allies doing the same at Port Moresby, both sides were building toward the pivotal battles that were about to take place on the ground, in the air and on the sea across in eastern New Guinea and across the Southwest Pacific.

Early May was to be a pivotal moment here, as was the middle of January in Borneo or the first week of March on Java. It was the moment when the invincible Japanese war machine would make decisive and simultaneous moves across a vast swathe of ocean and island from Port Moresby, about 870 miles to the east, across the Coral Sea to the islands of Tulagi and Guadalcanal in the Solomon Islands chain.

There was great confidence and no reason to believe that things would not go as they had at every turn for the past five months since the great simultaneous offensives on December 8. If the landings in the Solomons went smoothly, it would advance the Japanese pieces on the chessboard much closer to Australia's east coast. Japanese air bases here could threaten not only Australia, but its ocean supply lines from the United States.

Tomitaro Horii's South Seas Detachment, roughly 5,000 strong aboard a dozen transports, departed from Rabaul. The invaders of Tulagi had disembarked from one of the ships, and had gone ashore on Tulagi unopposed on the night of May 3–4, while the rest were bound for their amphibious landing at Port Moresby which was scheduled for May 7.

They were supported by the IJN 4th Fleet under Vice Admiral Shigeyoshi Inoue aboard the cruiser *Kashima*. It was the largest Japanese naval force assembled in one place since the operations across the Java Sea during the latter half of February. Directly supporting the Port Moresby invasion group was Rear Admiral Sadamichi Kajioka, with the cruiser *Yubari*, as well as the destroyers *Asanagi*, *Mochizuki*, *Mutsuki*, *Oite*, *Uzuki*, and *Yayoi*. Rear Admiral Aritomo Goto, meanwhile, commanded another covering group that included the light carrier *Shoho* and the cruisers *Aoba*, *Furutaka*, *Kako*, and *Kinugasa*. Also on hand was a carrier strike force comprised of the fleet carriers *Shokaku* and *Zuikaku* and commanded by Takeo Takagi who had led the virtual obliteration of the Allied fleet in the Java Sea, and who had just been promoted to vice admiral on the first of May.

The meticulous Operation *Mo* planning had called for the South Seas Detachment to secure Port Moresby by May 10, and Horii was confident that he could deliver. Japanese bombers would be conducting operations against Australia from Port Moresby by the morning of May 11. Before that morning, however, there would be other mornings and the unexpected, which always haunts the overconfident.

On May 4, just as the Japanese had gone ashore on Tulagi, they were attacked by USN aircraft from the USS *Lexington* and USS *Yorktown*, part of Rear Admiral Frank Fletcher's Task Force 17. As the two sides became aware of one another, and Fletcher deduced from intelligence sources that the long-anticipated invasion of Port Moresby was in motion, the opposing fleets searched for one another across the Coral Sea. Two days of maneuvering led to the joining of a remarkable battle on May 7. It was unlike anything that had yet been seen in naval history. The ships of neither side came within striking distance of the other. Throughout May 7 and May 8, the offensive battle was waged entirely by aircraft.

In the battle of the Coral Sea, each side lost a destroyer and several lesser ships damaged or sunk, but most of the attention was focused on the opposing carriers. The Japanese lost the light carrier *Shoho*, while the *Shokaku* was put out of action through battle damage, and the Zuikaku's aircrews were depleted in the fighting. The *Lexington* was fatally damaged and scuttled, while the *Yorktown* eventually limped back to Pearl Harbor for repairs. The naval battle was a statistical draw, but a strategic victory for the USN insofar as the Coral Sea marked the high-water mark in a great run of successes for the IJN.

A month later, during the first week of June, Admiral Isoroku Yamamoto prepared for what might have been a brilliant end run victory which, in turn, might have checked the USN in the central Pacific. He sent four fleet carriers to support the invasion of Midway, due north of

Hawaii. He had planned to include the *Shokakau* and *Zuikaku*, but after the battle of the Coral Sea, they were heading to Japan for repairs and were unavailable. If the battle of the Coral Sea was the end of the beginning for the IJN, the battle of Midway was the beginning of the end. All four of the Japanese carriers, *Akagi*, *Hiryu*, *Kaga*, and *Soryu* – each a veteran of the Pearl Harbor attack – were sunk at Midway. Things would never again be the same for the IJN.

The battle of the Coral Sea was also the high-water mark for the IJA in the Southwest Pacific. They would hold on in the Solomons, but as the hold began to falter, the momentum was never revived.

What then, of the invasion of Port Moresby, which was scheduled for May 7, and which was to be completed by May 10? As the battle began to unfold in earnest on that day, Admiral Inoue withdrew the invasion fleet. On May 7, with all three aircraft carriers preoccupied and embroiled in the great air battle, they could not support the invasion. Inoue decided that it would not be prudent to go forward with the landings without air cover. By the following day, one of the Japanese carriers was gone and the other two unfit for operations.

Inoue initially ordered a postponement to May 12, then to May 17, and finally the amphibious attack on Port Moresby, which was once just a matter of hours from happening, was cancelled. Inoue was relieved of his command and brought home to desk duty.

General Tomitaro Horii's South Seas Detachment, meanwhile, were not relieved of their duty. It was decided that instead of coming across the beaches, they would attack overland, across the Owen Stanley Mountains which form the jagged spine of the Bird's Tail. On July 21, Horii landed on the north shore of the Bird's Tail in the area of the villages of Buna, Gona, and Sanananda, with around 6,500 men. They then attempted to hike across the mountains on the rough, 65-mile Kokoda Track, a trail which climbs to 3,380 feet through some of the most difficult terrain on earth. Opposing the Japanese were small understrength Australian units – and the land itself.

New Guinea was such a difficult place to wage war that the troops found it a triumph when they managed to march a mile a day through its dense forests. These jungles, with their slippery hillsides tangled in forests and foliage where the sun had never shown, and where visibility is often measured in inches rather than yards, were literally hell on earth for most troops who dared to challenge them.

Being located barely south of the equator gives New Guinea a climate in which a veritable encyclopedia of tropical diseases can flourish. The troops discovered that malaria was almost routine and maladies such as dysentery were actually routine.

The Japanese continued to pour men and materiel into the Kokoda Track for months, eventually losing as many men as they had first committed to the futile campaign. One of them was Horii himself, who drowned crossing a river in September.

The IJA never reached Port Moresby. The momentum lost through the cancellation of the amphibious operation on May 7 was never recaptured. A month later, the battle of Midway guaranteed this. Australia was safe. If there had been an invasion of that country on the books, without Port Moresby, it was impossible.

On November 10, 1942, Winston Churchill went to the podium at the Lord Mayor's Luncheon in London with the news of the British victory against the German Afrika Korps at El Alamein. It had been a terrible three years for the Allies since the war had begun, with nothing but bad news at every turn. But El Alamein was, like the USN's improbable but glorious victory at Midway five months earlier, the demarcation of a high-water mark. There was cause for careful optimism, though it was also time to advise against unrealistic euphoria.

"Now this is not the end," Churchill cautioned. "It is not even the beginning of the end. But it is, perhaps, the end of the beginning."

Churchill made no mention of the Far East and the Pacific. The purpose of his remarks was to talk about good news for a change, and there was no good news from that side of the world. Nevertheless, at the same moment that he was speaking, the US Marines were giving up their blood, sweat, tears, and lives to end another Axis beginning on Guadalcanal, as were the Australian Diggers on New Guinea. It was on a stinking, narrow trail in a stinking, miserable jungle that the IJA was stopped in its tracks for the first time since December 8, 1941. After cutting through all that had opposed them like a hot knife through butter in battle after battle, for month after month, the invincibility was tarnished and beginning to fade. The Kokoda Track was not the beginning of the end for the IJA, but in this unlikely green hell, it was the end of the beginning.

CHAPTER 30

UNDER THE EMPEROR'S ROOF

By the end of March 1942 in most places across Southeast Asia and in the Philippines – except Bataan and Corregidor – the echoes of the sounds of war had faded. The jungles, villages, and cities were noiseless. These sounds had moved eastward to Kokoda and Guadalcanal. The British, Dutch, Australian, and American defenders of the prewar status quo who had survived were waking up in prison camps – in Southeast Asia or Japan, or even in distant Manchuria. The indigenous people of these formerly colonial lands were waking up to a new routine with their new colonial master.

Before the war, men such as Prince Fumimaro Konoe, Yosuke Matsuoka, and like-minded visionaries had spoken theoretically of a vast empire based on the idea of *Hakko ichiu*, the notion of "the eight corners of the world under one roof," which, for them was defined as East Asia under Japan's roof. In June 1940, Japanese Foreign Minister Hachiro Arita had articulated his idea of the Greater East Asia Co-Prosperity Sphere as a self-sufficient bloc of Asian nations led by Japan and free of Western powers. Now, two years later, it existed. By June 1942, there were 100 million indigenous people, spread across 2.8 million square miles, living beneath the Japanese roof.

In that booklet which every Japanese soldier had been given, entitled *Read This Alone: And The War Can Be Won*, they had been told that they had come as liberators. Those 100 million people who had been brought under Japan's roof in the space of half a year would "trust and honor the Japanese; and deep in their hearts they are hoping that, with the help of the Japanese people, they may themselves achieve national independence and happiness."

The pamphlet waxed colorfully that "Money squeezed from the blood of Asians maintains these small white minorities in their luxurious mode of life – or disappears to the respective home countries."

Of course, it was well known to all that the new master was no more altruistic than the former master. The war in the Dutch East Indies, for example, had been fought so that the oil wealth of that colony would disappear across the horizon, not to Europe, but to Japan.

As for "national independence and happiness," there were definite changes. With regard to "happiness," much was written immediately after World War II, and rediscovered in recent years, about the cruel Japanese occupation. There was the brutality of the Kempeitai, the military secret police analog of the Gestapo, who terrified Europeans. Then too, there were the armies of forced laborers, unhappily uprooted from their homes to build great engineering projects, such as the Burma Railway, to serve the "prosperity" of the Japanese vision of their Greater East Asia Co-Prosperity Sphere. In recent years, the enormity of the recruitment of brigades of "comfort women," to serve the "happiness" of the Japanese troops, has been revealed.

The notion of "national independence," in the context of the Sphere has received somewhat less attention in recent years. In 1940, Germany set about reorganizing Europe around Hitler's prewar vision for a Greater German Reich, a new reality designed for "a thousand years," by redrawing borders, erasing Poland, annexing smaller countries, dividing France into zones, etc.

In 1941, the vision of the Greater East Asia Co-Prosperity Sphere at it applied to Southeast Asia had been just that, a vision. In 1942, Japan began to actually formalize this vision into a political and economic reality. New forms of yen-oriented occupation currency were introduced, new constitutions were imposed, and Japanese administrators assumed prominent roles in governments at every level. British and Dutch executives and administrators were entirely displaced and Japanese became the official second language in each of the former colonies – including Singapore. Under the Asia for Asiatics doctrine, the new and Asiatic colonial master was being institutionalized.

In 1932, the Japanese had installed a puppet government in Manchukuo, complete with Puyi, the last emperor of China's Manchu (Qing) dynasty, as its puppet potentate. This arrangement had lasted for ten years and seemed permanent, so it was adopted as the template for parts of Southeast Asia. Indeed, it was only in Burma and the Philippines that Japan conceded to grant even a puppet form of "national independence," and this did not come until 1943. Of course, also within the Sphere, the Kingdom of Thailand had been a puppet of Japan, and a treaty-obliged ally, since its surrender on December 8, 1941, the first day of the war in Southeast Asia. Thailand would be repaid for its loyalty when Japan redrew the map to transfer the Malay states on Kedah, Kelantan, Perlis, and Terengganu to Thai sovereignty.

In Burma, the Japanese puppet leader was Ba Maw, a man whose anti-British credentials included not only prewar agitation, and prominence within the independence movement, but the fact that the Japanese had had to release him from a British prison when they occupied Burma.

A man with a similar background, and a similar dislike for the British, was Subhas Chandra Bose, a British-educated Indian attorney who had been an outspoken advocate of Indian independence since the 1920s. A member of the Indian National Congress, along with Mohandas Gandhi and Jawaharlal Nehru, he was much less inclined toward the non-violent tactics which became Gandhi's signature policy. In and out of jail in British India, Bose left the country in 1941 and made his way to Berlin, where he dined with Hitler and was the toast of the town for his outspoken anti-British rhetoric. In 1943, he relocated to Japan, transported by German and Japanese submarines, where he became the face of the Japanese effort to "liberate" India from the British.

In the early years of the occupation, the Japanese had considered unifying all of Malaya into a puppet state under Sultan Ibrahim II of Johor, the man from whose palace Tomoyuki Yamashita had studied Singapore on the eve of his attack. However, as the war progressed, more pressing concerns consumed the Japanese administrators and this project was never implemented.

In the Philippines, the political situation was somewhat complicated by the fact that the Americans had already set a date – July 4, 1946 – as the moment when they would end their colonial rule and grant full independence to the commonwealth. A two-chamber national assembly had already been established, and in 1935, in a national election, the Filipinos had elected Manuel Luis Quezon as president of the Commonwealth of the Philippines. He had fled the Philippines in 1942, and he died in exile in the United States in 1944 before the Philippines were liberated.

Shortly after the surrender of Manila, even as Americans and Filipinos were still fighting in Bataan, General Masaharu Homma disbanded the Commonwealth of the Philippines and set up the Philippine Executive Commission under Manila Mayor Jose Vargas. The puppet Republic of the Philippines was formed in 1943, heading off the American-promised independence date by three years. As president, the Japanese picked Yale-educated attorney Jose Paciano Laurel, late of the prewar Supreme Court, while Vargas became ambassador to Japan. Vargas later was quoted as having effused that "Japan is destined for sure victory and prosperity for ages to come."

While Burma and the Philippines were being granted quasi-independence, a sort of "dependent independence," based on the Manchukuo model, Hideki Tojo's headquarters in Tokyo made the decision to annex Malaya and the Indies to the Japanese Empire based on the Korea and Taiwan model. This clarification of status was implemented in May 1943, a year after the IJA's rampage of conquest.

———

As they settled into postwar reality as part of the Greater East Asia Co-Prosperity Sphere, the former Dutch East Indies were ruled by three regional rulers. Sumatra was ruled from Singapore by Lieutenant General Yaheita Saito, Tomoyuki Yamashita's successor as commander of the IJA 25th Army. Java was ruled by its conqueror, General Hitoshi Imamura, until November 1942, when he was succeeded by Lieutenant General Kumakichi Harada, who took command of the IJA 16th Army, now an occupation force. Borneo and Celebes were administered by the IJN.

In the Indies, there was a great deal more support for the Japanese and the idea of the Greater East Asia Co-Prosperity Sphere because there had been a more active prewar independence movement here than nearly anywhere else in Southeast Asia. According to historian Tom Womack, the Indonesians dutifully welcomed the Japanese with shouts of "Japan is our older brother," and helped the occupiers by eagerly betraying the hiding places of ethnic Europeans. Indonesian author Pramoedya Ananta Toer, in *The Mute's Soliloquy*, writes that "with the arrival of the Japanese just about everyone was full of hope, except for those who had worked in the service of the Dutch."

The lack of interest in talking about an independent Indonesia was perhaps because of the prewar independence movement. The zealous revolutionaries were interested in real independence, and the Japanese understood that the Indonesian leaders would never be satisfied as puppets, and could not be trusted not to bite Japan's hand if put into power.

Nevertheless, the Japanese did reach out to co-opt the would-be revolutionaries. The most important among these were Kusno Sosrodihardjo, who went by the single name, "Sukarno," and Mohammad

Hatta. As students, both had developed strong nationalist convictions and had dabbled in a broad spectrum of ideologies from Islamic to communist. In 1927, Sukarno was a founder of the pro-independence Partai Nasional Indonesia. By 1942, he was well known in anti-Dutch revolutionary circles, and was on the list of people in whom the Japanese had an interest. It was mutual. Sukarno saw the Japanese as his ticket to eventual independence.

As William Frederick and Robert Worden write in *Indonesia: A Country Study*, published by the Library of Congress Federal Research Division,

> Sukarno and Hatta agreed in 1942 to cooperate with the Japanese, as this seemed to be the best opportunity to secure independence. The occupiers were particularly impressed by Sukarno's mass following, and he became increasingly valuable to them as the need to mobilize the population for the war effort grew between 1943 and 1945.

In July 1942, Sukarno sat down with Hitoshi Imamura and struck a deal. In exchange for a public forum to promote his ideas, Sukarno was willing to delay independence and help the Japanese recruit forced labor. As noted in Chapter 24, the Indies became an enormous source of workers which Japan conscripted for infrastructure projects across Southeast Asia. Documents in the Library of Congress, cited by Frederick and Worden, note that at least four million Indonesians were conscripted as *roumsha*, or slave laborers. The two authors add that Sukarno's reputation was "tarnished by his role in recruiting *roumsha*," but the tarnish apparently wore off quickly after the war as Sukarno became the signature figure in the independence movement, and eventually he served as independent Indonesia's first president.

The Japanese never gave Sukarno the sovereignty that he craved, but in April 1945, Kumakichi Harada did create the Badan Penyelidik Usaha Persiapan Kemerdekaan Indonesia (Committee for Preparatory Work for Indonesian Independence) as a step toward giving his Indonesian subjects the sort of independence that the Japanese had allowed in Burma and the Philippines. This plan came only four months before the end of the war, and was therefore overtaken by events.

As the Greater East Asia Co-Prosperity Sphere became a reality, the Japanese sought to institutionalize this *Shintaisei*, or "new order," into a formal, permanent structure, just as Germany was doing within the redrawn borders. As in Germany, it was imagined that this new order would last for centuries.

In November 1943, to help give legitimacy to the new order, Hideki Tojo personally hosted an unprecedented pan-Asia economic summit conference. The two-day colloquium, known as the Greater East Asia Conference, looked a great deal like the later economic summits, such as the Association of Southeast Asian Nations (ASEAN) conference, held annually since 1976, and the East Asia Summit (EAS), a forum convened annually since 2005. Many of the territories occupied by Japan as part of the Greater East Asia Co-Prosperity Sphere were founding members of the contemporary organizations, although the present ASEAN embodies cooperation generated from within, rather than imposed from the outside. Tojo went to great lengths to make his puppet show seem as if it was not, but with him so obviously pulling the strings, there was no doubt that the conference existed only to project the legitimacy of Japanese regional dominance.

The conference was a who's who of Japanese-installed Asian governments. Zhang Jinghui, the prime minister of Manchukuo, attended. So too did Wang Jingwei, who had been installed as president of the Reorganized National Government of China. Naturally, both Ba Maw and Jose Laurel came, attempting to legitimize their rule on an international stage.

Thailand, as the only independent country in the region before the war, was unique among the participants. Prime Minister Plaek Phibunsongkhram, who had underscored the independence of his country by "resisting" the Japanese invasion for half a day on December 8, 1941, decided that to attend personally would cast him in too subservient a role. It would make him appear too much like Ba or Laurel, a mere puppet. On the other hand, Phibun did not want Thailand to be left out entirely, so he sent Prince Wan Waithayakon, who was a grandson of King Mongkut, and who functioned as a sort of diplomatic ambassador at large for the Thai government. After the war, Prince Wan landed on his feet, serving as Thailand's ambassador to the United States, and later as Thailand's foreign minister, and as president of the United Nations General Assembly, only 13 years after being part of Tojo's earlier international gathering.

Also present at the conference was Subhas Chandra Bose, the prewar Indian revolutionary, who had spent the previous few years in Berlin and Tokyo, and who was now the president of the Provisional Government of Free India (Arzi Hukumat-e-Azad Hind). While Ba and Laurel each presided over a country – albeit one that existed only because of the largesse and muscle of Japan – Bose's "Free India" was merely a conceptual country. India was still entirely under British control, so the presence of Bose at the Greater East Asia Conference manifested the desire by both Bose and Tojo for an unobtainable future ideal.

As with most multination summit conferences, it concluded with a joint declaration. It is no surprise that this incorporated the "Asia for Asiatics" rhetoric that Japan used to justify its conquests, or that the Allies, in their role as colonial powers, thoroughly condemned. The declaration read:

> The United States of America and the British Empire have in seeking their own prosperity oppressed other nations and peoples. Especially in East Asia, they indulged in insatiable aggression and exploitation, and sought to satisfy their inordinate ambition of enslaving the entire region, and finally they came to menace seriously the stability of East Asia. Herein lies the cause of the recent war.

The attendees agreed that through "mutual cooperation" they would "ensure the stability of their region and construct an order of common prosperity and well-being based upon justice."

At the same time that the Japanese were conscripting forced labor and comfort women from among the residents of the attending nations, the conferees agreed that

> the countries of Greater East Asia will cultivate friendly relations with all the countries of the world, and work for the abolition of racial discrimination, the promotion of cultural intercourse and the opening of resources throughout the world, and contribute thereby to the progress of mankind.

Today the Greater East Asia Conference is largely forgotten by history as being an anachronism long on irony, but short on substance. It was, after all, a delusional exercise by newly formed countries which would cease to exist within less than two years – which was sponsored by the Japanese Empire, which would, itself, cease to exist within two years. On the other hand, it provides a priceless insight into how the Japanese, especially Tojo, imagined the postwar world and the postwar reality within their Greater East Asia Co-Prosperity Sphere.

It took place in 1943, that critical year when the IJA had advanced as far as it was going to advance, and before the Allies had really begun to roll back Japanese territorial gains. It took place within an environment where it was still reasonable for Japanese planners to assume that the fantasy represented by the conference and its participants would continue indefinitely as the face of postwar Asia.

CHAPTER 31

THE BEGINNING OF THE END

On November 10, 1942, when Winston Churchill had spoken of El Alamein as the "end of the beginning" in the war against Germany, there was no one among the Allied strategic leadership who could envision speaking of an "end of the beginning" in the war against the Empire of the Rising Sun any time soon.

During 1943, though, a realization – a *cautious* realization – of this milestone finally seemed to have emerged, datelined New Guinea and Guadalcanal. However, through 1943, across the rest of Southeast Asia, the seas were still a placid Japanese lake, and the lands that lay beneath the flag of the rising sun seemed as permanently part of the Greater East Asia Co-Prosperity Sphere as Europe was still a part of the empire of the Third Reich. By 1944, the tide had clearly turned in the war against Germany in places from Salerno to Kursk. The "beginning of the end," while still not within grasp, could be seen on the distant horizon.

In Southeast Asia, the seas, the skies, and the land beneath those rising sun flags were still quiet. In Burma, though, two years after the Allied defeat in 1942, the British and Americans clung to a swathe of northern Burma, while numerous attempts by the Japanese to gain further territory had yet to yield real fruit.

Although the IJA was successfully holding the line against the Allies, their great offensives, which had so stunned the world in 1941–42 were a thing of the past – or were they?

———————

The man with the plan to resurrect the past glory of the IJA was Lieutenant General Renya Mutaguchi, one of the most experienced leaders in the service, having commanded the 18th Division in Malaya and Burma. In March 1943, he was promoted to command the 15th Army when Shojiro Iida was recalled to Japan for a desk job at the General Defense Command.

Mutaguchi had long been among that cadre of officers who advocated launching an offensive into India. If this had been done in 1942, it would have caught the Allies unable to mount much of a defense. In 1943, Mutaguchi was arguing that such an operation would be necessary in order to prevent the Allies, their strength now growing, from coming the other way.

Mutaguchi found an ally in his new boss, Lieutenant General Masakazu Kawabe, who had arrived in 1943 to take over as commander-in-chief of the newly formed Burma Area Army. Kawabe had graduated from the IJA Academy in 1907 in the same class as Hitoshi Imamura of the 16th Army, and two years after Tomoyuki Yamashita and Hideki Tojo. Like them, he had served as a military attaché to Switzerland after World War I, and later served in Germany. Until 1943, he had served in the Kwantung Army and in China, but he had not yet served in Southeast Asia.

The operational plan which they created, code-named *U-Go*, was approved by General Count Hisaichi Terauchi, who as commander of the Southern Expeditionary Army Group ran everything that the IJA did in Southeast Asia. He sent it on up the chain of command to Hideki Tojo, who also signed it off.

Specifically, *U-Go* called for a massive invasion of India, driving into the states of Manipur and Assam, across the Imphal Plain, through the Bramaputra River Valley and possibly threatening the state of Bengal with a drive to the Ganges River. At the very least, the Japanese expected to be able to cut the Allies' supply lines into northern Burma and capture Allied airfields that were being used for the massive airlift operation that carried supplies into China across the section of the Himalayas that Allied airmen called the "Hump."

U-Go was to be preceded by Operation *Ha-Go*, a diversionary attack launched from the western Burmese state of Arakan (now Rakhine), which was adjacent to the eastern part of Bengal that is now Bangladesh. Scheduled a month ahead of *U-Go*, the strategic objective of *Ha-Go* was to give the Allies plenty of time to relocate assets away from the Imphal Plain, where the opening phase of *U-Go* would involve a three-pronged effort to capture the city of Imphal in the state of Manipur. The attacking force would include elements of the 55th Division, which were commanded by Major General Tokutaro Sakurai and known as the Sakurai Force.

Defending Imphal was the British IV Corps under Lieutenant General Geoffrey Scoones, which was part of the British 14th Army, commanded by Lieutenant General William J. "Bill" Slim, who had commanded the Burma Corps in 1942.

Making a direct assault on Imphal from the east would be the Yamamoto Force under Major General Tsunoru Yamamoto. Utilizing troops from both the 15th and 33rd Divisions, Yamamoto would fight his way through the 20th Indian Infantry Division, based at Tamu.

Meanwhile, the remainder of the IJA 15th Division, commanded by Lieutenant General Masafumi Yamauchi, would circle north of Imphal and strike from that direction. The rest of the 33rd Division under Lieutenant General Motoso Yanagida would attack the veteran 17th Indian Infantry Division, then circle to attack Imphal from the south. Simultaneously, Lieutenant General Kotoku Sato's 31st Division would capture the neighboring city of Kohima.

It is significant that the operation also included the participation of the Indian National Army (INA), or Azad Hind Fauj. This organization, like Aung San's Burma Independence Army, originated with the prewar support and encouragement of IJA intelligence operatives and was composed of disaffected former British subjects. Of the two, the INA was by far the largest. The idea had begun in 1941 with Major Iwaichi Fujiwara, whose covert Fujiwara Kikan was a special operations project aimed at making contact with Indian nationalist and anti-British activists living in Southeast Asia, especially those involved with the Indian Independence League.

The largest pool of manpower for the INA was in the huge numbers of Indian troops serving with the British Army, who were captured in Malaya. Among them was Captain Mohan Singh, picked by Fujiwara to form the first iteration of the INA in 1942. According to Lieutenant Colonel G.D. Anderson of British military intelligence, as quoted by Peter Fay in his book *The Forgotten Army*, 45,000 Indian troops who had been captured in the Malay campaign were given the opportunity to join the INA, and all but 5,000 did so.

In 1943, with the rise of the colorful Subhas Chandra Bose, the president of the Provisional Government of Free India, the leadership of the INA was transferred to him. Because of Bose's popularity, this change proved to be an excellent recruiting tool and sizable numbers of new volunteers were added to the ranks of the INA. The exact numbers are not known because INA records were destroyed, but there were more than the Japanese had expected.

As planned, Operation *Ha-Go*, the diversion involving Saukrai Force, got underway on February 5, 1944, a month ahead of *U-Go*. After making initial gains, the Japanese found themselves pinned down in heavy fighting around Ngakyedauk Pass. In contrast to Japanese operations in 1942, the Allies now had air superiority, as well as the ability to resupply their troops on the ground with air drops. The Japanese were surrounded and on the edge of starvation when unauthorized and disorganized retreats began happening during the last week of February. Sakurai finally ordered an end to *Ha-Go* on February 26.

The failure of *Ha-Go* should have given pause to the plans of Mutaguchi and Kawabe for *U-Go*, but the main invasion of India nevertheless went forward on March 8. Major General Douglas Gracey's 20th Indian Infantry Division managed to hold Yamamoto Force near the Chindwin River until March 25, when Gracey began an organized withdrawal. The 17th Indian Infantry Division under Major General Punch Cowan also began its tactical withdrawal, escaping the clutches of the IJA 33rd Division. Slim's plan was to allow the Japanese to advance in order to extend their supply lines. With the Allies now in control of the air, and therefore of Japanese supply lines, this was a desirable tactic.

When he had originally proposed his plan, Mutaguchi had based his assumptions on his experiences of fighting the British and Indians in 1942. He did not seem to realize that his foe was now far better trained, better supplied, and better motivated than had been the Allied troops of 1942. Nor did he grasp the importance of the shift in air superiority from the Japanese to the Allies. During the battle, the entire 5th Indian Infantry Division was airlifted into the battle zone, something that would have been unthinkable in 1942.

Because the Allies were in the midst of preparations for an offensive of their own at the time, IV Corps was well supplied and well organized – and better prepared to take on a Japanese offensive than any Allied force in Southeast Asia two years earlier when the IJA was unstoppable.

The swift blitzkrieg that Mutaguchi imagined was never accomplished. Though IV Corps did not have the strength to throw Yamamoto Force back across the Chindwin River, they had the strength to stop the Japanese in their tracks, and this was done. Elements of the 33rd Division managed to get to within 10 miles of Imphal, but most Japanese troops never got nearly that close.

Meanwhile, Lieutenant General Kotoku Sato's 31st Division began closing in on Kohima on April 3, but wound up getting bogged down in heavy fighting. This continued until the middle of the month, when the defenders of Kohima were reinforced by the Indian XXXIII Corps. The Allied troops began a counterattack on April 18, which began pushing the IJA back. In fighting that lasted for the next month, Sato gradually gave ground before finally ordering his division to withdraw.

Throughout April, battles raged across the front, but on the first of May, Slim launched his counterattack. As with the Japanese advances in April, the Allied advances during May came slowly and at great cost. The Japanese and their INA allies felt the adverse effects of their long and difficult supply lines as they began to go hungry. When Sato had ordered the 31st Division to pull back, it was in search of something to eat.

When General Kawabe visited the front on May 25, the officers assured him that the battle could still be won – if only they could receive substantial reinforcements – but he could see that they were either delusionally optimistic or lying to him. The Japanese troops were just hanging on and spending most of their time scrounging for food. Attacks and counterattacks throughout June changed little on the ground, but the outcome was no longer in doubt. The Japanese attacked mainly because Mutaguchi was sacking officers who refused to order attacks. Finally, they just stopped communicating with the 15th Army commander. It was less about *gekokujo* than it was about despair.

Kawabe and Mutaguchi were now on the sharp and painful horns of a dilemma. For more than a month, both realized that *U-Go* had failed, but neither wanted to lose face by ordering a retreat in the IJA's last major offensive action in Southeast Asia.

Finally, with Kawabe down and out with amoebic dysentery, Mutaguchi broke the impasse and ordered the withdrawal on July 3. Because of the failure of *U-Go*, he was relieved of his command, recalled to Japan, and mustered out of the IJA. Kawabe was also brought back to Tokyo, but he got a desk job planning for the defense of the Japanese home islands.

In four months of fighting, more than twice the duration of Tomoyuki Yamashita's Malaya–Singapore campaign, the 15th Army captured no significant objectives and suffered 55,000 casualties, three times the number suffered by the Allies in the campaign. Their defeat in the Imphal campaign was the largest in Japanese history up to that time.

One is tempted to say that it was the beginning of the end for the IJA, but this had already occurred on the islands of the Pacific. It was more a desperate anomaly, a quixotic exercise by men who inhabited a mirage, madly refusing to acknowledge that these were no longer the invincible years.

CHAPTER 32

THE END

In August 1944, the IJA General Staff summoned the Tiger of Malaya to Tokyo. The architect of his country's greatest land war triumph in World War II had not set foot in Japan since the war had begun on the Southern Road. After his stunning victory in Singapore, in the moment of his greatest achievement, a victory that caused ripples of fear and respect for Japan around the world, General Tomoyuki Yamashita had been sidelined by the jealous insecurity of his old colleague, Hideki Tojo.

For two years, the crucial two years when the Empire of Japan most needed his skill, his cunning, and his strategic brilliance, Yamashita had been marking time in Manchukuo, 60 miles from Siberia, where there was nothing for a soldier to fight but boredom. He had been elevated to full general during his exile, and he had been given command of the 1st Area Army, but there was nothing for him and his army to do but await a Soviet invasion that never came.

Now, suddenly, he was needed elsewhere. So much had happened since he was last in Tokyo when the invincibility of the IJA was about to be proven in Southeast Asia.

So much had happened in the past few months. The American war machine, by now the most powerful the world had yet seen, had turned the tide in the Pacific. Their industry and their logistical apparatus confirmed that their armies would not run out of steam as had the IJA.

In June 1944, the Americans had captured Rome, landed in Normandy, and landed in the Marianas, the chain of islands that included Guam and Saipan. On July 9, they had defeated the Japanese forces that had defended Saipan. Everyone on the Imperial General Staff knew that from Saipan – and neighboring Guam and Tinian – USAAF B-29 bombers could bring the war to Japan's home islands.

Two weeks after Saipan fell, Hideki Tojo also fell. For all of the time since Tomoyuki Yamashita had last set foot in Japan, Tojo – his one-time friend, long-time colleague, and the man whom he perceived as being a professional nemesis for exiling him to Manchukuo during the critical years of the war – had reigned supreme. Tojo had ruled as the most powerful man – after Emperor Hirohito – across nearly half the circumference of the earth, while Yamashita bided his time on a front where nothing had happened, and where nothing was realistically expected to happen.

Tojo had been the minister of war since 1940, the prime minister since 1941, and chief of the IJA General Staff since February 1944. After Saipan, it all ended. On July 22, 1944, Tojo's colleagues called him in to the General Staff Headquarters and asked him to hand Hirohito his formal resignation. The generals knew the full meaning of Saipan. If there had been any doubt before, they now knew that the march of time had reached and raced past the beginning of the end.

On the day before Tojo resigned, Umezu, then the commander of the IJA's Kwantung Army in Manchuria and Yamashita's boss, had told Yamashita that Japan was entering a difficult and unsettled time, and foretold that soon Tojo would be gone. Now, a month later, as Yamashita walked up the steps of the General Staff Headquarters, it was to meet again with Umezu, who was now Tojo's successor as chief of the IJA General Staff.

———————

In 1941, when the IJA had embarked on Nanshinron, the Southern Road, Yamashita had been tasked with traveling that section of the road which was arguably the most important, that which terminated in the glittering jewel of Singapore. Today, once again, Yamashita was needed for perhaps the biggest defensive task outside Japan itself. Douglas MacArthur had promised, way back in 1942, that he would return to the Philippines. Now with the might and momentum of the United States being what it was, that return seemed imminent. Tomoyuki Yamashita was told that he would defend the Philippines from MacArthur. He was promised the full cooperation of the armed forces of Japan – including the IJN.

On October 6, 1944, Yamashita left Japan for the last time. After an overnight stop in Taiwan, he landed in Manila to take up the reins of his new post as governor general of the Philippines, and as commander of the roughly 250,000 troops that comprised the IJA 14th Area Army. The latter was the same 14th Army that Masaharu Homma had first brought to the Philippines in 1941, though it had gone through many changes and expansions, and it had been upgraded in status, becoming and area army on July 28, 1944. Yamashita arrived assuming that he had three months to prepare his forces logistically and tactically for the coming invasion. He had less than two weeks.

MacArthur's troops came ashore on the southeastern Philippine island of Leyte on October 20. Yamashita had anticipated the place, but not the time. Ordered to defend Leyte, Yamashita did so, but at a cost. By December, when it was all over but the mopping up of stragglers, the IJA had lost close to 50,000 men killed, and fewer than 900 who did not fight to the death and who were captured. Half of Yamashita's air assets were lost, and with bases in Leyte the Americans controlled the air. The naval battle of Leyte Gulf was the largest naval battle in history and a resounding disaster for the Japanese. Thereafter, the IJN essentially ceased to exist as a naval fighting force.

The Americans landed on Luzon, the largest of the Philippine islands, on January 9, 1945, coming ashore at Lingayen Gulf, north of Manila, where the IJA 14th Army had landed in December 1941. The Imperial General Staff demanded that Yamashita fight a single decisive battle, but he refused. As Yamashita said after the war, speaking with Captain A.

Frank Reel, one of the US Army officers charged with defending him at his war crimes trial:

> In view of the Leyte operations, I realized that decisive battle was impossible. Therefore I decided on a delaying action to divert American forces in Luzon so as to keep them from attacking Japan, as much as possible. I realized the American air forces and navy were exceedingly superior to ours, and also the firepower of the ground forces was superior and very mobile. I could not conduct warfare on flat land. Therefore I employed a delaying action in the mountains.

Yamashita's plan had been to withdraw from the city of Manila after destroying its harbor facilities. As with MacArthur in 1941, Yamashita wished to avoid costly and pointless urban warfare. He explained:

> I decided to put Manila outside the battle area. First, the population of Manila is approximately one million; therefore it is impossible to feed them. The second reason is that the buildings are very inflammable. The third reason is that because it is a flat land it requires tremendous number of strength [sic] to defend it. The army units evacuated Manila gradually in accordance with my orders [by the middle of December].

However, Yamashita ran into opposition from Rear Admiral Sanji Iwabuchi of the IJN. The Imperial General Staff had promised Yamashita that he would have authority over all Japanese forces in the Philippines, including those of the IJN, but Iwabuchi did not see it that way. Yamashita ordered Iwabuchi to take his roughly 15,000-man Manila Naval Defense Force, and join the IJA in evacuating Manila, but Iwabuchi refused. There was his pride. Most IJN officers felt that they should never take orders from an IJA officer, but there were also personal reasons. In his last shipboard command, he had suffered the humiliation of having the battleship *Kirishima* sunk beneath him, and felt that he must die in combat, in a blaze of glory, to redeem himself.

Instead of ordering his men out of the city, Iwabuchi ordered them to fight to the last man. As noted in Chapter 14, at the beginning of the war, the IJN naval infantry, the Special Naval Landing Forces, were an elite force. However, by 1944, these units had been depleted of their original troops, had lost unit cohesion, and had become dumping grounds for poorly trained misfits transferred in at random from other units wishing to be rid of them.

As MacArthur's troops converged on Manila during the first week of February 1945, the undisciplined and unsupervised IJN troops were still in the city. The result was nothing short of catastrophic. Knowing that they were going to die, they went on a well-documented rampage of cruelty to the civilian population, raping, torturing, and murdering Filipino adults and children before compelling the US Army to fight a street-by-street, house-by-house battle that devastated Manila. They and Iwabuchi died in a blaze, but not of glory. Yamashita had no sense of the dimensions of the disaster that came to be known as the Manila Massacre. He recalled:

On or about the 13th of February, I received a report to the effect that, while just an element of the Navy had evacuated the city, the majority still remained in Manila. I immediately sent an order to [Lieutenant General Shizuo Yokoyama] to the effect that, in accordance with our original plan, to evacuate immediately all the navy troops from Manila.

By this time, with the US Army in control of the approaches to Manila, communication between the city and Yamashita's headquarters in the mountains near Baguio was impossible.

Though he managed to maintain sporadic wireless contact with General Count Hisaichi Terauchi, his immediate superior at the Southern Expeditionary Army Group headquarters in Saigon, Yamashita was unaware of the full extent of what had happened in Manila until after the war.

Yamashita and his troops fought their delaying actions in the mountains of northern Luzon. Through the spring and into the summer of 1945, they battled the Americans, the weather, and a nightmare kaleidoscope of tropical diseases. It was the reverse of the campaign that Yamashita had fought in Malaya, or that Homma had fought here in the Philippines in 1942. This time, Yamashita and the IJA were on the defensive, cut off from all hope of resupply and growing hungrier by the day. The Americans, well supplied and well armed, continued to push the Japanese into the virtually inaccessible mountains and jungles. One by one, pockets of Japanese troops were overwhelmed, captured, or eliminated. Nevertheless, Yamashita remained in direct command of thousands of IJA troops who were still fighting their hold action in the impossible terrain.

On August 15, in the wake of the two nuclear strikes against Hiroshima and Nagasaki, Emperor Hirohito made his famous and first-ever radio address in which he ordered all Japanese troops on every front to lay down their arms. Yamashita and his immediate command had not heard this broadcast on their radios, but on August 19, they got a message from Terauchi's headquarters instructing him to "obey Imperial command ... cease fire and stop fighting."

A few days later, an American aircraft dropped a message from Major General W.H. Gill of the 32nd Infantry Division, inviting Yamashita to surrender. Ordering his troops to "disarm according to American orders," Tomoyuki Yamashita walked out of the mountains on September 2 and gave himself up to the Americans. Taken to Gill's command post at Baguio, he signed papers formally surrendering the 14th Area Army.

At the time he surrendered, Yamashita was not an isolated recluse hiding in a cave in the mountains. There were still more than 100,000 uncaptured Japanese troops in the Philippines, and around half of these were under Yamashita's direct command, roughly as many as were under his direct command when he accepted the surrender of Singapore. With all these, Yamashita might have held out for many more months, well into 1946.

Coincidentally, it was on that same day, September 2, that momentous events were happening 1,850 miles to the north. That morning, General Yoshijiro Umezu, the man who had sent Yamashita to the Philippines, traveled into Tokyo Bay to go aboard the USS *Missouri*, to stand opposite Douglas MacArthur on behalf of the Imperial General Headquarters, and surrender the armed forces of the Empire of Japan. Surrounded by dozens of Allied officers and whirring newsreel cameras, Foreign Minister Mamoru Shigemitsu signed the Instrument of Surrender on behalf of the Japanese government and Emperor Hirohito.

Both General Jonathan Wainwright, who had surrendered the Philippines, and General Arthur Percival, who had surrendered Singapore, were on hand to witness the ceremony marking the end of World War II.

The Allies were in Tokyo. Douglas MacArthur was Japan's emperor in fact, and he would soon be meeting Hirohito as though the erstwhile Son of Heaven was a mere mortal. The strategy that the Allies had pursued since they had pried the Japanese from Guadalcanal and New Guinea had been aimed at this moment. It had taken them up the island chains of the Pacific, ingraining names such as Peleliu, Tarawa, Saipan, and Iwo Jima in the global consciousness and on American historical memory. The Allies fully expected to launch the greatest military campaign in history to invade and capture the home islands of Japan, but the world had been spared the reading of Japanese place names associated with vicious, bloody battles. Soon, the Americans would be coming ashore to occupy and administer a defeated Japan – without firing a shot.

———————————

However, as the sun rose over postwar Asia, the once invincible IJA still held its positions across much of what it had conquered across Asia. No Allied army had recaptured Beijing, Hankow, or Shanghai. The United States had recaptured most of the Philippines, although those 100,000 Japanese troops had yet to be rounded up, but the soil of Taiwan had felt the boots of no invading army since the Japanese arrived in 1895 after the First Sino-Japanese War.

On the Southern Road, the Allies had recaptured Rangoon in May 1945, and Borneo in July. Elsewhere, nothing had changed since the days in 1942, when the IJA had been invincible.

THE END

Across the vast territory of Southeast Asia, IJA troops were still patrolling the streets and jungle tracks on September 2 and on September 3. The Japanese administrators were still at their desks. The war was over, but most of the Japanese soldiers in Southeast Asia had not seen an armed Allied soldier since they had disarmed them back in 1942. Even as the surrender was being signed in most of the areas which the IJA had conquered in 1942, the IJA had yet to *be* conquered.

In Malaya, the occupiers would have faced a British invasion, code-named Operation *Zipper*, which was scheduled for October 1945, with landings on the west coast near Kuala Lumpur. The British did arrive in that city on September 12 in the form of the British Military Administration, who took back their desks and accepted the surrender of Lieutenant General Teizo Ishiguro of the IJA. It would be weeks before the Japanese throughout Malaya would relinquish what Tomoyuki Yamashita had captured in 1942. During this time, though, they were still at war – with the resistance movement known as the Malayan Peoples' Anti-Japanese Army. Emboldened by Japan's capitulation, this force continued their fight in the form of reprisals until disarmed by the British at the end of 1945. Employing tactics learned during the Japanese occupation, the same guerrillas reformed a few years later to fight the British for independence.

In French Indochina, both the IJA and IJN were still in place on September 3, as they had been since 1940, maintaining bases for operations elsewhere and functioning as a *de facto* occupation force. All pretense of Indochina being a French colony ended with the collapse of the pro-Axis Vichy government in France, and in March 1945, Japan formally terminated French rule. As it had done in Burma, it installed indigenous anticolonial nationalists as puppet administrators. The Japanese carved Cambodia out as a separate kingdom, installing 22-year-old Norodom Sihanouk as its monarch, a position that he would hold, off and on, until 2004. In Vietnam, they used the prewar emperor, Bao Dai, as their figurehead, hoping this would offset the influence of the Viet Minh guerrillas, who had been fighting the French since 1941.

When the Japanese formally surrendered, the guerilla leader Ho Chi Minh declared Vietnam's independence, but on September 12, when the British and French arrived in Saigon to accept the surrender of the Japanese, they did so under the assumption that the Provisional Government of the French Republic, which had replaced the Vichy regime at home in France, would reestablish the prewar French administration of all Indochina. There followed several weeks of confusion in which British, French, Japanese, and Viet Minh were trading gunfire, with American OSS operatives, who had been using the Viet Minh as an intelligence asset, caught in the crossfire. As for the independence of Vietnam, that is another, very long and well-known story.

———————

In the Dutch East Indies, the Dutch expected to do as the British were doing in Malaya, and as the French were doing in Indochina. However, as in these other places, matters were complicated by local aspirations. Sukarno and Mohammad Hatta had declared the independence of Indonesia on August 17, two days after Hirohito had called for a ceasefire. The Japanese, who had undertaken an exhaustive effort to eradicate Dutch influence in the Indies, initially allowed their administrators to be replaced by Indonesians rather than waiting for the Dutch to arrive.

Declaring themselves as president and vice president of Indonesia, Sukarno and Hatta moved quickly to install their own people in municipal governments at every level, especially in Java and Sumatra.

The Dutch may have intended to pick up where they had left off before the war, but with or without the inconvenience of the declared independence, it was a daunting logistical and administrative challenge. The Netherlands were exhausted by more than four years of German occupation, and facing critical food shortages at home, and were unable to send an army of administrators and bureaucrats to the Indies. Therefore, they were compelled to rely on British surrogates to reimpose the prewar colonial paradigm. Under the Allied chain of command, the Dutch East Indies fell under the jurisdiction of the Southeast Asia Command, headed by Admiral Lord Louis Mountbatten of the RN.

Personnel under Mountbatten's command reached Batavia in late September to accept the Japanese surrender amid the confused situation which had arisen when Lieutenant General Yuichiro Nagano of the IJA 16th Army had handed the keys to the city to Sukarno. Now, Nagano was tasked with getting them back. The terms of the surrender dictated that the Japanese occupation government functions should be turned over to the British on behalf of the Dutch. Thus it was that in October 1945, the IJA went back to war, this time against the very people whom they had once nurtured as a future puppet government.

The IJA, who had captured Bandoeng, the beautiful art deco Paris of Java, from the Dutch on March 10, 1942, captured it from the Indonesians on October 3, 1945 and promptly handed it over to the British.

On October 25, the 49th Indian Infantry Brigade under Brigadier Aubertin Mallaby, landed in Surabaya in eastern Java. He met personally with Sukarno and negotiated a ceasefire, but was assassinated by an Indonesian gunman on October 30. This led to a major intervention by the British, widespread fighting throughout Java, and the beginning of a large-scale evacuation of ethnic European civilians from the island.

This situation presented Mountbatten with an unanticipated manpower problem. The British Army was stretched thin globally against the backdrop of a demobilization which began when the war ended. To address this issue, the British initiated the Japanese Surrendered Personnel program, bringing Japanese troops back into service under his command. According to Andrew Roadnight, writing in *History* magazine in 2002, there were around 35,000 fully armed, former IJA troops actually fighting under British command in Indonesia in 1945 and 1946!

They were no longer technically IJA troops, of course, but they were maintained in their wartime IJA unit structure. In November 1945, a very surreal moment came when a former IJA major named Kido was recommended by General Philip Cristison for a British Distinguished Service Order!

The use of IJA troops under the Japanese Surrendered Personnel program was not limited to Java. They were used in Malaya and unarmed former IJA personnel were being used by the Americans in the Philippines. In April 1946, when he made an inspection tour to Sumatra, even Mountbatten was startled to see armed troops in IJA uniforms seven months after the war ended.

"I, of course, knew that we had been forced to keep Japanese troops under arms to protect our lines of communication and vital areas," he recalled, as quoted by Philip Towle in *Japanese Prisoners of War*. "But it was nevertheless a great shock to me to find over a thousand Japanese troops guarding the nine miles of road from the airport to the town."

The legacy of the Greater East Asia Co-Prosperity Sphere was seen in millions of people who had watched their colonial masters replaced for three years by the Japanese. They were now unwilling to go back to being colonies of a distant European power.

The United States made good on a prewar promise of Philippine independence in 1946. In 1947, the British withdrew from both Burma and India, but they maintained their rule in Malaya through the 1950s. When the dust settled, except for Malaya, all of Southeast Asia that had been beneath the roof of the Greater East Asia Co-Prosperity Sphere was independent within a decade. Sukarno fought the Dutch until they finally granted Indonesia independence in 1949, and remained as president until 1967. Ho Chi Minh battled the French until they withdrew in 1954, and ruled the northern half of a divided Vietnam until his death in 1969.

Finally, in considering the final chapter in the story of the invincible years of the IJA in Southeast Asia, we turn to mighty Singapore. As with so much of Southeast Asia, Singapore, known now as Syonan-to, had survived the war without being recaptured.

General Seishio Itagaki arrived in Syonan-to on April 7, 1945. As a colonel, he had helped to engineer the 1931 Mukden Incident, and as a lieutenant general, he later commanded the Kwantung Army and he served as Japan's minister of war in 1938–39. He now came to take command of the IJA 7th Area Army, and to step into the shoes first worn by Tomoyuki Yamashita as the senior military man in the great fortress. Itagaki commanded an army in an area that was no longer an active war zone, even as the Pacific beyond his Southeast Asia jurisdiction was ablaze with Japanese losses. But dark clouds were forming. The IJA may have still ruled Malaya and Singapore, but the Allies now ruled the sea and the skies above. There were starting to be numerous air attacks, and the British had penetrated the Syonan-to harbor to sabotage Japanese ships.

Itagaki heard Emperor Hirohito's message on August 15, and so too did his subjects. The city state that had been strictly governed with the iron fist of the Kempeitai fell into a state of limbo, a void between one regime and the next. Prince Kan'in Haruhito was flown to Syonan-to on August 20 to explain the details of the ceasefire and of the formal surrender that would come on September 2.

The flag of the rising sun still flew over the neo-classic, 1920s Municipal Building, but as Itagaki stared out of the window of his office, he knew that the British would soon return to reclaim their great bastion and change the name back to Singapore.

The British fleet arrived in Singapore Harbor on September 4, two days after the ceremonies in Tokyo Bay, and Itagaki was taken aboard the HMS *Sussex* to meet with Lord Mountbatten and his staff, and to sign the surrender documents. British and Indian troops came ashore the following day to an eerie scene of empty streets patrolled by IJA troops awaiting their arrival. Soon, the streets were filled with excited civilians.

When the formal surrender ceremonies took place at the Municipal Building on September 12, the entire center of Singapore was thronged with people jockeying for a view of history in the making, with British Royal Marines now tasked with crowd control. There were cheers when Mountbatten and other Allied leaders arrived to inspect the honor guard, but jeers when Itagaki and six other IJA officers made their way up the front steps.

The ceremonial signing took just ten minutes and Union Jacks were hoisted on flagpoles throughout Singapore. Itagaki surrendered the IJA 7th Area Army, and signed on behalf of Count Hisaichi Terauchi. The commander of the Southern Expeditionary Army, and as such the commander of the IJA in all of Southeast Asia, Terauchi had suffered a debilitating stroke and could not attend. When he stood to leave the building, Itagaki had surrendered 680,000 troops.

The flag of the rising sun came down across Asia as the actual sun set for the last time on the Chrysanthemum Empire. With the fall of that empire, the reach into the Far East of other empires from across the world was also beginning to fade, and that became the lasting legacy of the Greater East Asia Co-Prosperity Sphere which the IJA had conquered and lost. Even Singapore finally became independent, nearly two decades later, on August 9, 1965. It will always be remembered as the nexus of monumental events and monumental emotions.

Singapore will always be remembered as the nexus of monumental events and emotions. In many ways, the fall of Singapore was the signature event on the Southern Road in 1942. It was an insurmountable challenge, surmounted in a week. It shocked the world and established the reputation of the man who achieved the victory, as well as the reputation of the IJA as a force to be reckoned with, and a force to be feared. It became a symbol that stood for the whole Southern Road campaign, a yin and a yang symbol of both devastating defeat and glorious triumph.

If Winston Churchill could describe the fall of Singapore as "the worst disaster and largest capitulation in British history," then was not its capture by the Tiger of Malaya the greatest conquest of the then-invincible IJA?

EPILOGUE

John Wilpers, a young intelligence officer with the Office of Strategic Services, knocked at the door of a residence in the Setagaya ward of Tokyo. Hearing a single gunshot from within, he drew his own sidearm and banged again. He and the rest of his five-man OSS and military police team wondered if they had arrived too late.

Bursting inside, they saw a man lying on the floor of a room that was being used as a home office. There was blood visibly trickling from the bullet wound, so Wilpers immediately went into action, applying pressure to the injury and trying to save the man's life.

General Douglas MacArthur, the Supreme Allied Commander, had issued orders for the arrest of 40 individuals in Occupied Japan who were considered to be war criminals, and the man who lay dying on the floor was at the head of that list. Wilpers intended to take him alive.

Hideki Tojo, once the most powerful man in Asia short of Emperor Hirohito, had been out of the limelight for the 14 months since he was relieved of his jobs as prime minister, war minister, and chief of the IJA General Staff. Unwanted then, as Japan's fortunes in World War II turned sour, he was now very much a wanted man.

He had not been hard to find. It was September 8, 1945. The war had been officially over for six days, and the American occupation troops were pouring into Japan. With them, and in some cases ahead of them, had come the journalists. They had found Tojo before Wilpers had got his arrest warrant, and were camped out around his home. He had already started to give interviews, but when he learned that the OSS was coming, he decided that it was time to depart the cruel world.

Under *bushido*, the samurai code of honor, *seppuku*, or ritual suicide, is considered an honorable exit for someone who is about to be captured by his enemies. Usually, it is done with a knife and great ceremony, but Tojo was in a hurry. Wilpers and his team, who had come to arrest the symbol of Japanese militarism, had cut it close, but they had arrived in time.

They had also left the front door open. As Wilpers fought to save the man in the pool of blood, the reporters crowded around him to watch. Tojo's shirt had been ripped back and they could see charcoal markings on his chest. As they later learned, these had been put there by a doctor so that Tojo would know the location of his heart. If that had been his target, he had missed.

At last, they heard him start to speak, and the Americans watched as two Japanese reporters jotted down what he was saying.

"What'd he say?" the American reporters asked in unison.

George Jones of the *New York Times* wrote down the words as an English-speaking Japanese journalist translated.

"I am very sorry it is taking me so long to die," Tojo said. "The Greater East Asia War was justified and righteous. I am very sorry for the nation and all the races of the Greater Asiatic powers. I wait for the righteous judgment of history. I wished to commit suicide but sometimes that fails."

It had, and Tojo was taken to a US Army medical facility, patched up and transferred to Sugamo Prison, a facility that had been used previously to house political prisoners.

Tojo survived to endure a war crimes trial, but others succeeded in cheating the tribunals. Fumimaro Konoe, the prewar prime minister and champion of the Greater East Asia Co-Prosperity Sphere concept, became involved in forming a postwar Japanese government under American supervision, but later came under suspicion. When he was ordered to turn himself in, he bit a potassium cyanide capsule, and passed from the scene on December 16, 1945.

Tojo was tried at the International Military Tribunal for the Far East in Tokyo, the counterpart of the International Military Tribunal empanelled at the same time in Nuremberg, Germany, to try the accused war criminals of the Third Reich. Tojo was convicted on seven of the more than 50 counts of his indictment, including waging wars of aggression in violation of international law and authorizing inhumane treatment of POWs. He told the court:

> It is natural that I should bear entire responsibility for the war in general, and, needless to say, I am prepared to do so. Consequently, now that the war has been lost, it is presumably necessary that I be judged so that the circumstances of the time can be clarified and the future peace of the world be assured. Therefore, with respect to my trial, it is my intention to speak frankly, according to my recollection, even though when the vanquished stands before the victor, who has over him the power of life and death, he may be apt to toady and flatter ... To shade one's words in flattery to the point of untruthfulness would falsify the trial and do incalculable harm to the nation, and great care must be taken to avoid this.

Hideki Tojo went to the gallows on December 23, 1948.

Meanwhile, the Allies, especially MacArthur, went to great lengths to ensure that Emperor Hirohito would be shielded from war crimes accusations. MacArthur writes in his memoirs:

> I had an uneasy feeling he might plead his own cause against indictment as a war criminal. There had been considerable outcry from some of the Allies, notably the Russians and the British, to include him in this category. Indeed, the initial list of those proposed by them was headed by the Emperor's name. Realizing the tragic consequences that would follow such an unjust action, I had stoutly resisted such efforts. When Washington seemed to be veering toward the British point of view, I had advised that I would need at least one million reinforcements should

such action be taken. I believed that if the Emperor were indicted, and perhaps hanged, as a war criminal, military government would have to be instituted throughout all Japan, and guerrilla warfare would probably break out ... He played a major role in the spiritual regeneration of Japan, and his loyal co-operation and influence had much to do with the success of the occupation.

What then happened to the others of note in this saga of the IJA? We turn back to November 1941 and to the Imperial General Headquarters conference when Tojo unveiled the assignments for the momentous journey down the Southern Road, and to those present who would take those assignments and prove their service to be, for a moment in history, invincible.

Count Hisaichi Terauchi, of the class of 1909 at the IJA Academy, was the commander of the whole of Southeast Asia as head of the Southern Expeditionary Army in November 1941. Holding the hereditary title of count (*hakushaku*), he had become a full general in 1935, and was promoted to field marshal (*gensui*) in June 1943. He suffered his first stroke on May 10, 1944, having learned of the Allied recapture of Burma. Still in feeble condition in September 1945, he missed the Japanese surrender of Singapore, but Lord Mountbatten came to him two months later. In Saigon on November 30, as the two noblemen met face-to-face, Terauchi handed over a *wakizashi* short sword that had been in the Terauchi family since the fifteenth century. Having been taken into custody, the count suffered a second, more serious stroke and died on June 12, 1946. The sword is still kept at Windsor Castle.

Lieutenant General Masaharu Homma, class of 1907 at the IJA Academy, had been given command of the 14th Army for operations in the Philippines in November 1941. He was constantly criticized by the Imperial General Headquarters for the sluggishness of his offensive, and for taking five months to conquer the Philippines. Relieved of command in 1943, Homma was forced into retirement and faded from public view. After the war, he was arrested for his role in the atrocities of the Bataan Death March. Rather than his being tried in Tokyo by the International Military Tribunal for the Far East, MacArthur ordered him to be extradited to the Philippines, where the Death March had taken place and where the witnesses were living. Having been convicted by the United States Military Commission, Manila, Homma was executed by a firing squad on April 3, 1946.

Lieutenant General Shojiro Iida, class of 1908 at the IJA Academy, commanded the 15th Army in the overnight conquest of Thailand and the significantly longer Burma operations. He stayed on in Burma as military commander for the colony until 1943, when he was rotated back to Japan for a desk job at the General Defense Command. He briefly commanded Central District Army in Japan before his retirement in 1944. In the summer of 1945, as the war was nearing its climax, he was brought back into uniform and sent to command the 30th Army in Manchukuo. Shortly after he arrived, the Soviets declared war, and swept across the border. Defeated in this action, Iida was captured and spent the next five years as a POW in the Soviet Union. He returned to Japan, where he lived until his death on January 23, 1980 at the age of 91.

General Hitoshi Imamura, class of 1907 at the IJA Academy, was given the assignment to command the 16th Army in Java, where he wound up swimming ashore when his transport ship was hit by friendly fire on the first night. A lieutenant general since 1938, he remained as head of the occupation force in Java until November 9, 1942, when he was given command of the IJA 8th Area Army, based in Rabaul. In this post, he commanded both the 17th and 18th Armies during operations in the Solomon Islands and New Guinea. Having been promoted to full general in May 1943, he was still in this job on August 15, 1945, when he surrendered to the Australians. He was charged with permitting the murder of POWs by troops under his command, convicted, and sent to Sugamo Prison, where he remained until 1954. Imamura died on October 4, 1980 at the age of 82.

Lieutenant General Renya Mutaguchi, class of 1910 at the IJA Academy, commanded the 18th Division in Malaya and later Burma, seeing more action than most division commanders in the IJA. He took over command of the 15th Army from Shojiro Iida on March 18, 1943 and went on to promote the ultimately disastrous invasion of India via Imphal. Relieved of this command on August 30, 1944, he returned to Japan and forced retirement. In 1945, he was reactivated briefly as the commandant of a military prep school. He was arrested as a war criminal in 1945 and extradited to Singapore to stand trial. He was released from prison in 1948 and returned to Japan, where he died on August 2, 1966 at the age of 77.

And then there was Colonel Masanobu Tsuji, whom John Toland described as "a brilliant maverick spirit [revered] as Japan's 'God of Operations,' the hope of the Orient." This mercurial character, who was the key technical planner of the Malaya–Singapore campaign, and the operations officer for Tomoyuki Yamashita's 25th Army, reemerged in Japan in 1948, having spent three years on the run, fearing war crimes charges which never materialized. In his 1952 memoir, *Underground Escape*, he wrote that he was based in Thailand at war's end, having just returned from Saigon and a failed attempt to sell a plan to "go underground in China [for up to 20 years] to open up a new way for the future of Asia."

When the ceasefire was announced, Tsuji did go underground, exchanging his IJA uniform for the yellow robes of a Buddhist monk. He slipped out of Bangkok as the British troops arrived, bound for Vietnam. Changing disguises and dodging firefights between the French and Viet Minh, he stole a car and drove to Hanoi. Here he remained from late November until March 1946, when he caught a ride on an American aircraft flying into China. In Nanking (now Nanjing) and elsewhere, he was employed by a series of Nationalist Chinese government agencies translating wartime Japanese intelligence documents related to the Soviet military and the Chinese Communists, about which he claimed to have become an expert.

Returning to Japan in May 1948, Tsuji writes that he kissed the ground, observing that "though the country was defeated, the hills and the streams were still left, together with the Emperor." He was elected to the Japanese Diet in 1952 and wrote several books, including his highly regarded memoir of the Malaya–Singapore campaign, *Singapore: The Japanese Version*.

Arthur Swinson writes, in his 1968 book *Four Samurai*:

> He still lived mysteriously, travelling on secret missions, and in April 1961, he went to Vietnam. Since this date he has not reappeared but information reaching the author from Japan indicates that he is back in uniform and serving as an Operations Staff officer under Vo Nguyen Giap. When one considers the ruthlessness and brilliance of the North Vietnamese operations, the hand of Masanobu Tsuji can be seen clearly.

Indeed, he was never seen again, and was declared dead in 1968. There is no evidence that he was ever a consultant to the North Vietnamese, although, with Tsuji's record, it is not beyond the realm of possibility.

———

Finally, we turn to General Tomoyuki Yamashita, class of 1910 at the IJA Academy, the Tiger of Malaya, who walked out of the jungle on September 2, 1945 and surrendered the 14th Area Army. He was taken to New Bilibid Prison in Manila and charged in connection with atrocities against civilians, especially in the Manila Massacre of February 1945 in which Sanji Iwabuchi's naval troops killed or injured countless civilians.

As with Homma, Yamashita was not tried by the International Military Tribunal for the Far East in Tokyo, but by the United States Military Commission, Manila, near where his alleged war crimes were committed. He was the first Japanese general to be tried, with his trial beginning on October 29, 1945. In later years, there has been a great deal of criticism of this trial, particularly of the court's rules of evidence. There were days of heart-rending testimony from victims of the atrocities, many of whom still showed the scars of mutilation. However, the prosecution was unable to present conclusive evidence showing that Yamashita ordered or knew about the massacre at the time it was happening.

Colonel Harry Clarke, heading Yamashita's US Army defense team, observed in exasperation that Yamashita "is not charged with having done something or having failed to do something, but solely with having been something ... American jurisprudence recognizes no such principle so far as its own military personnel are concerned ... one man is not held to answer for the crime of another."

When he took the stand, Yamashita told the court that he had not ordered the Manila Massacre, but rather had ordered the evacuation of Manila by Japanese troops. Referring to the massacre and to the accusations of cruelty to captured civilians in late 1944, Yamashita said:

> The matters which are referred to in the charges, I have known for the first time from the testimony of the witnesses before this court. And if such acts were committed by my subordinates, they are in complete disagreement with my own ideas. And if such did occur, I feel that they occurred at such a time and place that I could not have known of it beforehand. I have never ordered such things, and I have never condoned such actions, nor have I ever recognized such actions, and if I had known of them in advance, I would have taken every possible means to have caused them to stop. And if I had found out about them afterwards, I would have punished them to the fullest extent of military law.

Yamashita was convicted and sentenced to death by hanging on December 7, 1945. This was a cruel irony for someone who had in fact disciplined subordinates for similar actions in Malaya. His attorneys appealed to the United States Supreme Court, who refused to hear the case.

"My death does not matter," Tomoyuki Yamashita told John Deane Potter in Manila in their last conversation before Yamashita went to the gallows on February 23, 1946. "I know nothing except being a soldier and now I am no longer young. My usefulness to my country is over. I am too old to fight another war, so if the Americans wish to kill me, they will not be harming my country."

When Potter rose to leave him for the last time, Yamashita bowed politely and walked with him to the door. Several other generals were sitting in the corridor, playing a game with hundreds of counters which looked to Potter "like checkers gone crazy."

"That is a typical game of ours, called Go," the erstwhile Tiger of Malaya replied calmly when Potter asked about the game. "It is very Japanese indeed. The idea of so many counters is so you can take as much territory as you can from your opponent in the shortest time."

With this, the man born amid the ancient cedars of Shikoku went to meet his fate, and ultimately his executioner.

An Overview of the Japanese Order of Battle in Southeast Asia (1941–42)

(Ranks are as of the dates of the actions described in this book)

Southern Army (aka Southern Expeditionary Army Group)
(General Count Hisaichi Terauchi)
(Answered to: Imperial General Headquarters in Tokyo)

14th Army (Philippine operations)
(Lieutenant General Masaharu Homma)
4th Division (Lieutenant General Kenzo Kitano) (deployed after initial landings)
16th Division (Lieutenant General Susumu Morioka)
21st Division (Major General Kameichiro Nagano) (elements of the Nagano Detachment)
48th Division (Lieutenant General Yuitsu Tsuchihashi) (later redeployed to the Dutch East Indies)

15th Army (Burma operations via Thailand)
(Lieutenant General Shojiro Iida)

18th Division (Lieutenant General Renya Mutaguchi) (redeployed from Malaya)

33rd Division (Lieutenant General Shozo Sakurai)

55th Division (Lieutenant General Hiroshi Takeuchi)

56th Division (Lieutenant General Masao Watanabe) (elements redeployed from the Dutch East Indies)

16th Army (Dutch East Indies operations)
(Lieutenant General Hitoshi Imamura)

2nd Division (Major General Masao Maruyama)

35th Infantry Brigade (Kawaguchi Detachment) (Major General Kiyotake Kawaguchi) (detached from 18th Division)

48th Division (Lieutenant General Yuitsu Tsuchihashi)

56th Infantry Group (Major General Shizuo Sakaguchi) (detached from the 56th Division)

25th Army (Malaya/Singapore operations)
(Lieutenant General Tomoyuki Yamashita)

2nd Imperial Guards Division (Lieutenant General Takuma Nishimura)

5th Division (Lieutenant General Takuro Matsui)

18th Division (Lieutenant General Renya Mutaguchi) (later redeployed to Burma)

56th Division (Lieutenant General Masao Watanabe) (held in reserve, but not used)

GLOSSARY

ABDA	American–British–Dutch–Australian Command
ABDACOM	Alternate form of ABDA incorporating the word "Command"
AIF	Australian Imperial Force
ASHR	Argyll and Sutherland Highlanders Regiment
AVG	American Volunteer Group (the "Flying Tigers")
CBI	China Burma India Theater
FEAF	Far East Air Forces (of the USAAF)
HMAS	His Majesty's Australian Ship
HMS	His Majesty's Ship
HNLMS	Her Netherlands Majesty's Ship
IJA	Imperial Japanese Army
IJAAF	Imperial Japanese Army Air Force
IJN	Imperial Japanese Navy
IJNAF	Imperial Japanese Navy Air Force
INA	Indian National Army
KNIL	Koninklijk Nederlands Indisch Leger (Netherlands Army in the East Indies)
MLD	Marine Luchtvaartdienst (Netherlands Naval Aviation)
ML-KNIL	Militaire Luchtvaart van het Koninklijk Nederlands-Indisch Leger (Military Aviation of the Royal Netherlands East Indies Army)
MV	Motor Vessel

POW	Prisoner of War
RAAF	Royal Australian Air Force
RAF	Royal Air Force (United Kingdom)
RN	Royal Navy (United Kingdom)
SARFOR	Sarawak Force
USAAF	US Army Air Forces
USAFFE	US Army Forces in the Far East
USAT	US Army Transport
USFIP	United States Forces in the Philippines
USMC	US Marine Corps
USN	US Navy
USS	United States Ship
WPO-3	War Plan Orange, third iteration

BIBLIOGRAPHY

Allen, Louis. *Singapore 1941–42*. Newark: University of Delaware Press, 1979.

Attiwill, Kenneth. *Fortress: The Story of the Siege and Fall of Singapore*. New York: Doubleday, 1960.

Bayly, Christopher and Harper, Tim. *Forgotten Armies: Britain's Asian Empire and the War with Japan*. London: Penguin Books, 2005.

Bayly, Christopher and Harper, Tim. *Forgotten Wars: Freedom and Revolution in Southeast Asia*. Cambridge: Belknap Press of Harvard University Press, 2007.

Bell, Bowyer. *Besieged: Seven Cities Under Siege*. Philadelphia and New York: Chilton Books, 1966.

Bix, Herbert. *Hirohito and the Making of Modern Japan*. New York: HarperCollins, 2000.

Brown, Gary and Anderson, David. "Invasion 1942: Australia and the Japanese Threat." Background Paper Number 6 1992. Canberra: Department of the Parliamentary Library, 1992.

Bullard, Steven (translator). *Japanese Army Operations in the South Pacific Area New Britain and Papua Campaigns, 1942–43*. Canberra: Australian War Memorial, 2007.

Burton, John. *Fortnight of Infamy: The Collapse of Allied Airpower West of Pearl Harbor*. Annapolis: US Naval Institute Press, 2006.

Callinan, Bernard. *Independent Company: The Australian Army in Portuguese Timor 1941–43*. London: William Heinemann, 1953.

Campbell, Archie. *The Double Reds of Timor*. Swanbourne: John Burridge Military Antiques, 1994.

Churchill, Winston. *The Second World War: The Grand Alliance*. Boston: Houghton Mifflin Company, 1950.

Covarrubias, Miguel. *Island of Bali*. New York: Alfred A. Knopf, 1937.

Cull, Brian. *Hurricanes Over Singapore: RAF, RNZAF and NEI Fighters in Action Against the Japanese Over the Island and the Netherlands East Indies, 1942*. London: Grub Street Publishing, 2004.

Cull, Brian. *Buffaloes Over Singapore: RAF, RAAF, RNZAF and Dutch Brewster Fighters in Action Over Malaya and the East Indies 1941–1942*. London: Grub Street Publishing, 2008.

Dorn, Frank. *The Sino-Japanese War, 1937–41: From Marco Polo Bridge to Pearl Harbor*. New York: Macmillan, 1994.

Drea, Edward J. *In the Service of the Emperor: Essays on the Imperial Japanese Army*. Nebraska: University of Nebraska Press, 1998.

Edgerton, Robert B. *Warriors of the Rising Sun: A History of the Japanese Military*. Boulder, Colorado: Westview Press, 1999.

Elphick, Peter. *Singapore: The Pregnable Fortress: A Study in Deception, Discord and Desertion*. New York: Coronet Books, 1995.

Fay, Peter W. *The Forgotten Army: India's Armed Struggle for Independence, 1942–1945*. Ann Arbor: University of Michigan Press, 1993.

Frederick, William H. and Worden, Robert L. *Indonesia: A Country Study*. Washington, DC. Library of Congress, Federal Research Division, 1993.

Frei, Henry P. *Japan's Southward Advance and Australia. From the Sixteenth Century to World War II*. Melbourne: Melbourne University Press, 1991.

Friend, Theodore. *Indonesian Destinies*. Cambridge: Harvard University Press, 2003.

Gamble, Bruce. *Darkest Hour: The True Story of Lark Force at Rabaul – Australia's Worst Military Disaster of World War II*. St Paul, Minnesota: Zenith Press, 2006.

Gamble, Bruce. *Fortress Rabaul: The Battle for the Southwest Pacific, January 1942 – April 1943*. Minneapolis, Minnesota: Zenith Press, 2010.

Gill, G. Hermon. *Royal Australian Navy 1939–1942. Australia in the War of 1939–1945*. Canberra: Australian War Memorial, 1957.

Gordon, Andrew. *A Modern History of Japan: From Tokugawa Times to the Present*. Oxford: Oxford University Press, 2003.

Hack, Karl and Blackburn, Kevin. *Did Singapore Have to Fall? Churchill and the Impregnable Fortress*. London: Routledge Curzon, 2003.

Hara, Tameichi. *Japanese Destroyer Captain: Pearl Harbor, Guadalcanal, Midway-The Great Naval Battles as Seen Through Japanese Eyes*. Annapolis: Naval Institute Press, 2011.

Harries, Meirion. *Soldiers of the Sun: The Rise and Fall of the Imperial Japanese Army*. New York: Random House, 1994.

Hayashi, Saburo. *Kogun: The Japanese Army in the Pacific War*. Tokyo: Taiheiyo Senso Rikusen Gaishi, 1951.

Hsu Long-hsuen, and Chang Ming-kai. *History of The Sino-Japanese War (1937–1945)*. Translated by Wen Ha-hsiung. Taipei: Chung Wu Publishing, 1971.

Ike, Nobutaka (ed.). *Japan's Decision for War: Records of the 1941 Policy Conferences*. Stanford: Stanford, 1967.

Imperial Japanese Army. *Read This Alone, and the War Can Be Won*. Tokyo: Imperial Japanese Army. 1941.

Jacoby, Annalee and White, Theodore H. *Thunder out of China*. New York: William Sloane Associates, 1946.

Jansen, Marius B. *The Making of Modern Japan*. Cambridge: Harvard University Press, 2002.

Jeffreys, Alan and Anderson, Duncan. *British Army in the Far East 1941–45*. Oxford: Osprey Publishing, 2005.

Kirby, Stanley Woodburn. *War Against Japan, Volume I: The Loss of Singapore*. London: Her Majesty's Stationery Office, 1957.

Kirby, Stanley Woodburn. *War Against Japan, Volume II: India's Most Dangerous Hour*. London: Her Majesty's Stationery Office, 1958.

Kirby, Stanley Woodburn. *War Against Japan, Volume III: The Decisive Battles*. London: Her Majesty's Stationery Office, 1961.

Kirby, Stanley Woodburn. *War Against Japan, Volume IV: The Reconquest of Burma*. London: Her Majesty's Stationery Office, 1965.

Kirby, Stanley Woodburn. *War Against Japan, Volume V: The Surrender of Japan*. London: Her Majesty's Stationery Office, 1969.

Klemen, L. *Forgotten Campaign. The Dutch East Indies Campaign 1941–1942*. www.dutcheastindies.webs.com/.

Krancher, Jan A. *The Defining Years of the Dutch East Indies, 1942–1949: Survivors' Accounts of Japanese Invasion and Enslavement of Europeans and the Revolution That Created Free Indonesia*. Jefferson, North Carolina: McFarland & Company, 2003.

Lee, Clark. *They Call it Pacific*. Whitefish, Montana: Kessinger, 2005.

Lee, Henry. *Nothing But Praise*. Pasadena: Pacific Asia Museum, 1985.

Library of Congress. *Indonesia: The Japanese Occupation, 1942–45*. Washington, DC: Library of Congress, 1992.

Library of Congress. *Indonesia: World War II and the Struggle For Independence, 1942–50*. Washington, DC: Library of Congress, 1992.

MacArthur, Douglas. *Reminiscences*. New York: McGraw Hill, 1964.

Morison, Samuel Eliot. *History of United States Naval Operations in World War II: Volume III The Rising Sun in the Pacific.* Boston, Little Brown, 1984.

Morton, Louis. *United States Army in World War II, The War in the Pacific, The Fall of the Philippines.* Washington, DC: Center of Military History, 1953.

Percival, Arthur. *Operations of Malaya Command from 5th December 1941 to 15th February 1942.* London: UK Secretary of State for War, 1946.

Percival, Arthur. *The War in Malaya.* London: Eyre and Spottiswoode, 1949.

Reel, A. Frank. *The Case of General Yamashita.* Chicago: The University of Chicago Press, 1949.

Romulo, Carlos. *I Saw the Fall of the Philippines.* Garden City, New York: Doubleday, Doran, 1942.

Roskill, Stephen. *The War at Sea 1939–1945 Volume II.* London: Her Majesty's Stationery Office, 1956.

Ryan, Allan A. *Yamashita's Ghost: War Crimes, MacArthur's Justice, and Command Accountability.* Lawrence: University Press of Kansas, 2012.

Saburo Hayashi: *Kogun: The Japanese Army in the Pacific War.* Quantico: Marine Corps Association, 1959.

Saint Kenworthy, Aubrey. *The Tiger of Malaya: The Story of General Tomoyuki Yamashita and "Death March" General Masaharu Homma.* New York: Exposition Press, 1951.

Seagrave, Sterling. *The Soong Dynasty.* New York: Harper, 1985.

Sheehan, Neil. *A Bright Shining Lie: John Paul Vann and America in Vietnam.* New York: Random House, 1988.

Shillony, Ben-Ami. *Revolt in Japan: The Young Officers and the February 26, 1936 Incident.* Princeton: Princeton University Press, 1973.

Shores, Christopher. *Bloody Shambles: Volume One: The Drift to War to the Fall of Singapore.* London: Grub Street Publishing, 2002.

Shores, Christopher. *Bloody Shambles: Volume Two: The Complete Account of the Air War in the Far East, from the Defence of Sumatra to the Fall of Burma, 1942.* London: Grub Street Publishing, 2009.

Sims, Richard. *Japanese Political History Since the Meiji Renovation 1868–2000.* Palgrave Macmillan, 2001.

Smith, Colin. *Singapore Burning: Heroism and Surrender in World War II.* London, Penguin, 2006.

Smyth, John George. *Percival and the Tragedy of Singapore.* London: MacDonald and Company, 1971.

Snow, Philip. *The Fall of Hong Kong: Britain, China and the Japanese Occupation.* New Haven: Yale University Press, 2004.

Storry, Richard. *The Double Patriots: A Study of Japanese Nationalism.* Westport, Connecticut: Greenwood Press, 1957.

Sun Tzu, trans. Griffith, Samuel B. *The Art of War.* Oxford: Oxford University Press, 1980.

Swinson, Arthur. *Defeat in Malaya: The Fall of Singapore.* New York: Ballantine Books, 1970.

Swinson, Arthur. *Four Samurai: A Quartet of Japanese Generals.* London: Hutchinson, 1968.

Toer, Pramoedya Ananta, trans. Samuels, Willem. *The Mute's Soliloquy.* New York: Penguin, 1998.

Toland, John. *The Rising Sun: The Decline and Fall of the Japanese Empire 1936– 1945.* New York: Random House, 1970.

Towle, Philip, Kosuge, Margaret and Kibata, Yoichi. *Japanese Prisoners of War.* London: Hambleton and London, 2000.

Tsuji, Masanobu. *Underground Escape.* Tokyo: Booth & Fukuda, 1952.

Tsuji, Masanobu. *Singapore: The Japanese Version.* Sydney: Ure Smith, 1960.

Thurman, Malcolm Joseph and Sherman, Christine A. *War Crimes: Japan's World War II Atrocities.* Paducah, Kentucky: Turner, 2001.

US War Department. *Handbook of Japanese Military Forces, TM-E 30-480.* Baton Rouge and London: Louisiana State University Press, 1991, reprint.

Wigmore, Lionel. *The Loss of Ambon, Australia in the War of 1939–1945, Volume IV: The Japanese.* Canberra: Australian War Memorial, 1957.

Williams, Adriana. *Covarrubias.* Austin: University of Texas Press, 1994.

Willmott, H.P. *Empires in the Balance.* Annapolis: Naval Institute Press, 1989.

Womack, Tom. *Dutch Naval Air Force Against Japan: The Defense of the Netherlands East Indies, 1941–1942.* Jefferson, North Carolina: McFarland & Company, 2006.

Notes on Imperial Japanese Army Documents

IJA documents taken on the field of battle were collected by or for the Allied Translator and Interpreter Section (ATIS), who evaluated all such documents, translating and publishing those of immediate value. After the war, the ATIS compiled historical records and debriefed numerous IJA and IJN officers about their roles in the war. These documents were published by the ATIS, and are filed at the Center of Military History in Washington, DC.

IJA histories and reports were also compiled after the war by the 1st and 2nd Demobilization Bureaus. These units were staffed by former IJA and IJN officers and Imperial General Headquarters personnel operating under the direction of G-2, US Army Far East Command.

Further documents are included among the transcriptions and exhibits from the war crimes trials held by the International Military Tribunal for the Far East in Tokyo, but by the United States Military Commission in Manila. These records were originally in the custody of the Judge Advocate General but were later transferred to the Departmental Records Branch of the Advocate General's Office.

INDEX

INDEX

INDEX

357

INDEX

ABOUT THE AUTHOR

Bill Yenne is the author of more than three dozen non-fiction books, including *The White Rose of Stalingrad: The Real-Life Adventure of Lidiya Vladimirovna Litvyak, the Highest Scoring Female Air Ace of All Time* (Osprey 2013). His other works have included many military histories, as well as several military biographies, and he has contributed to encyclopedias of both world wars. General Wesley Clark, the former Supreme Allied Commander in Europe, called his recent biography of Alexander the Great, the "best yet." *The New Yorker* wrote of *Sitting Bull*, Yenne's biography of the great Lakota leader, that it "excels as a study in leadership." His dual biography of Dick Bong and Tommy McGuire, *Aces High: The Heroic Story of the Two Top-Scoring American Aces of World War II*, was described by pilot and best-selling author Dan Roam as "the greatest flying story of all time."

He has also appeared in several documentaries broadcast on the History Channel, the National Geographic Channel, and ARD German Television. He lives in San Francisco, and on the web at www.BillYenne.com